THE SEVEN-DAY
WEEKEND

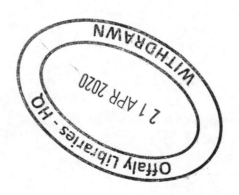

Contents

Acknowledgements

A good third of this book would be used up, and far too many trees, in thanking all who made it possible. Some would not sleep at night, however, if I didn't find it in the heart of this book to remember them. Such is the case of Sabra Chartrand, who made the sometimes frustrating aspect of editing feasible. My agent at ICM, Heather Schroder, was as usual invaluable, even making phone calls from her honeymoon hideaway (talk about a seven day weekend!). Suzanne Gluck, who started this project is also fondly remembered here, as well as Esther Newburg, always a watchful eye.

Then there are the personal supports, primary of which Fernanda, always exhilarated with progress, and constantly providing selfless encouragement. Also Bill Ury, Suzy Wetlaufer, Horacio Piva, Fernando Lottenberg, Noel Ginsburg who gave up their time to make wonderfully helpful comments.

I would also like to acknowledge the authors that I have quoted in this book; Marie-Henri Beyle Stendhal, Emperor Hang Djing Di and Lewis Carroll.

Last but not least, the Semco crowd, who gave hours of their time to this project. They are too many to mention, but know who they are – to them, a warm, warm Brazilian *abraço*.

This book is dedicated to Clovis Bojikian, Lord of the Semco Rings, father-figure, cuckold hen and eternal fire beneath the posteriors of authoritarians everywhere.

Forewarning

I am currently unemployed. Gainfully unemployed, as it were. To the lady in the Social Security window I'd have to confess that I've not looked for work in several months. Instead, I've used part of that time to write this book.

I've chosen the metaphor of the seven-day weekend as an anchor, dropped in the sea of novelty. Your first reaction may be dismay at the loss of your conventional weekend – after all, we naïvely define weekends as free time, personal days, idle hours. But that definition is already outdated. The traditional weekend ended long ago. This book faces that fact and uses it to explore making work more fun, to finding a balance between it and private passions, so both can be significantly gratifying.

To do that, we must re-organize the workplace, both physically and culturally. At my company, Semco, we've spent 25 years questioning the way we do things. When we started, everyone said we wouldn't last.

Now Semco employs 3,000 people working in three countries in manufacturing, professional services and high-tech software. But even now, I continue to hear that our experiments could never work anywhere else – Semco is too small, our structure is unique to the business we're in, our ideas could only work in Brazil. We plunge ahead anyway, defying the military and boarding school mentalities that are the backbone of traditional business structure. And we prove that in re-distributing the weekend across the workweek, our employees find balance and Semco makes money.

So even though Semco is in large part a sociological or anthropological experiment, we also make an excellent business case. We fit neatly into any MBA examination of success, because the right approach to employees always creates profit.

It's very simple – the repetition, boredom and aggravation that too many people accept as an inherent part of working can be replaced with joy, inspiration and freedom.

That's what I wish for everyone who reads this book.

Ricardo Semler
(Lying in a hammock with a laptop and my little boy, having fed the ducks at a nearby pond)
On a Monday in May, 2002

Part One

In Whack

1. Why are we able to answer emails on Sundays, but unable to go to the movies on Monday afternoons?

2. Why can't we take the kids to work if we can take work home?

3. Why do we think the opposite of work is leisure, when in fact it is idleness?

CHAPTER 1

What Planet Are We From?

ON A LEAFY SIDE STREET in São Paulo, Danilo Saicali approached the headquarters of Semco Corporation on the first day of his new job. Toting a briefcase and clad in a dark suit and tie, Danilo was poised to run Semco's New Ventures unit. He'd been a partner and CEO at Arthur Andersen and then at Amway, so he was bringing years of knowledge and seasoned authority to Semco, a 50-year-old company with annual revenues of $160 million. He'd be part of a close-knit team managing Semco's diverse businesses in machinery, real estate, environmental services, and as an investor in high-tech businesses.

But Danilo was joining a company better known around the world for what it doesn't do.

Semco has no official structure. It has no organizational chart. There's no business plan or company strategy – no two-year or five-year plan, no goal or mission statement, no long-term budget. The company often does not have a fixed CEO. There are no vice presidents or chief officers for information technology or operations. There are no standards or practices. There's no human resources department. There are no career plans, no job descriptions or employee contracts. No one approves reports or expense accounts. Supervision or monitoring of workers is rare indeed.

Most importantly, success is not measured only in profit and growth.

Danilo knew all this on his first day because he'd heard it from me, and I am Semco's major shareholder. Just before Danilo accepted the job, we sat down for what I call my 'scare off' meeting. Even people who understand our philosophies may not be prepared for what it really means to work at Semco. I briefed Danilo: He'd have no office, no permanent desk, no secretary, no parking place, no official title, no business cards.

3

Semco had agreed to pay Danilo a substantial salary for his talents, but we weren't prepared to give him his own desk. Money is one thing. But the rigid structures of the past are another.

Danilo was a little taken aback. But I'd seen that before. Fifteen years earlier, a prominent Brazilian politician, Senator José Macedo, invited me to the far north of Brazil for a conference. This wonderful self-made man had begun his working life as a soap salesman. By the time I met him, he was a billionaire in the flour, biscuit, beer and car dealership businesses.

I spoke to the conference for an hour about Semco and its strange practices, and then Senator Macedo opened the question and answer session. Sitting in the first row, he looked back over his shoulder at the hundreds of people who filled the hot, humid auditorium and asked: 'Mr. Semler, before answering other questions, can you please tell us what planet you're from?' It took several minutes for the room to quiet down – I can still hear the good-natured laughter to this day.

So anyone picking up this book may first ask, what is Semco?

I can't tell you. If you ask me to describe it in conventional business terms, I'd have to admit I have no idea what business Semco is in. For the last 20 years, I have resisted defining Semco for a simple reason: Once you say what business you're in, you create boundaries for your employees, you restrict their thinking and give them a reason to ignore new opportunities. 'We're not in that business,' they'll say.

Instead of dictating Semco's identity, I let our employees shape it with their individual efforts, interests, and initiatives.

But that, together with stories like Danilo's, may make Semco sound like a company with an offbeat management style that wouldn't succeed any place else. Nevertheless hundreds of corporate leaders from around the world have visited São Paulo to find out what makes us tick. Some, like representatives from the Royal Hospitals in Australia, schools in Finland, the Amsterdam police department and a few dozen private or public companies around the globe, have gone home and emulated us. But many more have gone away shaking their heads in bewilderment. At its peak, there was a 17-month waiting list for the bi-weekly tour of Semco (with each tour including 35 outside companies). At that point we cancelled the program because our workers were beginning to feel like animals in a zoo.

The visitors were curious about Semco because they want what we have – huge growth in spite of a fluctuating economy, unique market niches, rising profits, highly motivated employees, low turnover, diverse product and service areas. In short, sustainability.

Our visitors want to understand how we achieve that. How has Semco increased its annual revenue between 1994 and 2001 from $35 million a year to $160 million when I rarely attend meetings and almost never make decisions? When with a show of hands, employees can veto new product ideas or whole business ventures?

This book is intended to explain the straightforward philosophies and practices that make Semco one of the world's most unusual workplaces. Be warned – many of our basic tenets fly in the face of even the most progressive business owner or manager. Our architecture is really the sum of all the conventional business practices we avoid. It's easier to say what it's *not*, rather than what it is.

It's our lack of formal structure, the way we give up control so workers can follow their interests and their instincts when choosing jobs or projects. It's our insistence that workers seek personal challenges and satisfaction before trying to meet the company's goals. It's how we encourage employees to ramble through their day or week so they will meander into new ideas and new business opportunities. It's inherent in how we embrace democracy and open communication, and encourage questions and dissent in the workplace.

On-the-job democracy isn't just a lofty concept, but a better way to do things. We all demand democracy in every other aspect of our lives and culture. People are considered adults in their private lives, at the bank, at their children's schools, with family and among friends – so why are they suddenly treated like adolescents at work? Why can't workers be involved in choosing their own leaders? Why shouldn't they manage themselves? Why can't they speak up – challenge, question, share information openly?

If we have a cardinal strategy that forms the bedrock for all these practices, it may be this: Ask Why. Ask it all the time, and always ask it three times in a row. This doesn't come naturally. People are conditioned to recoil from questioning too much. First, it's rude and dangerous. Second, it may imply we're ignorant or uninformed. Third, it means everything we think we know may not be correct or true. Fourth, management is usually frightened by the prospect of employees who question continually. But mostly, it means putting aside all the rote or pat answers that have resulted from what I call 'crystallized' thinking, that state of mind where ideas have so hardened into inflexible and unquestioned concepts that they're no longer of any use. Employees must be free to question, to analyze, to investigate, and a company must be flexible enough to listen to the answers. Those habits are the key to longevity, growth, and profit.

João Vendramim, our 61-year-old director emeritus, once asked a worker if he'd ever considered a different approach to his job.

'He answered that his boss told him to do it that way,' Vendramim remembers. 'So I insisted. He told me that once he had done his job differently, but his boss reprimanded him. While trying to explain to his boss what happened, he said, "I was thinking that. . . ." To which his boss instantly replied, "Thinking? You are not supposed to think. I am the one who thinks here."'

'This employee will never try to think again at work,' Vendramim says. 'That's not very clever of us. If people are afraid, they don't innovate. We don't want scared people. We want everybody to know what happens everywhere at the company. We want them to question.'

Any parent of a toddler (as I am) understands the value of questions. When the child asks the first why, you give a careful, adult version of the 'right' answer. This is closely followed by a second why from the child. You then stutter a little, and respond with even more care. Now, after this second explanation, a third why makes its way from that tiny mouth. After that third why, no matter what the subject, there is only one solution: Buy the kid an ice cream.

It's the same way with most questions: Why do I have to wear a suit and tie, or why does that person make more than I do, or why does the company have to grow. Or why does the product only come in black, or why can't I exchange it after 10 days, or why do I have to stand in line for this or that.

None of these quandaries will hold up over three consecutive whys. The first and maybe second pat answers will break down by the third time they're questioned.

At Semco we spur people to question everything they hear – to undo, dismantle and restart every concept or instruction. We don't do it to sow contention, but because more than once it has led to new opportunities for us.

Rogerio Ottolia came to Semco because he wanted a free hand to question everything – even though we offered him less money than he was earning at his previous job with a company that specialized in biochemical analysis. We were considering buying that company, and one day I had a meeting scheduled with the owner. The man was too busy to see me, so Rogerio stepped in. We hit it off, and though the acquisition never happened, a week later Rogerio and I were negotiating his move to Semco. His boss immediately countered with a raise and a promotion to plant director. Rogerio thought about the factory he would be running.

'It wasn't a place that you'd call a clean and efficient factory,' he remembers. 'The people there had no idea what they were producing. The ones who assembled displays didn't have a clue where the display would be used. There was no association between what the company produced and what people did. How could I offer them a compensation package based on results if they didn't know what they were producing?'

Rogerio decided to take the promotion only if he had full authority to make changes at the factory.

'My boss stood up and gave me a hug, and told me not to worry about those peasants,' he says. 'That was enough for me to refuse the offer. I understood that I would be a toy. I could only be the director if I played the game.'

At Semco, Rogerio realized early that our supermarket scales division could also develop weighing systems for various industries. He made a bid for business with Alcoa, but lost. He tried again with a Brazilian group called Ultra. He lost again. The second time, Rogerio refused to take no for an answer. He asked why so many times that finally Ultra's lead engineer told him that although we offered a better price, we'd lost because we couldn't show experience or expertise. Rogerio asked yet another question – would Ultra give us a chance to demonstrate competence?

Only to be polite, the engineer agreed. Rogerio and a software engineer then spent an entire weekend creating a model of a 300-metre industrial scale from a supermarket scale design. After he took the model to Ultra, we won the contract. When the system was delivered, the Belgian engineers who worked for Ultra called it the most modern in all their plants. It became a prototype for other scales.

All because Rogerio insisted on the leeway to ask questions and follow his gut instincts.

I once had a weekly lunch schedule that would have made any maître d' smile. Three to five business lunches a week. One sunny day I asked myself why I was going to lunch with a particular executive. Because that way you'll be closer to the person, I thought. Why do I want to be closer to the person when all I want is a professional relationship? Because close personal relationships generate better business. Why? Because people will not see you simply as a business, and may overlook some deficiency in price, quality or delivery because they relate to you as a person. Why, then, shouldn't I use those two hours a day for improving price, quality or delivery so that the personal relationship at lunch is no longer necessary?

That's when I stopped going to business lunches. I've kept those dates to three to five per year. My relentless whys freed me from a grinding lunch schedule.

Sometimes why seems unnecessary. Its obvious companies should grow. Everyone agrees, right? But why?

The 'adult' response to the question would be career opportunities, global reach, and economies of scale. Again I ask, why? Why are careers better in a company that grows, rather than in one that does not? Why is profit necessary above a small percentage over sales? What happens when there's too much profit? Are there any studies (none that I've seen) demonstrating that companies that grow fare better than ones that don't?

Soon enough there are no easy, comfortable answers.

Why can be lethal to a business. If you pull on that string, you may unravel an entire company. Something must form the thread that runs through the whole enterprise – a unifying principle, let's say. That has certainly been Semco's experience – in my 20 years at the company, we've been a pump manufacturer, a machinery specialist, a service company, a digital ventures company. We've transformed ourselves many times while remaining in all of these businesses. But if you ask people what Semco is, their answer will be the same as it was two decades ago. They won't cite our ever-changing product line. They won't cite a mission statement. People will talk about shared ideas, a precept that existed 20 years ago just as it exists today. And that comes from the freedom to ask, Why?

Semco's glass and steel high-rise headquarters is a far cry from the gritty industrial shop floor that my father, Antonio Curt Semler, founded in 1954. It started not long after he moved to Brazil from Argentina, having emigrated before that from his native Vienna. He patented a centrifuge for separating oils, and with that started his own small machine shop, choosing its name from a contraction of Semler & Company. Soon Semco was a $2 million a year business.

Then, in the late 1960s, my father formed a partnership with two British marine pump manufacturers, and Semco quickly became a major supplier to the Brazilian shipbuilding industry.

For the next 25 years, Semco built marine pumps, and its name became synonymous with the shipping industry. It could also have been synonymous with rigidity and tradition. When I was still quite young, my father assumed that I would take over Semco. I wasn't anywhere near as certain. I had spent many youthful years in a rock band, and one miserable summer as an intern in Semco's purchasing department. After that, I could only wonder: How can I spend the rest of my life doing this? How can I spend my life watching people to see whether they clock in on time? Why is this worth doing?

When I voiced my worry, I was reassured with 'that'll pass, young man,' or 'I, too, was like you once.' I could only think, I'm too young to accept this as a universal proof. Instead, I wanted to know if it was possible to liberate people and free them from the elements of life that make it a drag, by creating an entirely new kind of organization.

The answer lay in relinquishing control. It was a deceptively simple principle because it would mean instituting true democracy at Semco. I'd never run across a truly democratic company (and still haven't).

Believing my family wouldn't let me do my own thing at Semco, I spent a year investigating a faltering ladder manufacturer. I was then 21, and preferred the prospect of a small, dangerous venture before a commitment to family interests. On the day I was to sign the final papers for the ladder company, my father called me and proposed a deal.

After much debate and negotiation, we agreed I'd take over Semco and he would step back and allow me a free hand to re-make the company as I saw fit. I was so young that no one at Semco took the news seriously. Clovis Bojikian, one of five senior Semco managers and our venerable human resources guru, remembers coming to Semco for an interview shortly after I took over.

'They put me in a room, and a boy arrived,' Clovis says now. 'I thought he was a messenger. He was about my son's age. He sat down and started to ask me questions, and it was Ricardo Semler.'

Within days of taking over, I fired outright two-thirds of my father's most senior managers. I then spent the next two decades questioning, challenging and dismantling the traditional business practices at Semco.

Twenty years later, I can honestly say that our growth, our profit or the number of people we employ are secondary concerns. Outsiders want to know these things because they want to quantify our business. These are the yardsticks they turn to first. That's one of the reasons we're still privately held. I don't want to be burdened with the 90-day mind set of stock market analysts. It would cost us our solidity and force us to dance to a tune we don't understand – the scoreboard of analysts constrained by pension funds, investment sharks and little old ladies in Oklahoma.

We don't need that. We generate enough of our own cash, and we're growing nearly 40 percent a year without public investment. Sure, we've been hounded to take our company public, but we've never been able to answer Three Whys that question the purpose of that process and the money it would generate.

Yes, we're successful by market standards – we've grown, we've made more money, and we've added employees. But that success means little to me if it's measured only in these terms. Sure, it's wonderful to have money. But it doesn't change what it takes to get out of bed in the morning, go to work, and perform a job day after day. When I started with my family's company, that motivation was missing completely.

By the time Danilo Saicali came along, I had not only detonated Semco's structure, I'd written a book about the experience and become zealous about shattering long-held, rarely questioned ideas of how organizations should be set up.

These principles have resulted in tremendous growth: Semco has gone from my father's peak of $4 million a year to $35 million in annual revenue in 1994 – and $160 million in 2001.

My father's 90 employees have increased to nearly 3,000. We've moved from industrial manufacturing to services to high-technology without giving up any earlier businesses. Semco workers make money for the company – and take a good chunk of it for themselves in a profit-sharing plan. Most importantly, they make it the kind of organization people clamour to work for and where turnover is negligible.

Semco's experience befits more than just business. It's germane to any organization where sociology and anthropology guide how people interact. Type is irrelevant, and so is size – that's why Semco practices have been adopted at schools, hospitals, and police departments around the world.

Along the way, I've lost sight of what defines Semco. I can no longer say exactly what it is, or where it is going. That's not because it's too big to manage or I've stepped back too far from day-to-day operations. It's because I don't want to know where Semco is headed. It doesn't unnerve me to see nothing on the company's horizon. I want Semco and its employees to ramble through their days, to use instinct, opportunity and intrigue to choose projects and ventures.

I do not remember the last time Semco leaders tried to guess what size the company would grow to be, or how many people we might eventually employ. We don't talk about these things, much less try to quantify them in budgets or business plans.

That doesn't mean we don't think about the future. We spend a lot of time in what we call, in portuguese, 'ideas that pour from the sky' (known elsewhere as brainstorming sessions.) There we hack the future to death. We ask why repeatedly. We just don't write anything down in black and white with numbers. That's because any written plan is dangerous. People will follow a plan like a Pied Piper – mindlessly, with no thought as to their final destination.

We often jot down generic ideas and broad numbers so we can visualize the dimensions of a new product or service. Then, we throw those notes away. At the next meeting on the same idea, we'll start over, without the benefit of the original notes. That way we cannot fall into the trap of 'fixed assumptions'. We're obligated to reconsider all the variables.

Sometimes our meetings are like scenes from an Ingmar Bergman film – we address the same subject again and again. When an executive is new to Semco, he or she will often stammer: 'But we already ascertained that at the last meeting,' or 'Are we going to question the assumptions once again, instead of forging ahead?' They'll initially be frustrated at revisiting notions that were accepted during the last debate. But if they listen to their colleagues asking why, they'll find that additional flaws are often uncovered, or a new angle is discovered.

In the 1990s, our philosophies attracted attention. Six thousand people have since written to us out of curiosity about Semco, and hundreds of newspaper and magazine articles have featured our company. BBC Television and dozens of other TV programs have profiled us. I've given nearly 300 speeches to companies, conferences, charitable groups, youth groups and universities such as Stanford, Harvard, MIT, the London School of Economics and INSEAD. Semco is a case study at 76 universities, and texts of our

11

organizational practices are required reading at 271 other schools. Sixteen Master's and Doctorate candidates have made Semco the subject of their theses.

And the first book about Semco, *Maverick!*, was on bestseller lists in 12 countries and sold 1.1 million copies.

All of this demonstrates a *bona fide* interest in Semco. But when visitors learn that our economic success requires replacing control and structure with democracy in the workplace – well, often those starry-eyed executives go home afraid or unsure, too wary to make it happen in their workplaces.

Fortunately, my convictions have borne results that business people value, and more importantly, can understand – sustainability, productivity, profit, growth, new ventures. These are all a by-product of worker balance.

And balance is what we seek when we ask why. Balance ensues when people are given room to manoeuvre – so they can find out where their talents and interests lie, and merge their personal aspirations with the goals of the company. Once employees feel challenged, invigorated and productive, their efforts will naturally translate into profit and growth for the organization. That's what the Semco way is all about.

But you still want to know – just what does Semco do? We have 10 companies, give or take. I'm not sure because they come and go; we've had a minimum of five for 20 years. We also have six Internet companies, so we could claim 16 units. But we don't know how many of those will survive, or in what form. As I write, one of our companies is studying a merger with its competitors, one of our very large units is looking to buy a competitor, and one is a partnership that is about to go public in London, which would make us minority partners.

At the risk of offering a description, Semco is a federation of businesses – with a minimum common denominator. All our business units are highly engineered, premium providers and market leaders in their niches. We haven't ventured into any of them by chance.

The first, the industrial machinery unit, is what's left of my father's original business.

It began with marine pumps and moved into industrial mixers. It now produces only high-tech mixing equipment – the kind of complex, engineered industrial mixers used for pharmaceuticals and at candy factories. We manufacture all of General Food's gum mixers, for example. These large stainless steel mixers operate with electronic controls; one system mixes the ingredients, cuts and wraps the gum. Costing from half a million to six or seven million dollars apiece, we produce only a few each year.

The second unit is SemcoBAC; it's our second-oldest unit, a partnership with Baltimore Air Coil in the US. Essentially we make cooling towers for commercial properties. For example, we installed ice tanks on top of the Citibank headquarters in São Paulo. With that system, the air conditioning runs at night, when electricity is cheaper, to create ice. The ice then generates cooled air for the building during the day. We also produce refrigeration for breweries, and a system called District Cooling. We generate air conditioning for three city blocks, for example, and everyone in that district pays for what they use.

The third company is Cushman & Wakefield Semco, our eight-year-old partnership with the New York real estate company of the Rockefeller Group. We began this association assuming C&W's business model – we managed buildings for our commercial customers. But Semco account managers had already been long-conditioned to look for creative ideas and opportunities. They began asking our clients if there was anything else we could handle for them while we went about managing their office towers. Some of the biggest were more than happy to shed other logistical responsibilities, and soon we were managing all of their non-core business. At Itaú Bank (a major Brazilian institution), for example, we now manage the 126 sub-contractors who provide everything from data centre operation to logistics, cleaning, security, taxis, helicopters, all the way down to maintenance of the bank's ponds and fish, and the flowers that are delivered every Monday.

The fourth business unit is Semco Johnson Controls; in 1995 we entered a partnership with this $16 billion world leader in facility management. Johnson manages large properties like hospitals, airports, hotels, and huge factories.

The fifth is a company called ERM. We added this unit in 1996 in partnership with Environmental Resources Management, one of the world's premier environmental consulting companies. The unit does environmental site remediation (identifying hazardous material leaks, determining where the material went, remediating the source, hiring another company to clean up the site), environmental intelligence (brainstorming and pre-planning environmental issues before they become a concern), and risk management (studies on retrofitting windows on Chunnel trains, of hazardous material transporters, and offshore platform risk assessment, for example.) But we've added services of our own. We also trade and broker carbon emission certificates and outsource management of environmental departments at large corporations, facets of little interest to our US and British partners. In fact, when the opportunity first arose, ERM told us: 'We're not in that business.'

Then we have Semco Ventures, our nod to the Internet and our high-tech ventures unit. It houses 14 projects, but only four have evolved into working companies. The businesses are diverse, like one that manages virtual trade fairs with software that enables participants to attend via their laptops. Another is called Mobius and tracks financial records, so that a cheque written two years ago can appear within 40 seconds on a computer screen. Another venture on the cusp of becoming a business is based in Goa, India. That unit will process accounting for companies in South America. Because of the 12-hour time difference between South America and India, employees in Goa will be able to process the accounts while it is night in South America. Managers in Brazil will get up in the morning and their books will be tabulated. Goa is a logical choice because it was once a Portuguese protectorate and many people there speak portuguese.

In the high-tech arena, SemcoHR manages the outsourcing of HR activities for large companies. By keeping top experts on staff who specialize in recruitment, selection, training, medical assistance plans, pension plans, and benefit management, this company creates value by having expertise that very few companies can afford to keep in-house. It makes it a very agile way for a client to eliminate HR headaches, and retain only a few strategists. SemcoHR doesn't provide any services – it thinks for the client and manages the outsourcers.

An important innovation is that SemcoHR manages anyone who works for its clients – and not only their traditional employees. It manages part-timers, the semi-retired, commissioned salespeople, individual consultants and independent contractors as if they were employees – a feature that will be more relevant in the future as companies deal with greater numbers of workers who are not formal employees.

We've had our share of high-tech failures – ideas that died before becoming reality, and even companies that we shepherded into operation and then watched go down the drain with much of the rest of the Internet boom. Still, we're cultivating several more (some of which date from the dot.com era) in the hopes they will become businesses in the near future.

Another company is Semco-RGIS, which provides inventory control. At Wal-Mart in Brazil, for example, we count and record inventory. At a typical store, we deploy 160 people with thigh-top computers. They're trained to count and to depress the keyboard without looking at the computer. The computers are also radio controlled, and every two minutes their contents are downloaded and transmitted to a central computer. There the numbers are continuously bench-marked against inventory from all Wal-Marts, as well as against inventory at other stores like Sears and JC Penney.

If there's an anomaly, an alarm sounds. For example, if an inventory-taker counts 67 televisions but inputs 670, the system will beep and question the number. Since we conduct these inventories when the store is open (unlike most others in the industry), we are counting while customers are in the store and picking items off the shelves. So our system also reconciles the inventory with the check-out registers.

Semco's 10 (11, 13 . . . who's counting?) units are very diverse; in fact, anyone looking at them might wonder how such industries came to be part of the same business. But a closer look will reveal a hidden synergy between our businesses – synergy that we reached by following our instincts. We find this synergy by satisfying three basic criteria when we consider a new venture. First, we look for complexity, which for us usually means 'highly engineered'. Everything we do has a high entry barrier of complexity. If a new business isn't hard for us and for others to break into, then we're not interested.

Second, we demand that in each of our markets, we are the premium player. We want to offer a high-end product or service. That means we're always more expensive because we provide the premium that stretches what the customer will pay. And third, we want a unique niche in the market, one that makes us a major player in any given industry. To us, this follows naturally from the first two requirements. We want to be only in businesses where our disappearance would cause our disheartened customers to complain loudly. They'd survive, but they'd have substantial difficulty moving on.

All of our products and services meet these criteria.

Our standards constrain us when it comes to new ideas, new partners and new products. ERM International is a good illustration. Its biggest business is site studies. But Semco doesn't do them, even though our managers point out that we could chalk up $30 million almost overnight. But the business is relatively simple, and relatively easy to break into. It doesn't meet our complexity requirements, and so it doesn't add to our sustainability.

There are other examples. Union Banco, another huge real estate management client, asked us to take over arranging and running their cleaning crews. Janitors. How hard would that be? Not hard at all, that's the problem. Is it engineered? No, not in the least. Theoretically, we could clean. But we hate cleaning. Nobody at Semco is interested in cleaning. So we wouldn't do it well.

Outsiders look for commonalities because it's accepted that a common interest is fundamental to growth. If Semco can do anything, why don't we own a farm or run an architectural design firm? Is it true that stand-alone businesses that lack synergy have a limited capacity to grow? Yes. Biology shows us that common traits or interests foster growth. At Semco, we've spent years trying to figure out what those are.

So we leverage the power of our units. For example, Wal-Mart has gradually become a customer of four of our units – because our employees took the initiative, asked why, and 'rambled' into a new idea. We asked, and we received. Wal-Mart now uses Semco to count their inventory, manage their cooling towers, administer buildings and warehouses, and conduct environmental site investigation and remediation.

Other clients like GM, BankBoston and Unilever have become customers of multiple Semco units. This isn't unusual for us. The point of entry may change, but our objective remains the same – synergy.

Whichever unit serves as the point of entry, it soon finds business opportunities for the others. Signing on with a client is usually our biggest hurdle, because we are more expensive than our competitors. Once a customer is onboard, however, we rarely have operational problems, we rarely abandon a customer, and they rarely leave us. Repeat customers represent some 80 percent of our annual revenue. I can count on my fingers the number of clients who have dropped us in 20 years of business.

*

When Danilo arrived at Semco with a briefcase full of documents and notes, he found a company with all these diverse units. He also found it difficult to do his job without daily reports and staff meetings – not to mention staff! He met employees who comfortably challenged themselves and their colleagues with a barrage of whys, and who expected him to be equally comfortable with having little control over them.

His first week at work was a bewildering search for a place to plunk down his laptop, a way to replace his two secretaries, for help in operating the copy machine. He learned the merits of arriving at strange hours in a first-come-first-served parking lot, and discovered that at Semco, if you want to call someone to your office – well, first, you don't have an office, and second, the call may or may not generate a reaction.

But he'd already discovered that the predictable structure at his previous companies did not ensure his happiness. At Semco, he is able for the first time to travel during the week to his mountain retreat. It's strange for him to sit barefoot in his shorts, meditating in the blue-green mountains over the next e-mail he'll send. Recently he asked people on an international conference call to hold on while he looked for some papers. He was speaking to several vice-presidents of a potential partner in California, and realized that the papers he needed were jammed under his golf bag. He excused himself, muttering while he lifted the clubs. The others were a bit bemused, maybe a bit startled. In any case, he found the papers, and the discussion resumed. The deal went through, so apparently the interruption did not scare the partners away.

Danilo needn't be embarrassed, or look over his shoulder. No one at Semco questions his productivity. In fact, we're paying him to ponder the mountains in the middle of the workweek. I know he'll begin asking a lot of whys. He'll come up with better ideas, ramble into new opportunities, be more open to change, be willing to give up control and take on risk.

Soon he'll find the balance between his personal aspirations and his professional goals that he lacked in his previous jobs. In the end, everyone at Semco will benefit. That's a pretty good reason to pay him – or anyone – to retreat to the mountains.

CHAPTER 2

The Traditional Weekend Ended Long Ago

SOMETIMES AT WORKSHOPS I conduct, I ask participants to write down what they would rather be doing at that moment. I've never had someone write: 'Nothing. I signed up for this workshop, so this is exactly how I want to spend my time.' They always write fishing, golfing, being with my kids, digging in my garden, or even answering my e-mail.

But shouldn't they say the workshop is the only place they want to be? Why is it a given that work is the last thing someone wants to do? Instead, we lament being robbed of freedom. We talk so easily about how much we value our free time – but rarely make it a priority in our lives. Few of us even know what free time is anymore, or how to be genuinely idle. Yet few people if asked on their deathbed about their regrets would respond: 'I'm sorry I didn't spend more time at the office.'

People believe the opposite of work is leisure. But it isn't, it's idleness. Work is activity, so idleness is inactivity. Any good Greek philosopher can explain that.

We no longer grasp the difference between leisure time and being idle. Western society is highly structured. If you go to the beach, you don't spend the day 'doing nothing'. Within half an hour you're reading, walking, swimming, fretting about your tan or over-exposure. Most of us have to keep one eye on our children while slathering on sunscreen and planning dinner. Idleness is really just a change of scenery: There's no true opportunity to sit back, relax and

19

let the mind wander. Even when we set weekends aside to 'do the things I want,' we often spend most of Saturday and Sunday engaged in chores, personal tasks and other obligations that may not be work but are still often things we don't really want to do.

An American study in 2001 on how children use their time showed that kids between the ages of three and 12 spent 31 hours a week with their mothers and 23 hours with their fathers. The kids spent more time with their parents than children 20 years before did, but the study found that the increase was due to the hours the kids spent sitting in traffic with Mom while she ferried them to football games, piano practice and day camp, or from errand to errand. Are those kids better off than their predecessors were? Is that idle, quality time for anyone?

And now, technology permits work to seep increasingly into the gaps between weekend activities. We can work at home, be tracked on our cell phones at the beach, read reports sent to us anywhere via e-mail. Technology has made us accessible 24-hours a day, seven days a week. It has no respect for the weekend, or for the sanctity of a Sunday afternoon. Once, it was possible to completely avoid contact from the working world simply by refusing to give out a home phone number. Now, e-mail is coming to TV! And when a football match is on and a telltale beeping announces an e-mail with an exclamation mark, will anyone be able to ignore the message and watch another 30 minutes of the game?

Technology has encroached so deeply into our lives that I believe we must make deliberate efforts to beat it back. I have an idea for a technology respite at Semco, but no one agrees to let me test it. It makes them nervous, so they're resisting.

Two hours of general computer shutdown. Semco Unplugged. That's my impish dream.

My idea is to have a half-day, every so often, when the company is unplugged. What would people do if the whole system was down on purpose?

E-mail, the contemporary manifestation of Gutenberg's printing press, permits instant communication across seas, deserts and mountain ranges. But it also changes the profile of our working lives, and we are not prepared for that. It makes communication more efficient, but it also makes it far too easy for anyone to find us. It frees up time – which we immediately fill with more e-mail. With e-mail, people are intensely and continuously involved in minutiae, and that creates a new form of information overload. People who still haven't mastered time management now have e-mail added to the demand on their energies. We face a glut of messages every day, but have come to believe we can't live without our electronic mail boxes.

That's why Semco employees are so wary of my idea to unplug their computers without notice.

Of course e-mail is often down at random for one reason or another – problems with hardware, the phone lines, a server. When that happens, anxiety rises very quickly, especially if employees have an outbox full of mail primed to be shot into the ether, or they're waiting for information to arrive from the cosmic e-mailman. Rather than exacerbating that anxiety, unplugging the company for half a day would restore the primitive practice of thinking about what we're doing instead of just yammering non-stop with the world.

Of course my plan is far from perfect. If people know that at a certain time on a certain day their electronic contact with the outside world will be severed, then they'll just organize their day around their crippled computer. They might not even come to work that day. Or they'll find other work to fill the three hours. The only way to experiment would be to unplug the system at random. But then we have to worry that it might happen in the middle of a dramatic and very important negotiation. So perhaps we would need to keep one computer terminal connected for emergencies.

And maybe people will line up for half a mile to use the emergency line, and I'll be pushed and jeered out of a job.

I don't know what form it will take, or whether it will start with half a day a month and then increase. I'm enthusiastic about the idea, even though I know it's still artificial. I may just be trying to fake a by-gone world.

Technology is a double-edged sword. We marvel at what man has produced, and are constantly amazed at the gadgets and break-throughs emerging from cyberspace. One moment it's wireless e-mail, the next it's bacteria-based electronics that warn you when your milk is no longer fresh. Now my fridge will automatically re-order things. What could be bad about that? (For the record, it sounds awful to me). But with our dependence on technology, we're standing at the top of a slippery slope – too soon we become slaves to gadgets and digital services. Does anyone know how to delete an e-mail without first answering it? Some people may have taken that plunge, but technology remains a step ahead – now some communications programs alert the sender the moment you have opened their message. George Orwell would be smiling.

My small, lightweight laptop computer hardly appears intimidating. But in fact, it has enslaved me, too. When I travel, I often leave things at home (Amex card included). I customarily forget socks, ties and cufflinks. But the only thing I am never without is a paper clip. It's the only tool that fits into the re-set button on the base of my laptop.

For all the high-tech sophistication of my portable computer, I am completely at the mercy of the software that so often causes my machine to freeze up. Not to mention how irate I become when my inanimate, ignorant computer blatantly accuses me of having committed illegal acts – thus finding itself under the obligation to shut me down without recourse! The only recourse is to poke at the re-set function. Oh, how I enjoy putting it out of its misery with a low-tech paper clip.

My experience is a nice way to illustrate how Semco makes a deliberate effort not to confuse progress with essence. For us, technology is simply 'nice to have'. Sure, we have our share of techies, high-end servers and fancy equipment. But we try to keep technology down to ancillary status. We have no such thing as a CTO, a chief technology officer. Just as we have done away with human resources as a department, we resist any effort to create a unit around technology.

Don't misunderstand, we don't shun technology. We adopted mini-computers, Fortran IV, Cobol and the other 'essential' languages of the 1970s, and then were among the first buyers of the IBM microcomputer in the early 1980s (or the MRPS mega-systems, or the Oracle 9i platforms). We stay abreast of technology. But it's never a priority, it's never handled through Master Plans and Programs, never receives separate storage space. Equipment and people are scattered all over, and each company has the freedom to use whatever hardware or machinery it wants.

Heresy! the experts will scream. Scale economies go out the window, specialization is lost. But no one ever accounts for the excessive specialization, or the diseconomies of scale. Sure, it might be better to combine several computer orders and buy from one source. But consider this: Wandering through Semco, one will be bewildered at the makes, brands and types of equipment littering the desks, server rooms and back offices. Samsung, LG, IBM, HP,

Toshiba, Sony, you name it. There's always someone with something new. It is very common for our US partners to gaze at new notebook computers or radio-controlled servers. They want – no, need – the newest thing. But because of their centralized, careful purchasing plans, they're always slightly behind the times (or lagging substantially). It takes a long while to make low-risk decisions in global companies. So they're almost always using outdated equipment, until they make the momentous decision to invest millions in purchasing committees, Master Plans and bureaucratic RFIs, (Requests for Information), RFPs (Requests for Proposal), and final bids.

Then their systems are brand spanking new for six months, whereupon they become obsolete and the whole enterprise must begin anew – but not too soon, mind you, because they have to justify and depreciate the purchase they just made. One of our partners in 2001 took months to decide between Compaq and Hewlett Packard – and as soon as the battle was over, HP bought Compaq.

This explosion of technology means we must re-gain the time we've lost to the merging of personal and work life. People should be allowed and encouraged to re-arrange their week, drop the traditional notion of a weekend, and divide the seven days among company time, personal time and idleness. Then they should look for wasted hours and days. Rush hour, for example. Or time spent trying to do two things at once. Hours intended for relaxing which are really filled with errands. It might be more efficient to run those errands on a quiet Monday – especially if you've spent part of Sunday answering e-mail.

Anyone who can eliminate the stress of an over-taxed schedule, arrange her work week so she can sleep according to her bio-rhythms rather than a time clock, and enjoy a sunny Monday on the beach after working through a chilly Sunday will be a much more productive worker.

Such redistribution should be undertaken to restore serenity and space to think. As lofty as this may sound, it will ultimately benefit organizations because employees will find equilibrium for their professional, personal and spiritual lives. This isn't just an avant-garde approach to running a company. It's a sound strategy for business intelligence and competitive savvy.

People have to learn for themselves that the inner connection, the care and feeding of their soul, doesn't come from working 60-hour weeks to acquire a radio, a TV, a cable hook up, cars or houses (and onward to the private helicopter and pilot). Or that once they acquire all these toys, they will necessarily be happy, contented, fulfilled. On the contrary. They'll be happy once they discover that those toys are not stepping-stones to nirvana.

Let's say you could remove the burden of work, declare every day a Saturday, and leave people alone with their toys and accessories. You wouldn't be granting them automatic peace and contentment. That's what is important to understand about 'the seven-day weekend'. That's what I mean when I say that people who lose their weekend haven't lost idleness.

Since work is so ubiquitous – since there's no getting away from it – we have to find ways to make it fulfilling. Consider religion. We're familiar with Western religion. Yet when most Westerners examine religious philosophy, a great many admire the ones they have no experience with, and to which they cannot relate – Eastern religions like Hinduism and Buddhism. They admire the adherents and decide that their philosophies are healthy for the soul. Look at that Tibetan monk, they say. Now there's a happy, content man, at peace with himself and the world around him.

But if Buddhist monks experience greater harmony than the rest of us, it's probably because of the symbiosis between their 'work', and their intimate beliefs and sense of purpose.

We all need that symbiosis. First we have to face up to the seven-day weekend, and re-organize daily life with that in mind. Sociologists might argue that eliminating fixed days and events, creating a world of constant and sudden change, would make people insecure. Even unhinged. But the seven-day weekend doesn't mean that regular Sunday lunch with the parents will cease to exist, or that weekly Mass will be on erratic days. People will maintain their important routines, just as they do now – without feeling that Sunday lunch is a burden they wish they could cancel. The rest of the time, they'll create other fixed events – like Marcio Batoni, the CEO of Semco RGIS, who has a regular Tuesday afternoon movie date with his wife. But instead of expecting – even demanding – that our extra work hours be traded for an equal amount of personal time, we accept our lack of freedom because of the Western 'work ethic'. Judeo-Christian culture teaches that good earthly works will lead to heavenly reward (Protestants promote this with fewer ritual trimmings than Catholics). It's probably a defence mechanism – believing thus allows people to feel gratified by working all the time.

We have to justify those long work weeks, the extra work on the Sabbath (either one). It'll be worth it in the end, when the heavenly payoff is doled out at the pearly gates, or at least upon retirement.

Semco is bucking not only the traditional business model – we're resisting a code of behaviour at the very core of Western culture. No wonder our ideals are hard for outsiders and other companies to embrace.

Take Danilo Saicali, for example. He's passionate about his house in the country. But in the months that he's been with Semco, he's worked from there only a handful of times. I urged him to exploit this freedom and work there often, but that's hard for him to absorb. In my experience, it's hard for everyone to absorb. Lately Danilo has begun working at his country house on Fridays, and if he sticks with that, he'll begin to eliminate his weekend.

People have learned to answer e-mails on Sunday evenings but they don't know how to go to the movies on Monday afternoon.

Balancing the two is important for anyone, under any circumstances, but becomes particularly critical when life takes an unexpected turn. Several years ago, João Vendramim lost his wife of more than 30 years to cancer. Magali Vendramim was an easy-going, friendly woman, and when she was first diagnosed, Semco's ideals became very real for Vendramim. His wife was immediately his first priority, compelling him by default into a flexible schedule.

'I'd come to work a few times a week, but even then I wasn't here,' he remembers now. He never felt guilty about it, and no one at Semco ever expected anything else. We supported his need for balance and a system that accepted it was already in place.

But João didn't believe he could live without his wife. He resigned from Semco three different times, and each time a troop assembled to dissuade him. On one harrowing occasion, João asked the company 'to just take care of my wife and kids – and leave me be.' That fateful year was filled with highly charged emotion. But the Semco way prevailed – we were all forced to deal with Vendramim's tragedy openly, and in the context of his whole life. It paid off. We managed to keep Vendramim, he managed to keep his head, and the long, difficult recovery from mourning was not made worse by rash decisions.

At Semco we insist that our people form new habits. They start by adopting one abiding principle at Semco – avoid routine, steer clear of habit. As such, we've actively eliminated some of the more familiar, dependable structures of most organizations. We tossed the rigorous nine-to-five, Monday through Friday schedule out the window. Notions of 'flexitime' have been around for decades, but almost always with a tit-for-tat approach. Workers could put in a ten-hour day for two weeks in return for Fridays off. They could come in at 5a.m. and leave earlier than their colleagues, as long as they put in eight hours each day. But for many people, there's virtually no end to the workday. The same Intranets, web access, modems, e-mail, pagers, cellular phones, and laptops that have ended the weekend have also eliminated the nine-to-five workday.

Márcia Fração started working when she was 13, after her father died. She came to Semco in 1986, and is now Rogerio Ottolia's deputy at Semco MAQ.

'In all these years, Semco never discounted a minute's worth of salary, even when I was late or absent,' she says. 'I take a reciprocity position. When Semco needs me I am there. When my brother got sick, I was gone for four days and Semco didn't discount a penny from my cheque. In turn, I haven't claimed overtime for the weekends I worked on a commercial exhibition. There's a virtuous circle in place that requires no overt declaration.

'At Semco, we only work, we don't have to show we are working,' she says. 'That's superfluous.'

We also dumped any requirement that employees work only in a specific office, factory or other piece of Semco real estate. And we are dismantling our own headquarters in favour of satellite and portable offices.

When Semco first introduced flexible work schedules and impermanent offices in the mid-1980s, virtually everyone predicted they'd fail immediately. Couldn't we see that people need regular hours and regular contact with each other – that they need to speak to each other face-to-face, to know when and where to find one another? They'd need a common meeting ground, the proverbial gathering around the water cooler (or cappuccino machine). Nowhere was this more obvious and critical than on the assembly line, the naysayers said. So when we expanded flexitime to include assembly line workers, all intellectual hell broke loose. That was taking it too far, we heard – we were ignoring the basic requirements of a shop floor. Of course an assembly line cannot have flexitime, people hollered. And we would ask: Why?

Wasn't it obvious? If workers weren't working at the same time, the assembly lines would grind to a halt. We know that, but so do the adults who work on it. And why would they jeopardize their output, their jobs? If they don't care that the assembly line moves or stops, then we have a much graver problem, and the sooner we find out the better. I was confident that our assembly line workers would implement the flexitime schedule in a way that kept operations running smoothly. But others were sceptical. To our surprise, no one was more sceptical than the Metalworker's Union. They held us up for almost six months with constant debate over what we were really up to. During one memorable meeting, the union director told us that he thought he'd figured it out. It was like this, he explained: Labour law in Brazil says that every employee has the right to be five minutes late, every day, without penalty. Now, if the worker had the flexibility of coming in between 6:00 and 9:00 in the morning, how would he make use of his five minutes leeway?

We were at a loss to answer that.

In the end both the union and our middle management approved flexitime on an experimental basis. Both wanted a careful, monitored test. It was agreed that a committee would meet twice-a-day for the first month, once-a-day for two months thereafter, and finally twice-a-week for a year, to deal with all the inevitable problems, stoppages and conflicts.

That committee never met. The day before the program began, people turned to their left and right and asked what time the others would be coming in next morning. End of story.

Now Semco employees are free to customize their workdays, to come in earlier or later than traditional schedules. The hours they work are determined by their self-interest, not by company dictates. They're the best judges of the amount of time and the proper place necessary to get their job done.

Yet people continue to assume that chaos would ensue if everyone were left to choose their own work time. Journalists tell me that newspapers wouldn't appear on some days, doctors say that operations would be cancelled due to an anaesthetist who didn't show up, actors say that their play's curtain would never go up, and transport specialists warrant that the subway would never run.

Nonsense.

Do we really believe that responsible adults, whether interested or not, committed to the company or service or not, would simply not show up after promising to do so? That a journalist who understands the urgency of headlines will go to the movies while the presses are

27

standing still, waiting for his submission, that the woman who studied anaesthetics for years will simply roll over in bed, thinking that the patient should have taken more care with his cholesterol? Or that actors who choose the theatre will leave the public hanging, and a subway car driver will shrug and take his granddaughter to school while 45,000 people stand on the platform, looking into a dark tunnel for a train that never arrives? Come on. What a disheartening view of humankind.

The same doomsayers raised their voices when we first proposed 20 years ago that people could work away from the office. That won't succeed either, they said.

Social scientists wondered whether people would be able to work far from one another. What would happen to tribal instincts in the absence of a meeting ground? People who worked at home would slowly lose their sense of community. People would lose their bearings if they couldn't interact to update themselves.

There are two false dilemmas in those arguments. The first is that home will replace the office as the only work location. That's just not true. Our people work in Semco's satellite offices and 'at home' (meaning wherever they want – the house, a café, a park). They move around all the time, and when they do they meet with whomever they need to as soon as they begin to feel out of touch (which I doubt happens so frequently).

The second false assumption is that business or the work environment is the only tribal affiliation people have. Anyone who works at home will find they actually belong to four or five 'tribes'. And, of course, they can meet by the water cooler any time, by going in to an office for a short while each day, or for several full days in a row.

Besides, there's no getting around the inevitability of working away from the office. In 1990, only four million people 'telecommuted' from home or somewhere else in the US. By 2000, there were 23.6 million telecommuters.

In the early 1980s (two decades, or a tech-light-year ago), I was already working three half-days a week at home. Given that summers in Brazil can be sweltering, I was often sitting in shorts by the pool, with stacks of yellow telexes at my side. In the beginning, I was constantly vexed when a messenger showed up with the office mail pouch – when the bell rang, I would sometimes pull on a pair of trousers, just to look more professional. I kept imagining the young man going back to the company and roaming the corridors with the

28

gossip that the boss was sunbathing while everyone else was toiling in the dark hell of the greasy machine world.

After a while, I figured that everyone already knew I worked at a garden table in my shorts, and I stopped worrying about it. Clearly, I was still getting my work done. Slowly, more of our directors started working from home (or elsewhere). Then our middle-managers, followed by ordinary employees.

In any event, the traditional office will never disappear completely. There will always be a certain percentage of people who cannot work at home – they don't have the space, they have kids in the house, or someone noisily vacuuming, or they don't have the discipline to stop watching TV. For these, satellite offices around town are part of the solution.

It all started when Eugenio Singer, the CEO of ERM, could no longer face the two-hour drive to work from his home in the São Paulo neighbourhood of Alphaville.

'He decided to rent a room near his home in Alphaville,' remembers Cecília Negrão Balby. 'This was before we had an office there. So ERM inadvertently opened the first satellite office for the company. (In a way, they also pioneered our non-territorial office. 'We kept Eugenio's office empty at the main building, so I was always in there when he came to work,' Cecília says. 'We would regularly share his table or he would let me work alone in there.')

The decentralized office system has several advantages. Some are obvious. Imagine working five hours after lunch before heading to the parking garage for a 60-minute drive to a restaurant. You'd arrive at about 7p.m. A Semco worker could leave at 3p.m., drive 15 minutes to the satellite office closest to the restaurant, read a queue of e-mails, and then saunter slowly to dinner at a quarter to seven. She wouldn't have those e-mails hanging over her head, and perhaps might even enjoy a part of a beautiful day before arriving fresh to meet husband and friends.

Another advantage is even more powerful: We've done away with another layer of control.

'If the boss doesn't really believe in freedom at work, at least he won't be able to look at his people with reprimanding eyes,' says João Vendramim. 'Sooner or later, that kind of boss will be the one to leave.'

With satellite offices, a boss' control is eliminated. If employees can come in anytime, work anywhere, and take sole charge of their hours, how can they be controlled? At Semco, managers are concerned with the essence of what employees do for the company, nothing more – certainly not the 'boarding school' issues of who arrived at what time, wearing what clothes, and left when, to go where. So it all comes back to that hardest of all reforms – relinquishing control. And giving it up happily, no less.

Managers who came of age in the many decades since Henry Ford, believe that 'you get what you see' – and they have to see their employees at work. But cost and technology mean that even satellite offices will someday be passé. People will work wherever they are. Companies hoping to recruit the best and the brightest must demonstrate that they trust employees with the freedom to work anywhere. They must assume that they're buying talent and dedication, not what the Brazilians call 'butt-on-chair time'.

Those old timers can learn a thing or two about this from newcomers. Young workers take for granted some of these 'radical ideas' – that they'll have freedom to balance their work and personal lives, that they'll be able to shift their work and leisure time around, that they can customize their jobs so they remain interested and inspired.

José Carlos Reis de Magalhaes was just 23 when he came to work at Semco. He'd only recently graduated from one of Brazil's top business schools, and was working at an important and aggressive investment bank, managing its Internet ventures in the construction industry. An uncle of his introduced us, and I learned to call him by the nickname everyone uses, Zeca. I immediately recognized Zeca's passion for work. He reminded me of myself at his age. Very quickly I wanted him to help launch Semco Ventures, our high-tech unit. When he quit the investment bank, his infuriated bosses couldn't understand why he would leave an established, venerable organization for a start-up. But Zeca already felt something those older executives had yet to learn – that status, power and even money are sometimes not enough to make a job interesting. Or maybe it was just that he wanted to have lunch with his girlfriend occasionally. It's not unusual for Zeca to work 12-hour days. That makes it hard to find time for friends or family. But he regularly has long lunches with his girlfriend. 'Only because I work at Semco,' he says. 'Nowhere else could I do that without feeling guilty.'

No one tracks when Zeca puts in his 12 hours – often they're in the middle of the night. It's up to him. Shortly after he started at Semco, the Brazilian tennis champion Gustavo Kuerten played in the Roland Garros finals – (France's Wimbledon, where Kuerten was twice champion). An avid tennis fan, Zeca thought nothing of taking off whole days during the tournament. He didn't philosophize over whether it was right or wrong – and he didn't ask permission. The matches were played in the middle of the day, so Zeca simply made it clear he'd be home watching TV and would work at night instead (maybe). He didn't miss a match – and his work didn't suffer either. On the contrary, pursuing his hobbies (or his girlfriend) mean balance to him.

Francisco Alves Pereira is a shop floor manager at Semco Processes, and he likes to stay home on the days before a new project begins. A big man who is rarely without a pair of safety glasses slung around his neck, he prefers to think in comfort and solitude about how he'll set up the factory floor and how to configure space for assembling new machinery. He makes those decisions, not an engineer (a good example of how democracy blurs the traditional lines between blue and white-collar workers).

Once Francisco figures out how he wants to assemble a new machine, his team settles on an arrival time. Each project can have a different workday schedule. Usually they choose an early start-time, to avoid São Paulo's horrific traffic and get to and from work earlier than other commuters.

Francisco works with a group of six others, but often hires ex-employees for short-term projects. He looks for multi-skilled workers, people who can offer services or parts to Semco. His unit out-sources as much as it can. 'People tell me what has to be achieved, what machine has to be assembled, but how it will be done is my business,' Francisco says. He's had offers to work elsewhere – for more money – including from a former boss who worked at a biscuit machine factory that once belonged to Semco. Francisco declined, saying, 'I like the environment at Semco. I wouldn't want to risk this at a traditional company.'

Traffic isn't the only reason for elastic work schedules. By the same token of bio-rhythms, if I demand that a worker show up at 8a.m. even if she is someone who regularly sleeps until 9, all I will get is a couple of hours of her least productive time. And if I'm closing down at 6p.m., I'm sending her home just as she's hitting her stride. Her best hours may be from six to eight. Someone else may be alert and prolific after a 20-minute catnap in the afternoon.

If I insist on standard work hours, I may be sacrificing a certain amount of employee potential every day. By encouraging uniformity, I lose productivity.

By changing the rules, we remove the obstacles that throw people's lives out of whack. When we tell people they're free to work closer to their homes, to come to the office only when they need to, to work odd hours or take a weekday off in exchange for having laboured on a Sunday, we're really telling them that there are no rules when it comes to finding a balance in their lives. Everything at Semco that is designed to foster change, innovation and freedom is really there to help create that balance.

This is where Semco's *Retire-A-Little* program comes in. By most standards, this is going to sound cuckoo. But it takes life cycles into account when planning how to spend a lifetime. It expands on my conviction that we should redistribute the work week by providing a way to redistribute the time devoted to an entire career.

It goes like this: If you plot the curve of human health, you easily see that the climax of physical capabilities is in the 20s and 30s. The downturn is heaviest after 60. On another graph, you can plot financial independence and see the height is usually between 50 and 60. On a third graph, idle time naturally peaks after age 70.

The sad conclusion is that when you're most fit to realize your dreams, you don't have the money for them, and when you have the most time and money on your hands, you no longer have the stamina. Aren't we avoiding the obvious? Shouldn't this system be replaced with one that allows for a 'best of' practice? Best of physical abilities with best of work performance and best of family balance. Let's shift some of the strengths of youth to the days of old age, and vice versa – and use the business organization to do it.

Our *Retire-A-Little* program addresses the ironies inherent in our life cycle like this: You acquire from the company as much early retirement time as you wish. Say, 10 percent of your time. Let's say that amounts to an afternoon per week, and that the company sells it to you at something below par value.

Now, Wednesday afternoons are yours, to pursue those interests that you would ordinarily reserve for retirement. Fishing, weaving, gardening, studying. Your paycheque comes with a slight discount, but you've authentically and unarguably bought back some freedom from the boss.

If everyone knew how to spend an afternoon in the garden (and enjoy it with a clear conscience!), maybe the buying and selling could be done away with. In that case, company work could be accomplished on Sunday. With the 'seven-day weekend,' that kind of exchange would be inherent. We're not there yet, however.

In the meantime, with *Retire-A-Little*, you've bought time, and received it, so the transaction is complete. But Semco adds another dimension to it. You receive a voucher for work after your retirement. So, if you took off 100 Wednesday afternoons, you are now entitled to redeem such vouchers after your retirement. In essence, by showing up with your voucher and saying: I'd now like to work one Wednesday a week, for two years, and receive proportional pay.

You've effectively exchanged early retirement for later work. You mountain climb on Wednesdays this year, and you think about our new product on Wednesdays ten years from now.

It's too early to know how we will deal with the offshoot issues that this program raises: Will people fret that the company may not exist when they retire? Will our finance people worry about too many people showing up in a decade for work that we no longer have? I can think of many reasons to hesitate – as I could have for every one of the 30 or so innovative ideas we put in place in the last two decades. Like everything else at Semco, *Retire-A-Little* is chiefly designed to push boundaries and test the future today.

I've created quirky practices of my own to combine work with personal goals, and to pick and choose my hours and work places.

I have a habit that I call e-bike. I need a daily hour of exercise, and an hour or so just to keep up with the Joneses of e-mail. From the 134 e-mails I receive on average each day (last six months' statistics), about 40 must be answered. So I retreat to my gym, where I have an exercise bicycle equipped with a sturdy platform for my notebook computer. I plug in and pedal for 60 minutes into the galaxy of e-bike. Fitness purists may say I'm not dedicated enough to my exercise, and the people who receive my mails know that my 'handwriting' shakes and that I don't correct typos. But I get off that machine feeling four pounds lighter, half of that from my brain alone.

This is one way in which I strive to find a balance between technology, well being, work and personal life.

I do this at 6a.m. I don't actually like to wake up that early, although I love being up at that time, once I've groaned and moaned my way out of the bed, past the mirror and down the stairs for an espresso (no sugar). The day begins peacefully; the city shakes off its indolence, the dull roar of the metropolis rumbles in the distance, and

I often think of my father and his early rising habits. I remember sitting on the edge of the bathtub at 7a.m., watching my father shave and listening to him describe the important issues that would fill his day. I was a pre-teen at the time, and the problems he dealt with meant very little to me. Maybe I was a good listener, maybe he just needed to talk, but I vividly recall the ambience, the sharp, exact strokes of his razor, the sound of the scraping on the skin and the long faces he pulled as he made his skin taut. These images and sensations fill my mind on many days as I shave after e-bike.

Years before e-bike, I sojourned with the extraordinary Spanish architect Santiago Calatrava. I had asked him to design a studio home on the water for me. I'd bought a piece of rock by the pounding sea, a mere hour from São Paulo, and the studio was meant as a work space where I could spend a night. It was intended for those days that call for sea air and the rush of waves on the cliff, but still hold a lot of work that must be done.

Calatrava is a maverick in his field. He studied engineering after his first drawings as an architect were dismissed by contractors as unfeasible. He is now a professor at the ETH in Zurich, one of the world's leading engineering schools. His designs of harp-like bridges in Spain, his Montjuic Olympic communications tower, the TGV station in Lyon and the new Museum of Modern Art in Milwaukee are all testaments to his unusual talent.

I cite Calatrava here for several reasons: Firstly, because he has found an enviable equilibrium between technology and art, personal life and work. It's enough to hear his dissertations on Michelangelo, cris-crossed with explanations on the marvels of aluminium tension relief plastics. Or to see him bundled up with one of his three kids, speaking italian, swedish, swiss-german or spanish, indiscriminately, as he prepares them for school in the lakeside house in Zurich where he keeps offices upstairs.

In order to spend as much time as possible with his family, he wakes up at 4:30 and goes down to the empty, dark hall, where he works, sketches and thinks until breakfast time. At eightish everyone is awake, and he spends quality time with them. He walks and skis, and then only returns to work in the mid-afternoon, through to dinnertime.

The rest of his time is like that, wherever he is, and he has offices in Valencia and Paris, as well as work in places from New York to Kuala Lumpur. He is extraordinarily productive, there are books filled with his intricate and mind-boggling projects, and he is still in his forties.

With this example in mind, I took to waking up at 5:30, which has now crept to 6a.m. By 7:30 I have my e-mail up to date, and have fired away dozens of messages, read the on-line news of the local newspapers, the *Financial Times*, the *Wall St Journal*, as well as the odd on-line Sotheby's catalogue, wine rarities journal or palm tree society newsletter.

Having become notorious at Semco for two huge wastepaper baskets under my desk, to symbolize what I think of all the paper that comes my way, I am an avid deleter. If the message cannot be answered by anyone else, and if small disasters will occur should I not answer, I reply. Otherwise, I fill my computer's bottomless, invisible wastepaper basket with furious quantities of discarded e-mails. Recently I emptied my recycling bin to find I had dumped 11,455 into the garbage can in the sky.

My replies are mostly monosyllabic. Sometimes people will scroll up and down for the answer to their two page memo, only to find that there is a little word up there that says 'OK'. No name, no signature, just 'r' sometimes. I make immediate decisions about everything that comes in, and don't leave e-mails for later. Otherwise they pile up malignantly, relentless and unforgiving, giving me that high school homework depression.

I rarely did my homework, for that matter, but learned back then that stress is the difference between your expectations and your reality.

After jacuzzi and breakfast, it's still only about 8a.m. People are stalled on the highways, and I'm ready to think. There will be two, or four, or maybe six important tasks for the day. Some people think there must be many more. But I remind them that those four important tasks a day equal a thousand important things per year, or ten thousand tasks by the time your kid is ten-years-old. Nobody can have that many important tasks to perform. When I finish the ones I've set out to do, I'm finished for the day. If I'm done before lunch, lucky me. Since I don't 'do' lunch, I usually eat at home. The lunches that I indulge in are no different on weekdays or weekends. The same leisurely pace, the same time for a cigar. After all my leisurely lunch only takes an hour or so and I would use up more than that in traffic having lunch with a business associate.

My weekday and the weekend have been interchangeable for almost ten years. I take my son bicycling any day of the week, and we also go to the lake to feed the ducks – even though he eats most of the old bread himself, to the chagrin of the confused water birds. It might be Tuesday afternoon or Sunday morning. Most of the time it would be difficult to say.

I definitely have a hard time knowing what day of the week it is.

I drive to the mountain ranch on Thursdays, or Saturdays, and return on Mondays, or Wednesdays. What difference does it make? I answer e-mails on weekends early, usually at the same 6a.m.

People question whether this doesn't take the joy out of the weekend. It could, surely, but I've transported joy to every weekday. I'll go to a movie on a grey afternoon, or for a hike in the hills early on a Wednesday. And even with the volume of mail I get, I've never heard someone from Semco complain that I'm slow to reply – very rarely does it take longer than a day to receive an answer to an e-mail that was sent to me.

Ah, well and easy, if you own your company, some will say. But it doesn't take family wealth, a mountain retreat or being a CEO to achieve this schedule or pace in life. It's simply a question of choice: To find balance between the personal and the professional. My work, my responsibilities and Semco don't suffer because I regularly walk down a country lane, puffing on a cigar as I gaze at the horizon. That's when ideas come to me. That's also the time the Semco crowd dreads most. God forbid that man is walking with a cigar, they think. That's when I get subversive, with dangerous notions such as stringing hammocks in the office and banning e-mail on random days.

Everyone in an organization has such choices – but most don't realize it. We are caught in routines that eat up the precious time we need for thinking. People accept rules, even when they no longer exist!

Fifteen years ago, Semco adopted a two-week paid paternity leave policy for new fathers. Not a single father has made use of it. The same is true for a policy that allows people to take off Monday mornings if they've been out of town over the weekend. It's supposed to help them avoid the mad rush of traffic returning to the metropolis. Very few people use it, even when we remind them and badger them in e-mails and circulars.

Freedom is no easy thing. It doesn't make life carefree – because it introduces difficult choices. It's much easier for people to give into a familiar system in which they don't have to make any decisions.

Recently we invited people to bring their kids or spouses to work on occasion. Chaos, many said! There will be children hanging up phones in the middle of conference calls, toddlers throwing milk into the web servers, wives who become jealous when they see pretty girls in the office, husbands who will not like the look of his wife's boss. On and on. Silly. No such things happen – or if they do, one can always call back, wipe off the server, explain the bosses and colleagues – and get the parties to meet each other.

Stress relievers, such as golf before a conference call, or a break on the beach between inventories, are vital. Executives who are embarrassed to take these breaks or the company that frowns on them are anachronistic. Stress is a major disruption, and its effects, such as burn out, are grim reapers for talented people.

How to deal with every day stress? I spent many years setting my watch five minutes fast. I thought that was so smart. I'd increase my chances of being on time, and also give myself a little boost of relief at the last minute when I 'realized' I had five minutes to spare.

I know people who started out innocently enough, like me, and now set their watches 15 or 20 minutes ahead.

Recently at Semco I gave a talk called 'The Merits of Omission'. I recommended that everyone set back their watches. It works like this: Suppose you're in stuck in traffic on the way to an appointment. Gridlock, horns, lights that go red, green and red before you can inch ahead. Soon you're ready to punch numbers into your cell phone to let people know you're going to be late. However thoughtful, it doesn't change the fact that several people are waiting for you to arrive.

Some fixed variables are at work here. First, you may be one of those people who are always in a rush, always late. I used to be chronically tardy, a bad habit that worsened when I moved close to our head office 10 years ago. I was only one traffic light away – too close to arrive on time. So I was constantly rushing into the office out of breath and long after the people who lived across town were already seated.

Peter Kuhlman, an executive at RGIS, remembers a time I explained why I missed a meeting. I was waylaid at home, I said, waiting for a physical therapist to treat a back problem. The man never arrived – and I found out later that he'd gone to the wrong house and given a massage to the wrong patient! Peter, of course, considered this the lamest excuse he had ever heard. In truth, my neighbour's name is also Ricardo, and my street number is 304, and his 204, and someone in his house was changing massage therapists at the time. But I concede that this is a long shot.

Another fixed variable is that once late (and fuming as another car cuts in front of you and traffic refuses to move) there is very little you can do about it. Sure, you can kick yourself every four minutes for not having left earlier. You can also think up wilder and wilder excuses – traffic no longer impresses anyone, anywhere in the world. (For years I thought São Paulo led the world in traffic snarls, until I experienced Bangkok gridlock. It took me an hour and twenty minutes to drive to an early meeting just ten blocks from my hotel. I asked what time I should plan to set out for the airport that night. 'If I were you,' someone said, 'I'd leave now.')

So there you are, thinking of what to say. First you stick to the real events that took place in your life recently – which you could borrow for the occasion. 'So sorry, gentlemen, my son decided to play hide and seek with my car keys.'

As you realize how flimsy they are, they become more substantial. When you finally decide to enter with a grave demeanour, putting on your 'mother-in-law in a coma' face, you know you're suffering from traffic grand delusion.

That's just a form of modern life stress, but it needn't be. Imagine the same situation with your watch set back 15 minutes. Now, you are sitting in the same mess, glancing at your watch on occasion, relieved there's still time left. The delays are the same, your reaction is the same, but now you are surprised to see that you're late when you pass the clock above the secretary's desk. Even better, you may never find out because your hosts are gentlemanly and don't mention it. No stress, *voilà*!

You will accuse me of being facetious and cavalier about making other people wait. But I am very rarely late any more. Punctuality is a mind-set. It has no relation to watches – there are always plenty of clocks around, or people with watches to consult. I stand by my belief that stress is the difference between your expectations and reality. You feel stress because of something left undone, or a place not reached. (Whether you leave on time on the next occasion has no bearing – stress is not cumulative and does not learn from itself.)

This is true for the pedestrian and the sublime.

Suppose you are a 41-year-old woman who cannot get pregnant. Stress. You are a five-year-old who forgot his knapsack at home.

Stress. You have 152 pages to copy and the customer is waiting on the other side of the fax machine. Stress. You wave at your neighbour in the suburbs every day, and his company Lincoln Continental reminds you that he's two management echelons above you, and four years younger. Stress. You rush through the house because you can smell the pie burning in the oven, and knock a bottle of red wine onto the white carpet. Stress. You get my drift.

The list of stressful activities includes going on vacation – there's the expectation that it will be perfect, of how many things need to be arranged before you leave. Not to speak of the stress when you are about to return, and start to fret over the work or mail or errands awaiting you. No wonder there is so much shouting at airport counters.

Lack of information adds to stress, too. It's a sub-set of the above hypothesis. When you feel some strange pain in your stomach, or cannot see well through your left eye, nothing relieves your stress like the doctor telling you that it's just a virus going around.

Another source of stress and disappointment is the expectation that the workplace is an extended family. People want their jobs to provide a sense of belonging, to feel they're taken care of, to bond with colleagues. But they're looking for characteristics the company can't supply. They should keep the company role in perspective. The first expectation to kill is that big families are fun and supportive. Romantic, but untrue. Anyone with a big family can tell you there are always people they don't like among their own relatives. Yet large numbers of family-owned and mid-size businesses foster this notion. They do this because the image of 'family' is an image of loyalty, mutual support and shared culture.

The fact is, you don't have to like people to work with them. And finding compatibility of purpose at work does not require surrounding yourself only with those you like. You can admire people, even if you don't like them. There are several managers at Semco that I would never have lunch with – I don't empathize with them at all – some I downright dislike. But that is irrelevant, because I still respect their style and performance.

We all need to find ways to design workplaces that can respect co-habitation. The seven-day weekend creates another important issue: privacy. Because technology has made it impossible to delineate between personal and work communication, Semco has taken a unique position on e-mail, privacy borders and personal rights. It's one that angers techies and lawyers.

Consider the privacy of communications. If someone opens a letter of yours, or listens in to your phone conversation, they can be sent to prison. Is it acceptable for a company to monitor an employee's private conversations? What if that company reads all e-mails, can access personal files, and maintain a careful record of what websites and chatrooms a worker visits, whether he has a lover, how his sister is doing?

Some in the legal world seem to believe in the rather sinister dogma that we all relinquished our rights to privacy when the Internet was invented. They seem to believe that all personal information belongs to a company because it owns the hardware involved. In that case, it should be legal for companies to tape record all personal conversations that occur in its offices. Tapped phone lines, maybe even cameras in the bathrooms and microphones by the drinking fountain. After all that's company hardware being used, yes?

Recently GM and Xerox fired dozens of employees for sharing pornographic web links. They weren't trading in paedophilia, or committing criminal acts. They were just looking at pictures of sex. But where does morality come into businesses? Doesn't attempting to enforce one management group's moral code take us back to living by boarding school rules? So who gets to choose the morals we all play by? At Semco we've decreed that IT cannot and will not have access to people's e-mails, and that it is none of our business if employees want to join chat rooms or shop on the Internet for gifts during work time.

Recently I spent an afternoon working at one of our city satellite offices. I barely recognized anyone, and thus sidled up to a woman I knew. Four of us worked at one table, and true to my Gemini personality, I listened in to their conversations more than I should have. (It's not really eavesdropping when four people at one round desk are less than a meter from one another.)

The mix of business and personal talk impressed me, as did the amount of chit-chat in between spreadsheets. One girl was cold-calling, and my sympathy grew for her pleas for attention. All she seemed to say was: 'Yes – I understand, yes – I see, hmmm – OK, I'll call back.' I have no idea what she was selling, she never got as far as her sales pitch. After a while, she turned to her notebook computer and pounded away furiously. Feeling empathetic, I asked her whether she was taking out her frustration in an e-mail to her boss. She replied nonchalantly that she was using the time to bawl out her boyfriend –

to cheers from the girl on my left, a fundraiser from the Semco Foundation, who said she does the same thing when she's turned down by potential sponsors.

This led to cappuccino time for all. I was introduced to two of the people, and asked the girl – Márcia – whether she felt at ease using the company Intranet to send and receive private mail. 'Of course I do,' she retorted without a thought. 'They said there is no snooping in this system.' I countered that the people in IT could read all her mail if they decided to overlook the official policy. 'Oh, but they'd get crucified if it was found out,' she replied. Hmm . . . by whom, I wondered. Maybe they would.

It is hopelessly outdated to expect people to live freely in their personal lives but to comply with company rules during work hours. It reminds me of a father declaring that his children can do whatever they want when they grow up, but must abide by his house rules while they're under his roof.

Well, Semco employees have moved out of the house, away from Mom and Dad, and they're adults with the right to the freedom they've been promised all their lives. They should be treated like the adults they are, not as adolescents who require a big brother and a bishop rolled into one.

Not to mention, if we want people to do only company work while they're in the office, shouldn't we also have corporate police to make sure they're not working on company business on weekends? And what if they surf porno sites at home, or on their notebook computers on weekends? Server monitoring makes it entirely possible – and eerily easy and commonplace – for companies to peruse the entire lives of their workers.

Add to that credit card and shopping information or central records in government agencies, and you have all the trappings of the end of privacy.

At Semco, we guarantee our people that corporate eyes will never spy on them, regardless of what lawyers and techies say is permitted or commonplace. We hand workers their freedom and encourage them to find balance in their lives. How they choose to spend their time, how they use technology, how they communicate with the outside world, is a part of the balance.

On the days that his idol is playing a crucial tennis match, Zeca arrives flushed at the office in the afternoon. We can all see that he's spent the morning screaming and shouting at his television. But he doesn't have to be in leisure mode to soar. People complain that working near him can be distracting – he gets up, walks around excitedly, gestures constantly. When he finally clinches a deal, he's all over the office, beaming and stuttering.

It is just as well that he usually sits next to Jorge Lima, the CEO of our mobile outsourcing unit. At a recent board meeting, Jorge excused himself tersely after receiving a message on his cell phone. We all knew what it was about – a small open bid (with nine contestants) for services at AIG – the insurance giant. His pallor changed immediately and as he left the room, we commented that he looked like he'd just heard that someone had died.

We carried on with our agenda, and then Jorge erupted into the room. Joy radiated from his face. 'We won, we won,' he shouted. A smile that shone from ear to ear remained on his face for the rest of the meeting.

These glittering mementoes of a career are worth more than any gold watch we could give Zeca or Jorge, or anyone at Semco, and they come from equilibrium.

I, for one, have for decades looked for the balance that leads to happiness. For example, I've always played several instruments and felt very connected to music. As a child I would sit quietly while my mother, a concert-level pianist, played by ear – her eyesight had been severely affected by eight pregnancies (of which only two succeeded). We shared a love of music.

I spent ten years of my life playing in studios and rock bands. Yet I would dearly love to be a symphony conductor, no less. I enjoy the synergy generated when everyone in a group is intent on the same objective.

But even without a symphony of my own to conduct, I often experience life's highs. When my 3-year-old son kisses me on the lips, or when I read novels by Peter Carey, W.G. Sebald or Arundhati Roy, when the sun rises at 6a.m. over the fog in the mountains, or when I hear Pablo Casals play the cello. It happens when I feel love intensely, when I smile to myself after writing something intriguing, and even when I think I've found a new product or service. It hits me when I think I've discovered the solution to something (I'm often wrong, but the 'eureka!' moment is blissful).

Everyone has exhilarating moments, and accumulating as many as possible should be every collector's dream. Imagine a notebook with a tally of heart-soaring moments, a list that would prove they'd happened and could – if needed – be shown to everyone as evidence of the width and breadth of the experiences.

The Sufi poet, Rumi, created intense moments with his celestial writing almost every day of his life; Mozart was equally prolific. We all have our moments as well, but they are far more rare. The kind of soaring heart I refer to is launched only every few weeks or months, for those of us who are not Rumi or Mozart.

These highs are the equivalent of standing on the summit of Mount Everest. But it's easier to achieve that feeling while listening to Led Zeppelin or Mozart during rush hour than hiking up 25,000 feet with frost-bitten toes.

When I think of my soaring moments, the times every week or so when I suddenly feel silly and don't care what other people think, I remember that I was probably listening to Rachmaninoff or Sibelius in the car.

Rather than constantly talking about 'passion' – serving customers passionately, filling in blue forms passionately – organizations should make it possible for employees to feel exhilaration once in a while. Let them get involved to the point that they shout 'yes!' and give each other High Fives because they did it their way – and it worked.

People are free to soar when they find equilibrium between their personal and work lives. For most, life is out of whack. Fortunately, all they have to do is use the time granted by the seven-day weekend to restore balance.

Part Two

Success And Money Are Distant Relatives

'In our calling, we have to choose; we must make our fortune either in this world or in the next, there is no middle way.'
Marie-Henri Beyle Stendhal

1. Why do people have to stick to a career choice they made as an unprepared adolescent?

2. Why doesn't money buy success if almost everyone measures their success in cash?

3. Why do billionaires greedily accumulate money, only to donate it to ethereal concepts such as world peace?

CHAPTER 1

Topping Off The Tank

SOONER OR LATER, pursuing personal or company goals must tap somehow into what I call the 'reservoir of talent'. Everyone has a wealth of instincts, interests and skills that combine to form their talents. Some refer to it as a 'calling'. Whatever its name, this reservoir can be deeper and more diverse than even the holder himself realizes.

The best way to ensure job satisfaction over the long run is to exhaust that reservoir or to answer the calling. After all, no one works for money alone.

When asked, most workers will tell you there's living, and then there's making a living. People need more than a paycheque in their lives to gratify them. Yet most cannot figure out how to reconcile living with earning a living. How to make them one in the same? It would certainly be a happy combination. But only a lucky few can do so. The rest haven't found a way to insert their passions into their jobs. And that's why the vast majority of people don't really like what they do all day.

But people don't come to work to produce an inferior product. To come late and leave early. To be bored and insubordinate. They must come to work for some reason, some kernel of interest that attracted them to their particular field or profession as a means of earning a paycheque. So let's create an organization that can find out what that is, and exploit it.

The first principle to accept is that if an employee has no interest in a product or project, then that venture will never succeed. I'd rather find that out early on, so I can either fire someone, let him resign or move him to another area, another project. But to other companies, this suggests anarchy. So workers are compelled to do jobs they are not excited about. But that almost guarantees the company or product will never excel.

I want people who are excited by their work. If they don't know how to create that passion, I want to help. I can't do that simply by taking their frustration and wrapping it up in an action plan. Sure, that gives me a written plan, but it also gives me an added burden: I'll have to follow up on people. Is there a bigger activity in business than following up on people? 'Did you do what I told you? But you committed yourself!' How many times a day do people regret the commitment they've made?

I'm not interested in the results of action just for the sake of action, and that is what it means to commit yourself to something you don't want to do. That's not to say people can't be reluctant to try something new – that's not uncommon, but mature or experienced workers understand that and know that once they get involved, they enjoy the challenge.

Employees must be reassured that self-interest is their foremost priority, one they must take care not to replace with company or other interests. We advocate that out of corporate self-interest – an employee who puts himself first will be motivated to perform. At Semco this is considered a form of corporate 'alignment'. Without it, a company has to institute programs to pressure, exhort and compel people to do their jobs. Soon they'll be singing company songs, organizing into support teams, reporting to assemblies for pep talks.

Ever-increasing hours and money are spent on motivational training. Why do people need so much self-help?

At Semco we look for the source of the problem. If the people aren't motivated, they don't need to sign up for motivation training – they need a different job! They might rotate to another position, go to work in a different office, participate more in project meetings, or find another way to work for us on a part-time, commission or representative basis. We can adapt if they can.

None of that is necessary if employees can pursue their self-interest and fulfil the company's agenda at the same time. They'll have found the compatibility of purpose that is so critical to gratification, and the results will be twofold: While they're busy satisfying themselves, they'll satisfy the company's objectives, too.

But first we must acknowledge that it's human nature to lose interest in anything after time. It's a fallacy for traditional companies to boast they want people with 'passion' to work for them, because people cannot be passionate about doing the same thing over and over. That's particularly true about companies that are highly departmentalized. Even more so if the company spells out job parameters. Those are highly crystallized organizations, and trying to spark passion in one of those is frustrating for everyone.

Often companies that make a big deal about passion in employees are really just putting a gloss on a marketing program, or worse, a mission statement with pasteurized phrases. Passion is very rare, and it's a stretch to find it in an office job. It's a disservice to expect all workers to feel passion for their jobs. It sets up an expectation that cannot be met. And it's handling an important part of life with a cavalier attitude.

The danger is that people will look at their jobs and themselves and find they have no passion. Or they'll compare themselves to others and come up short. And then they give up before they've even started, or find themselves unhappy with a job that previously felt okay.

It's like taking a rubber band and stretching it too tight. It'll snap.

Instead, companies need to understand that interests tend to be cyclical. At Semco we offer incentives to employees to move around different jobs and departments. It's another means for them to dip into their 'reservoir of talent,' and to develop independence. If they're moving around following an inner radar, then they won't rely on the company to tell them what to do.

Unfortunately, our society conditions us to accept boredom from an early age – we're taught to expect it in school.

Employees need the latitude to try different jobs because many of them emerge from an education system that compels them to make career and training choices at a very young age, when they have little information about professions and no experience.

By the time we go to work, most of us don't question that it's an inherent part of life. Those who do end up fleeing conventional jobs in favour of becoming painters and writers. Those who stick around simply learn to live with boredom. But that's a huge waste of human potential. People who run away take their 'reservoir of talent' with them. Others who are bored aren't drawing on theirs. So a company like Semco either misses out on the best people, or doesn't get the best out of the people it has. We often have to compensate for society's conditioning by letting people ramble around the company, exploring interests.

As a consequence, the company will ramble with them into

opportunities and new businesses. Auro Alves is a sales and technical assistance manager at Semco, but he began his career with us as a truck driver. He'd driven a bus in São Paulo before joining Semco, and expected that he'd spend his life as a heavy-duty commercial driver. But less than five months after coming to Semco, he moved into product acquisition, and eight months after that took a job as a junior buyer. He got involved in union activities, and discovered that he liked being a leader, and that other workers liked his management style, too. He had a knack for coming up with new ways of doing old tasks at Semco in order to involve more people. He saw that rapid change is an inherent part of Semco, and he learned to adapt. His natural talent, creativity and enthusiasm won him the support of his co-workers, and soon he was made a manager in charge of spare parts and new product sales.

In the time he's worked at Semco, Auro has also taken dozens of courses, each of his own choice – he's studied english, spanish, computers, negotiation techniques, sales methods and customer care. He's had offers to work elsewhere, but turned them down because he says Semco allows him to grow. He still works a nine-hour day, but he spends much of it explaining his decisions to his workers. He enjoys being challenged with questions – worker participation is 'part of the package,' Auro says.

Most importantly, Auro isn't finished exploiting his own 'reservoir of talent'. He has a five-year plan of his own (even if the company frowns on them.) He owns a beach house in Peruibe, and he spends almost every weekend fishing and getting to know the local people there. He plans to move there one day and run his own 'virtual business' as a supplier or consultant to Semco from the seashore.

Job rotation exposes workers like Auro to different challenges, but it also limits the kind of tribal alliances that pit workers against each other. When people change jobs, they're forced to work in a new environment and sometimes even cross over to another tribe. Moving around limits tribal affiliations that are detrimental to democracy, communication and innovation.

Another element of job satisfaction is stress – and stress levels are highest where balance is lowest. That's often a reflection of the difference between expectation and reality.

If an organization sets expectations too high and then fails to meet them, stress levels will obviously skyrocket. The carefully cultivated balance between individual aspirations and company goals will be upset. That's less likely to happen if people are in charge of setting their own expectations.

Moises Assayag conducted some of his personal quest at Semco – and in the end, did not find what he was seeking. But his experience proves my point.

At 6-feet, four inches, Moises towers over most people, bearing down on them with eagle-eyed intelligence. The olive-skinned son of a Lebanese immigrant, Moises began his career as a cost assistant in the backwaters of Northern Brazil, in the state of Bahia, where people are known as 'mañana types' (procrastinators). In Moises' case, this is obviously unfair. Moises did well at work, and transferred to Rio de Janeiro to attend night school in economics. When he graduated, he took one year off to wander around Europe, and then earn a post-graduate degree from the London School of Economics.

Back in Brazil he went to work for a large construction company, managing its stock market portfolio and institutional investors.

One day in 1999 he answered an ad from Semco. We were looking for a junior CFO for our Cushman & Wakefield Semco operation. He was soon one of six finalists facing one of our quirky all-inclusive interviews, where the candidates come together before an audience of Semco employees.

Bojikian remembers how we got started conducting 'collective interviews'.

'In the past, when no one inside the company fit the qualifications for a position, the human resources team would contact a head-hunter. A bunch of *curriculum vitaes* would appear in a couple of days. The human resources people would pick three or four candidates and invite them for interviews with the company directors. Like that, a person would be chosen for the job. It'd be quick, but it wasn't always the right solution.

'After getting hired, the person would have to adapt to the company,' Clovis says with a slight smile. 'At first, people would look at them with questioning eyes: Why is he working here? Is he someone's friend or relative? Can he do his job? Demonstrating the answers would take time. After several months they'd adapt. Or not, of course.

'We decided to use that time in a better way, instead of hiring people quickly and letting them adapt by themselves,' he remembers. We started like this – when a manager needed a new employee, he selected three candidates from the ones presented by the human resources department. After that, a group formed by employees who would work directly with the new hires, interview them and choose one of the three. 'Just like that, employees started choosing their bosses. If they don't like them later, they are the ones to blame,' Clovis says, partly in jest. 'Another advantage of this method is that the person being interviewed gets to know the people who will work with them in advance. This person can also ask all sorts of questions of the group.'

The employees interview the candidates, asking anything they want. Then they score each one. The finalists participate together, breaking into each other's sentences, proving one another wrong, and generally creating unnerving havoc for all involved. When someone is hired, 'the new employee would already be integrated, and their colleagues would know their limitations and qualities. And people also feel committed to the new person. After all, they helped choose him.'

Fate can turn on input from the workers, too. More than once, a director in a hurry found what appeared to be a perfect candidate, and then simply tossed two more names into the ring to complete the requirement for three applicants.

'Many times, one of the candidates without the required quali-fications got hired by the team of employees,' Clovis laughs.

Critics deride the whole process because the finalists have already passed several complex tests. They complain that a free-for-all would favour the candidate with the most 'air time', that notion derived from graduate business school classes where MBA students are rated by how often they wave their hands in the air to speak out in class.

But we still prefer the collective interview because it exposes management candidates to their future employees, and Semco people to their potential bosses.

The highest scoring candidate for the junior CFO job, (and the man who was ultimately hired) was not Moises Assayag but Carlos Pitta. His claim to fame was silence. Not once did he cut in. He spoke only when something was asked of him. Initially he appeared shy, but we learned that Pitta is simply perfectly capable of sitting in a three-hour meeting without once opening his mouth. His work is always impeccable, and he never says anything incorrect. He just believes, as he's said many times, 'flies don't enter closed mouths.'

The MBA finalists at our collective interview were all 'air time' experts and were all ready to aggressively promote themselves. Pitta beat them, though by all appearances he was just another monastic accountant. Only his coloured suspenders gave away that Pitta was a tough, big-city controller, and not a Tibetan monk.

Of all the finalists, however, Moises Assayag was the obvious choice for the job. He spoke magnificent english, which Pitta did not. He was the most impressive candidate. He waved his arms about when he talked, and looked people straight in the eyes. He was quick as lightning, and full of humor. His responses were right on the money. So we decided he was not the guy.

In fact, he was much too flamboyant, curious and electric to warm the junior CFO's chair. What were we to do with him? We are of the opinion that assembling special people is more difficult than finding something for them to do – or, as is our case – letting them find something profitable to do. We'd become famous for hiring people without having a job for them.

So I argued for hiring Moises and putting him in sales at Cushman & Wakefield Semco. Sales! people would exclaim – he has never sold a pencil in his life! That's what qualifies him, I would insist. We need to find new ways to sell, and make more solid pitches to customers. Moises would bring new flair to sales. Since he wasn't trained in the old ways, he wouldn't be stuck in the rut they created.

In the end, some saw the wisdom of that, while others just caved.

'It took three or four months to create a place for me,' Moises remembered later. 'I had a private secretary at my last job, and none here. I was lost. I got no support, and I felt like an astronaut. I had no roots. For a long time I asked myself, could I go through this? Was it really what I was thinking or not? It took me a couple months to adjust.

'When things don't work the way you're used to, it's a shock,' he added. 'You have to change the way you do things. But there's more freedom here, and an open environment. Every day that I get older, I care more about those things.'

Moises then spent a few years selling. He never became an ace at closing deals, even though he more than covered his salary when he single-handedly landed a contract to manage Hong Kong Shanghai Bank's large headquarters. And he settled into 'the Semco way.'

'I saw former peers from my previous company, talking about how it takes three days to get this or that approved, and so-and-so has to see everything, and it all seemed so sluggish,' Moises said. 'It would be very difficult to go back.'

But by 2002, Moises was discouraged with his own job. His voice was not being heard, and José Alignani, the CEO of Cushman & Wakefield, was doubtful about him, too. But others in the company were plotting to take Moises from Alignani and the Cushman & Wakefield Semco operation. They wanted him at Semco Services, the start-up company that was going to manage all non-core activities for companies, or at Ventures, to find new high-tech businesses.

But no one actually made an offer. While this strategizing went on in the background, Moises was becoming more disillusioned. Suddenly he made a decision. He told several colleagues, who kept it to themselves out of respect for his privacy. Moises decided that he was going to stay on at Semco only if the money was particularly good. He asked for additional benefits, for an increase in salary, and for a company car. Alignani procrastinated, and so did various directors. After a couple of months, Moises resigned. It turned out to be the same week that Semco Services made the decision to name him sales director, which would have put him in the running to be CEO of that new company.

It was too late, however. Moises did not feel Semco Services was the right solution any more. Now the Semco Services people were not confident of his motivation. Any chance of recovery fell through.

I sent Moises a note saying how much we were going to miss him, and reminding him that a slew of key Semco people had left us, only to return a few years later. I was sure that this would be his case.

The point of Moises' story is that happiness at a job cannot be bought with more money. That strategy always leads to the street.

Semco is loaded with people who could make much more else-where. Paulo Doneux, for example, worked at Semco for 11 years, quit and then came back five years later.

'None of us are here for the salary,' Paulo said one afternoon in Semco's non-territorial office, surrounded by a group of colleagues. 'I wanted a basis for comparison when I left. The level of competition between people is higher at other companies. We're competitive here, but it's fair play. There's respect here for colleagues. The philosophy, the group of people, the respect, the openness, the opportunity to spread ideas are all reasons to come back.'

Rubens de Oliveira left, too.

'I wasn't making the money I wanted. I left looking for a better salary,' he said. He found the money, but not satisfaction. After three and a half years, he came back as director of business development at ERM.

'My real motivation had become an interest in this international environmental company,' Rubens remembered. 'It's a big job to manage this business, but the real challenge is to blend the Semco and ERM cultures.'

At Semco, he had the freedom to make changes that would maximize not only ERM's potential, but also his own as a manager.

'We've changed strategies – we've gone from production to engineering, applications, business development, assembly and final testing,' Rubens says of ERM. 'We moved to outsource, and several former workers have started their own companies. We feel out the new trends and follow them rapidly.'

Marcia Palmeira left a communications company for a part-time job at Cushman & Wakefield Semco because she 'didn't like the rigid hierarchy' where she was.

'I've had opportunities to leave and make much more,' she says, 'but at Semco I can say what I think. I love to fight with Ricardo Semler by e-mail.'

Perhaps Henrique Oliveira, a shy, quiet applications engineer, put it best: 'I came here and found that everyone trusts you. There's a lot of space to give your opinion and make decisions. It's very important to my personal growth and development. That's the main reason that keeps me here.'

José Alignani could also easily make more money somewhere else. He's turned down several head-hunters. He doesn't stay with Semco out of charity, though. He's been with Semco for 19 years, in five different jobs, in four different business units – and there may be more ahead. He enjoys a level of challenge and independence he would have a hard time finding elsewhere, regardless of the pay.

Alignani says that he's 'been happy 90 percent of these 19 years.' Even if that is a bit much, it's a fact that happiness is the biggest tiebreaker there is. And Moises will have to look for that again, having learned that money won't replace it. It's also hypocritical to describe work as the passion of happy, eager individuals who create a wonderful product. In the vocabulary of many Eastern languages, words for 'work' are associated with sacred activities and hint at perpetuation and noble occupation. But even in those cultures, much work is boring, unfair and unfulfilling.

Workers have to want – and get – more from us than money.

Marcio Batoni and João Vendramim are two of the dozen or so Semco directors who have been at the company for some 20 years. Both have extraordinary schooling and business experience, and both are worth their weight in gold in the marketplace. However, when we ran into a long downhill cycle in the early 1990s, they survived due to a unique arrangement whereby the top Semco executives (known around the office as the Five Musketeers) pooled their salaries and withdrew equal sums at every end of the month.

I didn't agree with this plan, but that didn't matter – they went ahead and did it anyway. Some of them earned $120,000 per year; others $80,000. They had substantial bonus programs, but the times were difficult, and no one was hitting bonus status. To weather the storm, they redistributed the total so each received $105,000. 'We saw ourselves as a very united group with no difference among our responsibilities,' said one of the directors, José Alignani. 'We were all fighting for the company and believed the compensation package of all should be the same.'

From that moment on, Marcio and João were in trouble. Despite the fact that, for a year and a half, both lived on no more than $1,500 a month, a mere fraction of their former incomes, they chose not to look for other work. They did not to send out a single résumé. They preferred to wait out the storm, for two reasons: Firstly, they felt they wouldn't fit into any other culture after many years at Semco, and thus they wouldn't know how to cope at companies where there was no extensive freedom. And secondly, they believed that salaries were not everything, and they wanted to enjoy the substantial benefit they derived from quality of life, freedom, creativity and the sense of belonging that were paramount at Semco.

After that year and a half of slim pickings, Semco still couldn't pay five first class executive salaries – we were laying off a third of all employees in the Collor crisis period. So for many years, those five executives shared the total salary that Semco could afford – the equivalent of salary for three executives. Salary sharing lasted for many years, and was only discontinued when two of the Five Musketeers were managing very large units, the company was doing much better, and they all felt the method was no longer necessary.

Today, both Marcio and João are CEOs. As CEO of RGIS, Marcio earns 10 to 20 times more than he made during the meager years. He's running a young business with all the stresses of a start-up, and often attends to a dozen inventories a night and spends countless dawns at supermarkets. But his sense of satisfaction is enormous – making it all worthwhile.

Marcio owns five percent of Semco RGIS, a multi-million dollar company that has grown 40 percent per year. We all hope the financial end result will be even more rewarding. But there was no sign of this when he worked at home, without a specific job, wondering how he and Semco would survive.

We always hope that on their own, people will find something that matches their calling. Of course it doesn't always happen. However, we also need people to carry out uninteresting tasks – and sometimes the person who only wants a dignified, nine-to-five job, to make money to meet other ends, offers us a mutually beneficial arrangement. At least for a time. So we don't search only for motivated workers (not to mention for those with 'a passion'). We need all kinds, and if motivation or passion isn't there, much of the blame is ours.

Fortunate are those who find their calling early, and who find a place to develop it. Work is a noble undertaking for a doctor with an ideal, a fireman with courage, a mailman with stamina, a businessman with ideas or excess energy. But there are also people who work in the doctor's office, or in the administrative department of the fire department or mail system, and on assembly lines. Most of them are not answering a calling.

Those people constitute the vast majority of workers in the world. That isn't to say that a factory worker, a bank clerk or a shop assistant cannot be happy at work – but the chance is slim that they are exhausting their 'reservoir of talent'. It's my theory that the slow and measured exhaustion of that reserve is what makes a life worthwhile.

Scuba diving offers an easy analogy. You are given approximately one hour's worth of air in your scuba tank. You want to remain submerged as long as possible, to swim, roam and marvel as much as possible. And if you manage to get stuck in a cave, it's always nice to have a little bit of air left in the tank. Yet there are people who resurface in half the time with an empty tank. They breathed too hard and too fast. Usually they're tense and must teach themselves to breathe slowly and steadily. (Anyone with an introspective and patient character is the best candidate for this and presumably big city lawyers and stockbrokers are the worst candidates.)

On land, we each have a life's worth of air. We can consume it quickly and then fret about all the things we didn't have time to do. Or we can pace ourselves.

Too many people never learn this. They find no balance between work and personal life, and before they know it their opportunities are gone too. Receiving a gold watch after 30 years at an automobile manufacturer is dreary compensation indeed. Then there are people who make their jobs coincide with their calling, no matter what. Clovis Bojikian, our human resources icon, is such a case. After defying the military regime as the director of a highly avant-garde school in the Philosophy College of the São Paulo University (he was eventually removed by the authorities, prompting the students to occupy the buildings in protest), Clovis ran the human resources department at the Ford Motor Company's main plant in Brazil for 18 years. He came to us when we engaged a head-hunter to find a new job for my father's long time general manager. The head-hunter found the general manager a position as president of the German pump manufacturer where Clovis was HR director. He and Clovis clashed immediately, and the German company offered to let us hire Clovis.

Clovis' first job at Semco was as our HR director, back when we still had such a position. Now Clovis and Flor are all that remains of a human resources department that once had 90 people. We decided the department really had no reason to exist. The first human resources departments date to the turn of the century and were known as sociology departments. They blossomed because managers are uncomfortable dealing with personnel issues. In the early days at the Ford Motor Co., one of the first sociology managers was a Detroit chief of police. Over time these people claimed human resources techniques as their own, and it became accepted that managers couldn't recruit, train, place ads, hire head-hunters, do career plans or employee reviews.

Yet these are some of the most important issues a manager faces. But they were in a separate department. We decided that Semco couldn't operate that way. Whatever problems managers had at first dealing with personnel issues had to be solved at the source. We retained two people in human resources to be our eyes and ears to the outside world on the subject. They have become technical experts, and they advise our managers.

Clovis and I hit it off famously, and spent the first two full days just talking about ideas and projects. Only after he'd started work in earnest did we realize that we had never discussed his compensation package. That was in 1984. At the time, I was just beginning to make dramatic changes at Semco. I had fired many of my father's senior men and was hiring my own people. It wasn't easy to find people who shared the democratic ideals I wanted to promote. This was particularly true among candidates for the position of chief financial officer (CFO). But Semco desperately needed a magician to make the numbers work, so I hired the best traditional CFO I could find. He also happened to be an autocrat. Clovis had a lot of trouble with this man's management style, but he wasn't perturbed enough to leave Semco. However, bad luck dogged Clovis – he lost all his savings trying to help a relative who was drowning in debt. When another company offered him a job as human resources director with a 70 percent salary hike, he couldn't afford to turn it down.

It was painful to lose him but Semco couldn't match the offer. Clovis promised to help me find his replacement, but after interviewing a dozen people, I decided I'd never find someone who fit as well as Clovis. No one would fill the job until we could afford to pay Clovis's salary.

A year and a half later, Semco's fortunes had improved. I invited Clovis to dinner with me. He was tired of looking after the career fates of managers who were well able to take care of themselves. There was no challenge to his work, and he derived little satisfaction from it. The money had helped him right his financial boat, but it was no compensation for the drudgery of his job.

As we ate, we talked about his coming back to Semco as a director. We didn't discuss salary directly, but since he was returning to a bigger company, his pay would be closer to what he was earning where he was.

Shortly after his return, the dramatic changes that we were making at Semco caught the attention of Brazil's media. Journalists who discovered Semco also discovered Clovis, and the magazine and newspaper articles were followed by many attempts to poach him. Debt-free, Clovis refused these offers without considering them – even one to become human resources director at the biggest media corporation in Brazil with a salary three times what he earned at Semco, and another from the biggest services group in Brazil at double his salary. He rejected them all out of hand. Instead, he stayed at Semco without even asking for a raise (and he didn't even mention the offers until months later). He knew our numbers and it was crystal clear to him that we couldn't pay him more. He was earning something much more valuable than money.

'At Semco I was living the most exciting time of my career,' Clovis remembers now. 'The changes we were proposing were revolutionary. Our shop floor workers were participating in company policy and decisions at a level never seen before. I felt honoured by the other offers, but I didn't even consider leaving.'

Clovis has always had an affinity for blue-collar employees, and always said he could do more for them than for office workers. As Semco grew, our offices became fancier and employee facilities got nicer. We never made a deliberate distinction between white- and blue-collar workers, but humans tend to be tribal, and because of that, blue-collar workers from the factory floor just didn't hang around drinking coffee in the staff lounge. As the offices expanded and were updated, the factory remained the same.

All of which fuelled Clovis' dream of a rest space for the shop workers in the garden outside the factory. He was always occupied with other tasks, so it took years to get around to it. But finally, a 1,000 square foot area was set aside, an architect was hired and sketches were produced. They included a kiosk with a barbecue area, a coffee machine and a refrigerator. The garden had benches and shaded rest areas.

When I saw the sketches, I remembered an old dream of mine of hanging hammocks for worker catnaps. The body's natural biorhythms make an afternoon nap almost essential – yet modern societies have done away with the practice of the 'siesta' (though Brazil, like the US and the UK, never enjoyed them). Even though medicine has long known that afternoon naps are natural, Western culture has mocked and derided the need to sleep during the day as a sign of laziness and lack of discipline. The National Sleep Foundation in the US says only 15 percent of workers are allowed to doze on the job, even though the vast majority of people get less than the eight hours of sleep most of us need.

Initially my idea for hammocks was seen as another of my quirks, or a gimmick. A month and $30,000 later, the entire garden, with hammocks, was ready. It has been used prodigiously since. The garden slowly brought people around to reconsidering their productive moments, their need for silence and to recharge their batteries. Now there are people there most of the day.

*

Clovis likes to tell the story of a shipping and receiving clerk named Antonio Santos who once thanked him for the new flexible working hours available on the shop floor. Antonio's group had decided to start work well before morning rush hour to avoid traffic. In return, they left for home much earlier. Antonio was ecstatic because for the first time in his life, he could pick up his granddaughter from school. He'd never been able to pick up his own children, and sharing those moments in their lives was lost to him forever. He was more moved by the unexpected freedom to be at the school, waiting for his granddaughter, than he was about beating rush hour.

Having the power to change people's lives for the better was worth more to Clovis than a triplefold raise at another company. It happened to him more than once, too. Another time, a worker's wife actually phoned Clovis to ask what he'd done to her husband. For the first time in his life, her tough and autocratic husband was listening to his children. He took their feelings and opinions into account when making decisions. Clovis realized that the man was simply reproducing at home what he experienced at work. He knew it was a better system, and he realized it made him feel better about himself, as well. In that way, Clovis actually also helped the man's children. For both Clovis and the worker, a calling was fulfilled.

Executives must give up control and trust the power of talent. Only then will a person's calling emerge, and only then will that person – or his boss, or a colleague – find the right niche for him. Our inventory unit, Semco RGIS, can tell some extraordinary recruitment stories that merge talents with their real calling. The current general manager of the São Paulo District (our largest) began his work life as a waiter. Marcio Batoni, the CEO, ate regularly at a nearby Italian cantina, where his waiter was a particularly sharp man named Alex Guedes. One day, Marcio asked Alex if he'd like to try a new job. Alex said yes immediately – and rose quickly at Semco RGIS, in spite of a fairly autocratic leadership style. But Marcio stood by him, and he became the top dog in our biggest district, leading 160 people at a time during Wal-Mart inventories.

Alex wouldn't have lasted if he hadn't been good, in spite of Marcio's support. True, leaders are often chosen because they have technical or program expertise, and not because they're particularly skilled at leading others. Then they have to run a number of other employees, help those people feel good about their work and do their jobs well, and deal with customers and contractors. A bad boss

61

creates a morale crisis. At Semco we ensure that a poor supervisor does not become entrenched by asking all employees to evaluate their managers every six months. The results are posted for everyone to see, and the group holds a meeting to discuss what they might want to do about them.

That way, the only legitimate source of power in a company is talent, because it generates followers. As João Vendramim has discovered, 'it isn't true that bosses have no control of their people at Semco. The difference is that we want people to be bosses due to their knowledge and leadership qualities, and not due to their titles.'

We have been known to place ads reading: 'We have no openings, but apply anyway. Come and talk about what you might do for us, and how we might create a position for you.'

We're always looking for alternative ways to bring people into the company and to connect callings and talents with our needs. This started at a time when Semco needed new blood but we couldn't afford to add to the payroll to get it. The first ad emanated from our technical areas, and was titled 'Engineering Partners'. We made it plain there were no openings, but we offered to show interested people around the company for a day and then accept proposals for a way to work with us: for a fee, a commission, through sub-contracting, percentages, by the job, whatever might work. Hundreds of people responded, and visited our factories and offices over a two-day period. We accepted proposals of work from 35 people, and eventually hired two of them as employees.

One of the proposals came from a man with decades of experience in machine maintenance. He wanted to overhaul our machinery to operate more efficiently. He suggested a 'success fee,' or a percentage of the money we saved in operating costs. His work demonstrated the wisdom of outsourcing, and it was so successful that it was ultimately applied to other parts of our engineering areas – project design, planning, drafting, and machinery maintenance were all eventually outsourced. Other people came onboard as sales engineers, product application specialists, or as part-time draftsmen. Many did not last; several left when they found a better full-time job. But some remain at Semco to this day.

On another occasion, we posted flyers around São Paulo in search of people to take inventory for RGIS. Adrisia Moreira started with RGIS when it launched, and one of her first projects was to find enough competent people to train as over-night auditors at our inventory sites. Marcio Batoni, her boss, simply told her to find the people – he didn't tell her how to do it. Adrisia decided the most efficient way to recruit 100 people quickly was with posters. This clashed with what our hiring specialists favoured – they thought it gave Semco a bad image. But it worked – with one unusual result. A woman who found Adrisia's name and phone number in her husband's pocket refused to believe he'd jotted it down from an employment poster. She called Semco to threaten Adrisia, so that for a while, Adrisia never left the office without a few colleagues by her side.

After having described our collaborative interviews, and our careful, exhausting hiring process, I have to add that we've had our share of seat-of-the-pants hires. That's because sometimes the collaborative interview process that generally works so well for us runs headlong into someone's instinct – and into one of Semco's philosophies: It's better to beg forgiveness than to ask permission.

In early 2002, Jorge Lima needed an operations manager for Semco Maintenance, another new start-up. As it happened, José Alignani mentioned Semco Maintenance to an acquaintance at Xerox named Luiz Claudio Sá. He passed Luiz's name on to Jorge, who called Luiz at Xerox to set up an interview. They talked comfortably on the phone, buffered by their mutual friendship with Alignani. After 20 minutes, Jorge offered Luiz the job. Luiz hung up and 15 minutes later quit his Xerox job. The next day he reported for work at Semco Maintenance.

Not everyone who applies to work at Semco gets far enough in the process for a 'scare off' meeting where they hear about our unconventional practices and philosophies. Some are scared away before they're done with their first interview. Marcio Batoni, the CEO of Semco RGIS, says 'in some cases, it's harder to work in a company like this.

'I've seen many, many good professionals who have left this company, not because they have other opportunities, but because it's hard to work here if you don't have the entrepreneurial spirit,' Batoni cautions. Some of them couldn't condone subordinates with an equal voice, or the expectation that they'd cultivate respect through their actions, and not have it bestowed on them by title or their box on an organization chart.

But that's just democracy at work. Traditional companies recruit and hire for a function within the organization, one that is usually described in detail in a job outline and accompanied by a list of academic and career prerequisites. Their first priority is filling those requirements. Ours is in hiring people who will find a 'click' between their life purpose and the company's.

Does that mean that we should take a back seat, and invite into Semco as much talent as possible? Well, if you can never be too rich or too thin, then it stands to reason that you can never have enough talent, either. But in fact, you can. And too much talent can sometimes be the same as having three surgeons in an operating theatre – there might be a lethal level of strict worldviews, and ego, in the room. The question of too much talent has to be considered in the light of the issue of calling and how it makes for an especially talented professional.

Imagine, for a moment, such a surgeon. She battled to get into medical school, to keep up with the studies and exams, to survive a hospital residency. Finally, after much apprenticeship, she is operating and has a clinical practice.

When she gets called in the middle of the night, or is beeped in the midst of a racquetball game, her passion and excitement for her profession keep irritation to a minimum – she loves her racquetball but is also genuinely attached to her patients and to medicine. She wants to know what's happened to her patient, whether his new antibiotic worked, whether he's feeling better.

Excitement and energy are even more critical at the operating table. Imagine the surgeon arriving downbeat at 5a.m., the upcoming operation just another one in a long line, all part of day-in, day-out drudgery. Would you like to be lying on the table?

Or picture a weary cellist at a concert. Or a mailman who doesn't much care which mailbox the package goes into.

Where are the surgeons, cellists or even mail deliverers – the star performers – at 99 percent of companies? Why is it that church groups, amateur choirs or chess teams have such a high degree of commitment, when companies have to train, re-train, motivate and re-motivate all year round – just to keep people from biting off customers' heads over the phone? And why do those same bored or bitter phone attendants leave the office fed up with their workday only to transform into joyful choir singers that very evening?

Could it be that 'calling' is difficult to reconcile with office or factory jobs? Do nine-to-five jobs somehow naturally attract people who have no calling? Is the majority of humanity stuck doing jobs that are unfulfilling? Managers and executives certainly can't say that – we can't tell people they're doing a job because they're the part of humanity that has no greater purpose.

But is it perhaps unrealistic to expect that modern production methods be compatible with excitement? Are we just kidding ourselves when we hope that all of our employees will jump from their beds on Monday morning, excited with what awaits them at the job? Do we just train them enough to do what needs to be done, and re-awaken them from their boredom every so often with tricks, campaigns and subtle threats?

I'm always sceptical of companies that search for 'passion' in their employees, who portray their workforce as a happy, smiling family that cannot wait for you to bring your needs or problems to their doorstep.

The truth is closer to this: Most of the people who look for common office or factory jobs do not have a calling for what the work entails. They just need a job, to keep themselves and their family thriving so they can otherwise pursue their real calling. Is it a waste of time to deal with these people, therefore? Not at all, because they still have a reservoir of talent worth discovering. They just have to be given the opportunity to discover it themselves.

CHAPTER 2

Too Much Talent Is As Bad As Too Little

INSISTING THAT ORGANIZATIONS should add as much talent as possible is a simplistic cliché too often blindly followed. I've even created a silly formula for this equation: IQ+EQ+SQ-EGO.

For decades, IQ has created an artificial (and loaded) baseline for intelligence and capability. More recently, evaluating EQ, or the emotional content of intelligence, has become popular. Now SQ, or spiritual quotient, has been added to the equation. I mix the three together, and then subtract ego (I know I'd be in trouble with psychologists because ego includes most of the above, but I need a bit of poetic license for this homegrown theory).

Ego can outstrip normal self-esteem, especially when early or continuous success fires it up. If talent is like a fire, ego is gasoline. The combination can be explosive. People with high opinions of themselves can clash with others, or be abrupt or abusive. Circumstances like e-mail shorthand can exacerbate that – it's easy to rub people the wrong way with a curt reply or an unnecessary blind copy.

As such, it's important to keep egos under control. They're the reason that massing talented people in one department often backfires.

Business leaders speak constantly of the need to attract as much talent as possible. They are always referring to exceptional qualities, to the uncommon. They never mean night watchmen, travelling salesmen that visit the same customers every week, or draftsmen who draw what others designed.

Imagine situations where you'd like to see as many talented people

66

as possible working together, for example, when you need that operation. After you've visited the proverbial 'second opinion' surgeon, and then a third, try to fulfil your wish of having all three join up as a team and operate together. The sum of IQs would be wonderful, but the EQs and EGOs wouldn't let it happen.

The same is true in organizations, and was patently clear during the dot.com cycle. As soon as the start-ups formed, the founders were always reduced to just a couple per dot.com. Why weren't there 100 great companies with 15 talented founders in each – instead of thousands with one or two apiece? Because too much talent leaves little room for more. The first two talented executives push out the others.

I know people who have applied unsuccessfully to *Médecins Sans Frontières* (Doctors Without Borders). This French voluntary organization provides medical care and emergency relief in war-torn parts of the globe. An admirable organization filled with idealists. Thus the barrier to entry is high. The group is most wary of candidates who see the work as a route to their own salvation, who throw themselves into humanitarian projects in distant lands to escape their own shortcomings or emotional hang-ups. In other words, people who couldn't find balance at home.

Organizations seeking people with a 'calling' are often very selective. *Médecins Sans Frontières* is not looking only for qualifications like a medical degree. Instead, they understand that emotional balance and clear goals are more important.

An MBA applying to a business organization for a job is very much like a doctor looking to *Médecins Sans Frontières* for work. Companies should be as selective as MSF. At Semco, we look beyond qualifications like Ivy League credentials. We want interpersonal skills, and emotional and spiritual quotients.

We look for people like Ivan Maluf, who won a drawn-out competition for a financial controller's position at Semco. Ivan is quick, tough when necessary, and essentially a numbers man. But he is also a storyteller, and has attended courses on storytelling as an expertise. He dedicates himself to poor children in slums, where he goes to tell stories on weekends (or maybe weekdays, since no one tracks what he does from Monday to Friday).

In his spare time, Danilo Saicali runs a non-profit organization for the São Paulo State governor's wife, that provides shelter for street kids. And Rogerio Ottolia, the CEO of MAQ, has pursued a 'personal dream' of getting involved in Brazil's political and economic scene. He started by joining the Brazilian Association of Industry Machinery, where he created a technology fair focused on mixing processes and packaging. The fair was a big hit, and Rogerio was elected president of the food and pharmaceutical industry sector.

'I've always been interested in politics,' Rogerio says. 'I started as the Semco representative. Lately my group has taken over direction of the whole association. I'm responsible for international relations, and that's one of my passions.'

There's more at stake than Semco or technology fairs, however – Rogerio's group helped break a stalemate between Brazil and Mexico over import-export taxes. These extracurricular passions, whether grand political vocations or simple early morning tai chi groups, are the kind of characteristics (the SQs) that count when we hire new people.

But none of this is taken into consideration in business graduate work. Like doctors with shining clinical credentials who become a major liability on the ground in Zambia, MBAs who have fulfilled only the rituals of schooling need to be tested as team players.

Some years ago we hired a shining MBA named Robert Kinney. He was the son of an Englishman who had emigrated to Brazil. Tall, very handsome, well dressed, and a gentlemen in words and action. Another whiz kid. He had gone to college in Europe, and then done an MBA at Wharton. He came back to Brazil at 24, and by the time he was 26 he was running a small chain of restaurants in the centre of Brazil. General Manager by 26!

That chain was subsequently sold and Rob wanted to come back to his hometown. He was now 29. I'd known him for many years, and immediately snapped him up.

We were just starting our maintenance business, and it required broad vision and the ability to organize quickly, to choose the right people, and to position the product with precision. Rob had done all of that at the hotel chain.

The business was meant to serve as an outsourcing partner to hotels, hospitals, plants and the like. It would service machinery and supply parts, thus eliminating major headaches for those organizations. We'd offer 24-hour service, parts on hand, and specialized labour.

So Rob went off into the field. The first thing he did was list all available parts and their prices, hire good technicians and train them, and announce the business to the market.

After the first three months, our CFO, José Violi, got nervous. Rob insisted that his plan not only took time, but also depended on in-depth attention. He was designing new uniforms, hiring secretaries, re-organizing the area and the warehouse, and generally using up a heck of a lot of Violi's cash flow. By the sixth month we had a beautiful computerized warehouse, impeccable mechanics, and nattily uniformed assistants manning the phones. The only thing missing was customers. The computerized warehouse was quiet, the mechanics were trying to look busy, and the manned phones weren't ringing.

By this time Violi was about to have a fit. An old adage at Semco had always been to make people put up businesses in a shoe string fashion, using street smarts to guide them. But the boss (me, of course) wanted to move Semco to a more scientific level of precise operating routines and computer-controlled systems, and Rob had arrived with the perfect credentials.

To make a long story short, we thanked Rob for his time. It then took us more than a year to bring the parts inventory down to a manageable size. All the uniformed girls looked for an honest job somewhere else (several within Semco) and the mechanics were pushed out into the streets to find customers. We lost a good half million dollars on this operation, and learned never to leave MBAs to their own devices.

During the dot.com phase, we saw a lot of similar projects. It was MBA heaven! All bets were off, all semblance to market or business sense was abandoned as ignorant, outdated and passé. Everything was going to happen as per business plans that shone with figures, graphs and absurd assumptions, that passed for a new, new way of seeing the world. Rob would have done well in the dot.com world, if it had lasted.

Now, Rob was by no means a bad manager, and were he willing to make less money, we would have been able to merge him with our people who had street smarts.

I once did a course at Harvard where the professor, Gordon Donaldson, spoke of RLC. He said businessmen and women had to have RLC, which turned out to be Rat-Like-Cunning. But RLC and MBA don't go together.

Sure, we have our quota of MBAs – Ricardo Raoul, for example, who attended the best schools in Brazil, and holds a string of credentials from Harvard and Stanford. But like our other MBAs, he always reported to good old Violi, who has almost no formal training whatsoever. And when I need someone's opinion about a balance sheet, or which direction to take, or what's to be done in a difficult situation, Violi's the man. For me and for the MBAs.

Just look at the investment banks – the major employers of MBAs – to see the price that is paid for poor emotional qualification. They hire the 'best and the brightest,' those who excelled at the aggressive business school game, the ones possessing the highest proportion of raw brainpower. These MBAs are gathered side-by-side in large offices and given highly individualized and often mercenary goals to achieve.

Soldiers of fortune, they sell their time and weaponry to the army that pays best. Their allegiance is legendarily weak – they pay homage but only to themselves. This doesn't mean they are egomaniacs. It just means that they have a finely honed concern for their own interests. Most of them do not believe in a job for life, and manage their careers with as much precision as the market will allow. They thrive on working and playing hard, with 'hard' being the key word, unfortunately for them. This is why fast cars, drugs or drinking, and double-dealing became so common in the investment bank arena. So what is wrong with an army of mercenaries, as long as the end result is achieved? Well, end result has to be defined. If it is 'make as much as you can, as fast as you can,' then nothing's wrong. Mercenary armies are constantly assembled and dismantled.

If an organization wants sustainability, as we do at Semco, these soldiers can never form the backbone of our company. They might make good catalysts, or temporary workers. But their excess of talent and self-concern will lead to temporary success. The investment banks and their huge swings of fortune are proof of that. One moment they reap hundreds of millions of dollars in windfall profits, the next they are being liquidated, merged or acquired. And this creates no balance, no sustainable synergy between talent and the company's needs.

The way we organize our companies, of course, is what makes it possible for workers to find a balance. At Semco, one of the best examples came from a cleaning woman that talked to Rogerio Ottolia, who at the time was CEO of our digital scale factory. He asked her exactly what her job was. Without missing a beat, she replied: 'I build scales'.

She knew her work contributed more to Semco than just her efforts with a broom, a bucket and a pushcart. She didn't feel pigeonholed or labelled, or compelled to stick to an anonymous job description. She identified with the reason our scale factory exists. Maybe one of her suggestions will save Semco money or spark an idea for a new product.

That's not so far-fetched when you realize that like everyone at Semco, including the cleaning staff takes part in a monthly meeting that analyzes the company numbers. There they learn what our revenues and payroll are, why we are different from our competitors, why profit is rising or falling. Anyone can enrol in a course in reading balance sheets that is administered by the left-wing Metalworker's Union – we inaugurated the first almost 16 years ago, when talking to a union director was reason enough to be considered a communist.

Multiply that cleaning woman's attitude by the total number of employees at every level, and that's a lot of opportunity for a company to grow, profit and endure over the years.

So why do we go to work, if not for the money? To make the life-trip worthwhile, to feel alive with purpose. Nothing has bothered philosophers and peasants, bankers and nurses, bus conductors and Shiite Mujahedin more than the question: Why are we here? As much as I'd like, I cannot even begin to answer that. I can say that the query has taken me to Tibetan monasteries and Coptic hermitages, through years of therapy, and into no end of meditation, Zen seminars, cloisters, intense reading and lectures. After which I am glad to report that I've learned a lot and discovered nothing, yet. It's the process that provides the satisfaction.

First, work has to be customized to people's talents. That may sound obvious, but it's more than matching a résumé to a job description. Take Jorge Lima's obsession with pursuing customers.

Jorge once spent an entire week riding the elevators in a financial institution, in hopes of running into a recalcitrant director. He knew that if he could meet the director, his talents would rule the day. Jorge was running an operation for the institution, and he needed more freedom. But the director wasn't cooperative. So Jorge took to riding the elevator up and down, counting as he went along. On one of those limited voyages from heaven to hell and back, in which he counted 17 roundtrips, said director finally stepped into the elevator. Jorge struck up a conversation, and the rest is history. They are personal friends to this day, several years later. This talent for ferreting out a target is rare, and sometimes leads to trouble.

Jorge once had a target in view, a very difficult potential customer. This bank director was humourless, curt, aggressive and abrasive. He was universally feared within the bank. Jorge had tried a cold call, in the hopes of offering this man our services. After many failed attempts, Jorge learned that a mutual friend provided armoured car services to this bank director's department, and the friend arranged for a meeting.

The friend advised Jorge to be quick and to the point, and to refrain from his usual smiling, warm conversation, any physical contact, any 'instant intimacy'.

Jorge arrived, was kept waiting, and was finally let in to see this man, who barely raised his eyes. Jorge's interpersonal skills and his invitation to lunch extended the 15-minute interview. At a restaurant, they both had a beer, and the man loosened up. Soon they were talking about how some men needed to hang 'bimbos' on their arms.

They laughed as they pointed to some overdressed Versace ladies. Jorge then guffawed and beat his thighs as the most extravagant of the women walked in. 'That,' he exclaimed, 'is the queen of all bimbos!' He roared with laughter as the bank director got up – he could see the man was going to play along and say something funny to the woman. Instead he brought her to the table, and Jorge's heart sank as the bank director introduced her as his wife, Cristina.

Jorge stuttered, in a cold sweat, about how the term bimbo meant something else in the town where he was raised. The bank director turned nonchalantly to his wife. 'You, see, honey, Jorge here also thinks you're a bimbo!' Jorge excused himself, went to the men's room, threw cold water on his face and called his wife on his cell phone to ask her what he should do.

She advised him to go back and pretend nothing had happened, which he did. In the end, he got the contract.

But talent, or the obsession that comes with a particular talent, is not the same as doing something exceptional, despite the widespread belief that this is so. There are talents that few of us imagine possessing. I don't mean playing the violin like a world-class musician. I mean the ability to stay awake, night after night, in the dark and silence, watching a blue-tinged monitor in a night watchman's cabin. Or being an orderly in a public hospital in the developing world, cleaning latrines, making beds for the sick, taking out contaminated supplies. These are talents of great importance to all of us.

I realize that many people who fill these jobs have no option; that 'someone has to do it'. But among the countless people who work simply to earn a living, there are many that find a niche for themselves. Plenty of jobs are full of 'no talent required' tasks. But that doesn't mean they don't require skills.

When my father arrived in Brazil from Austria in the early 1950s, he started his company from a kitchen table in a downtown apartment. The very first employee he hired was Roberval Couto. Roberval was with Semco until he retired. He would drive our gringo visitors to and from the airport, and though he spoke no english, he had painstakingly learned to tell one and all that he had picked up my birth certificate when I was born in 1959.

The interesting thing about Roberval was that he started as a messenger – an 'office boy,' according to the politically incorrect term of the time. After 35 years and many opportunities, he had become, lo and behold, an office boy. And that's how he retired. But ask anyone to point out a happier person, and they would be hard put to find one who matched Roberval's ample smile, springy step and waving hand. He would proudly tell me how he could deliver a letter more quickly by ducking under a parking garage, by-passing traffic through side streets or taking the service elevator from the mezzanine floor. And he'd giggle at the thought of the other messengers waiting in line.

Roberval had a talent. Both for what he did and for being happy – and these obviously merged. And there is no greater talent indeed. Every time we tried to augment his income or promote him – in our mind, to increase his chances of 'success' – he would laugh and say: 'Oh, no, you won't catch me being an office clerk. Excuse, me, I've got to run.' We simpletons thought that sticking him behind a desk would improve his life. Meanwhile, he taught us the meaning of success.

Few are as fortunate as Roberval. The sum of human talent left untapped would surely be staggering if it could somehow be quantified. It's no wonder that companies campaign so relentlessly to motivate employees. Campaigns are necessary because boredom, repetition, and company constraints that block the 'reservoir of talent' snuff out natural inclination.

Boredom is expected among workers the farther they are from the top of an organization chart. Mid- and lower-level jobs are fractured and thus tend to be repetitive in nature. Yet managers don't think it unreasonable to expect someone to maintain their level of interest and activity for many years. After all, companies pay people to do repetitive jobs.

The result, of course, is that people will often take refuge into the proverbial 'nine-to-five' job attitude. They'll settle at an activity level and never budge from it. When employees do only what their job description instructs, they can cripple a company.

For decades, unions have striven to change working conditions, building solidarity among workers and harnessing collective indignation over the poor terms imposed by Big Business. Henry Ford said: 'Why is it that every time I ask for a pair of hands, a brain comes attached?' (This from the man whose first human resources department was called the sociology department and was run by an ex-prize fighter and policeman from Detroit.)

Take the long, bitter, winter strikes at The Big Three vehicle manufacturers in the Mid-West in the mid-1980s. Remember workers on the picket lines marching back and forth in the cold, day after day, sometimes for months on end? Were they stomping in the snow for extra money? Were their demands for negotiation really only salary demands?

I calculated the raises that workers were demanding during one of these particularly long strikes, and compared it to what management was willing to cede. The net difference was 1.8 percent. To the company, this meant tens of millions of dollars a year. To the worker, it meant the price of a small television. Who would stomp around in the freezing cold for three months to buy a small TV? Is worker dissatisfaction and frustration really over money, or over indignation at not being heard?

Jacques Nasser, former CEO of the Ford Motor Co., had to deal with his company's policy of axing five to 10 percent of the poorest performing employees. It's a philosophy that mirrors the curve grading scheme of business schools, where 'surely' ten percent of your managers and employees are sub-performing at any given time, and must be shed like dead wood.

Even from a purely financial point of view, isn't it wiser to discover what's wrong? Instead of wasting the time, effort and money already invested in the employee, repeating that investment on a new worker, and running the risk that the next person may turn out to be an under-performer as well?

Lucia Kobayashi is a good example of this. A daughter of Japanese immigrants, Lucia is a funny, optimistic woman whose blue hair makes it easy to pick her out of a crowd. She chose a career in marketing, and joined Semco during the infamous dot.com era. But she failed to produce as much as was expected, so her contract wasn't renewed. She was in the bottom 10 percent.

Since we believe in giving people time and opportunity to prove themselves, another unit about to launch new software for construction companies hired Lucia. Lucky Lucia – that project became known as the *Kursk*, after the Russian submarine that tragically sank with all hands aboard. Lucia was then hired to provide marketing to new ventures in a group formed by Danilo Saicali.

After a few months, that group realized that Lucia was not the right for them, either. They didn't renew her contract. But we still didn't want to let her go. Her managers felt she just had to find the right spot, so they made it known she was available.

Then I hired her. Poor Lucia. I can be quite a pain in the behind when I want something exactly as I want it. After an infamous request (I wanted to visit two hotels in Rio, but one was open only from Thursday to Saturday, while the other had conventions during the week. I wanted to meet the owner of one, who was there only on Saturdays, and have lunch at the other hotel on Sunday. I wanted to use the airport nearest the second hotel, but needed a car that was only available at the airport closest to the first), she gave up and decided to move to Japan.

But another Semco unit that sells software offered her a marketing job, and she's been there since, doing nicely. What can I say? She might retire at the company, and might still move around until she finds something that even better suits her blue-hair style. But she's been in the bottom 10 percent several times already, and would have been thrown out by the Fords and GEs of this world long ago.

In his long career at Semco, Marcio Batoni, has started five different, consecutive businesses, all of which went bankrupt. You'd think he'd be sleeping on the street – except for the fact that he made himself – and us – millions on the sixth try.

Organizations rarely believe they're to blame when an employee underperforms. But if the organization doesn't provide the opportunity for success, then people falter. At Semco we accept that every individual wants and needs a worthwhile pursuit in life. It's up to us to provide the environment and opportunity for their gratification.

So we resort to a series of programs and practices like job rotation, reverse evaluation and self-management. They're intended to help people tap their reservoir of talent and to preclude the need for 'weeding out'. We never assume there are weeds among us.

As with any microenvironment, our ecology has to be balanced. Compare it to Mao Tse Tung's war against disease-carrying pigeons. The snakes deployed to control the pigeon population were wildly successful – and left the Chinese with a snake problem.

It's the same with people. Purging 'dead wood' inevitably creates another problem – people find themselves working in a reign of terror, their fear of mistakes smothering their creativity. But a system should learn from its mistakes. Process is paramount to knowledge, and mistakes are powerful catalysts for the process.

Former GE CEO Jack Welch once told a store manager who was curious about the dead wood removal plan: 'Yes, you should indeed fire two out of 20 salespeople immediately.' This makes sense to hard-nosed executives: Watch out for competition, it's a tough world out there, let's get moving. But it's really just fear as a management technique. It spawns a regime of micro-terror and veiled threats: Stay busy, keep your numbers up, or we'll have your ass.

Anyone who has been through an MBA program knows how this feels. At the end of the first year, the under performers are dismissed from the program. Shy and thoughtful students are at an automatic disadvantage since evaluation normally includes 'air time'. In turn, these mild-mannered intelligentsia do well on the tests, but don't usually share their work or study tips with others – after all this is a competitive environment. As a result, MBAs are aggressive, individualistic and terror-tested. They're underexposed to teamwork, ego control, soft tactics and meditation. And when the corporate behemoths park their scouts outside ivy-covered brick walls, the tough-minded students within are already well steeled for the relentless career drive that awaits them.

But what, in the end, do they want? A job that gives them . . . what? An Audi for the city, a Range Rover for the mountains, diving and skiing equipment, an apartment in a flashy district, $50 bills to slip to maître d's? Of course not. They may enjoy these mementoes of what a confused society calls success, but they didn't get to

business graduate school by being simpletons. They also need gratification, to feel they've exploited their talent. Very few companies
offer that option. Very few new MBA graduates can identify which
organization dangling job offers will meet their long term need to
breathe slowly from their talent oxygen tanks, taking in the scenery
as they go along at a manageable pace.

I once knew a Brazilian who was graduating from the Harvard
Business School. His living room featured a large wall chart with
vertical and horizontal grids detailing the 14 job offers he was
considering. The chart was rich with information like salary and
benefits, insurance, geographical location, company statistics. A
scoreboard of his success.

But it was also gibberish. Not only had he reduced his opportunities to a jumble of numbers, he had also assumed that his decision
would be based on a complex mathematical model. But he left out
the most important consideration – his 'calling', and the chance that
one of the jobs above all others would let him maximize his talents
and satisfy his identity.

There was no place for these gut feelings in his calculations.
Instead, he relied on a decision tree model, which transforms
assumptions into statistical percentages. For example, if geographic
location were important, it would have a weight of two points out
of 10. The globe would then be parcelled into zones with ratings. By
multiplying the rating by the weight, he'd assign a value to the
location. The next step would be to calculate the chances that the
job location would change. And the chance that the job would
provide global opportunities. Each of these would generate a new
outcome.

Take this process and apply it to 15 items, each with three to five
criteria, add factors and weights for each of those calculations,
relative values and orders-of-importance, and you have an idea of
how long this young man stayed awake before making his decision.
And of his confusion.

In the end my Brazilian friend took a job with one multi-national
only to see it merge with another company four months later. He was
sent to another country, in another job, but left the business two
years later. Today he's working for his fourth company – exactly
when he calculated he would be in Phase II-C of his career in the first,
defunct corporation. So much for statistical charts. He's still chasing
an elusive idea about the perfect job, framing it all around his MBA

and technical background, while the air in his tank is seeping uselessly away.

At Semco, we abolish manuals, procedures and policies so that people are free to improvise, to soar, and to collect the moments of happiness that constitute genuine success. Because of our careful mix, because of the self-selection process that goes on, Semco has less than one percent turnover. We rarely fire anyone. In 2000 and 2001, a total of three people (out of almost three thousand) quit on their own.

To keep turnover low, we put mechanisms in place at Semco that remind employees to 'make sure that you are where you want to be, and make sure that this is what you want to do.' Because if they're not sure, we'll bend over backwards to find a completely different area or completely different type of work for them, just as we did for Lucia Kobayashi.

This is not from altruistic motives. It's purely selfish. Unless we click with a worker, unless he latches onto something he is passionate about, our productivity won't be high. If someone is bored in their job, they should be able to move on to something else, even if it means giving several options a try. Few organizations make an effort to find out whether a person has a 'calling'. At Semco we try to encourage the process with several different programs.

We created one that allows people to act like entrepreneurs within Semco. Called *Lost In Space,* this program assumes that young recruits don't know what they want to do with their lives. (They don't know, or they're mistaken.) The program is designed to help them decide by letting them migrate through the company for a year. Do what you want to do, we say, move where you want, go where your interests take you, work for one, or three, or six different units. At the end of the year, anyone you've worked for can offer you a job, or you may seek an opening in an area that interests you.

If neither happens, thank you for your year. We started this program because of my firm belief that under our current education and economic system, a post-adolescent or a 22-year-old college graduate is in a poor position to make the life altering decision of choosing a career. Eighteen-year-olds are unduly influenced by what their parents expect of them, particularly when it comes to education and profession. So at that tender age, they choose a fork in life's road. Then they go to college. There they specialize. And it might not have been what they really wanted.

In our *Lost in Space* program, Rafael Tinoco, an 18-year-old computer hacker genius, is free to spend a year at the company doing as he wishes while hopefully making himself interesting and useful to us. The difference between Semco and other companies is that we seat young employees like Rafael in our non-territorial offices. Mutual contamination is guaranteed. When the teenager is seated next to our old-time directors and surrounded by people of all backgrounds and ages, everyone will learn. When they share a cappuccino, or overhear each other's conversations, learning takes place. A training program or apprenticeship in a marketing or finance area only isolates a young person. How do we know where their real talent or real interest lies if they're constrained to one subject matter? And if they work in a designated spot, then senior people in the company might interact with them only at specific times, and then only for a few minutes or only by coincidence. When everyone sits together in non-territorial offices, they necessarily interact all the time.

Rafael's current interest lies in holography. Who can say what that will lead us to? Probably nothing, since we cannot currently envisage any connection with what we do. But the kid may change his interest, or find a niche for us in holography. The only thing I know is that we all will learn very little if we have pre-conceived notions of training, careers and business models that compel us to say 'this is the way we do things'.

How many kids like Rafael were thrown out the window during the dot.com phase? We hope to incorporate as many of them as we can. Our old-timers should be able to rub business sense onto them – and they should rub refreshing zero-base concepts onto us. And this rub-a-dub should take both of us into the future, instead of re-editing the past.

Some *Lost in Space* programs don't end as we'd envisaged. Sergio Vezneyan was such a case. One of our first lost-in-spacers, this lanky, timid and seemingly confused young man came to us from engineering school. At first, no one really knew what to do with him, even though he had impressed people during the selection phase, and even though no one was supposed to do anything with him. Marcio Batoni was Sergio's mentor, meaning he was there to show him the Semco ropes, if Sergio asked. Sergio didn't ask much. He spent one month in each area, and quickly impressed people with his insights. His sharp mind was immediately apparent. At the end of his *Lost in*

Space year, after ten stints in different areas, he had six job offers within Semco.

He decided to take none of them, and went off to Europe to study further. Once there he was snapped up by Browns, a large shoe selling concern. He was their European director in Paris by the time he was 29, and then moved to back to Brazil. Shortly thereafter he received an offer to be the sales director of one of Brazil's giant companies, and is there to this day. So it's a two-way street – we have to like the spaceman, and he or she has to like us. Sergio visits us on occasion and says he has fond memories – and that's nice . . . but we like to keep our good ones!

Another program called *Rush Hour MBA* assembles every Monday at 6p.m. It started as a productive way for people to use the time they would otherwise spend sitting in São Paulo's excruciating rush-hour traffic. Instead of impatiently wasting two hours in commutes from one side of the city to the other, people could attend lectures and classes in our headquarters that would last until rush hour had ended. They'd still have to drive home, but the ride would be much shorter and they'd have new learning to think about on the way.

The program started on a very small scale but swiftly became popular. Volunteers lead each session and suggest topics or bring up business trends, articles they have read, or subjects in the media. People with expertise expound on articles from the *Harvard Business Review*, McKinsey reports or last week's *Financial Times*. Now it includes people at Semco who are enrolled in training or graduate courses. They update their colleagues on what they've learned in more formal settings. We hoped that *Rush Hour MBA* would ignite change because it would prompt debate and new ideas. But it should also help people develop their calling.

Other companies have similar executive education programs. General Electric operates a huge one with an enrolment nearly the size of a respectable graduate business school. It has professors on staff and a pre-set curriculum. Naturally, we want our program to be more free form, more loosely structured, more 'rambling' than that.

I have my own resolution to study two hours a day. I want to further my own education, but I also mean to do it without rhyme or reason. In some respect, the goal of the *Rush Hour MBA* is the same. I may study Jupiter today, and the Spanish Inquisition tomorrow. Anyone concerned with structure might say there's no discipline to that. I believe the two hours is my discipline. It won't count for anything because no school could grade my efforts. But after a year in which I may have studied a little biology, a little astronomy, a little history, I'll be better educated and better able to apply my knowledge to what I do everyday.

This method also ensures I'll remain interested. If there were some control over how I studied, I'd probably give up once compelled to stay on a subject that bored me. That's the problem with control. It can cost the learner his interest. Like the movie says, if you make it interesting, they will come.

Another example is our internal hiring program called *Family Silverware*. The motivation here is to give preference to people we already know. It can create problems, because talented employees are always aware they can move to where the challenges are. Their managers are sometimes frustrated because while they are hoping the worker will maximize his potential with them, other managers are constantly dangling better jobs in front of them. In hiring, we give internal candidates a 'discount' over external candidates – usually a 30 percent rebate on the score necessary for the winning candidate. This differential makes up for the advantages our internal people have: They know us, we know them, and we believe they can grow into the qualifications if they set their mind to it. That's worth 30 percent. And, mostly, it makes it possible for people to change areas entirely, to try something that they might like better – and dip into their reservoir of talent.

That's how José Violi became our CFO. He had none of the usual qualifications, yet he rose from within and surpassed people with wildly superior formal qualifications. Everyone quickly learned to respect the tiny, timid man who in minutes can cut through a complex business plan to get to its essence.

Without Violi we'd be in endless hot water . . . and yet, he'd have a hard time being hired at another company. He doesn't flaunt his power, doesn't market himself well, and is always ready to say he doesn't know something.

We can't train people to turn them into what we want. Mostly because we want nothing. We don't favour training manuals. Nor do we ask people where they want to be in five years time. We want them to amble and ramble. If they happen to be on a fixed path, we'll gladly help them train for that – on demand. But instead of formal training, we encourage people to ask a colleague for explanations, demonstrations and guidance. Information in any organization should be information on demand.

Henrique Oliveira, the food engineer in our machinery business unit, was hired after a collective interview with ten people from across Semco. Most of them were people he'd eventually work with, and Henrique said the process helped him decide whether he 'wanted to work with them, too'.

Formal training was not part of the job once he started, however. 'People always ask questions, they ask if you are available, they ask for help. I hardly ever get an order. The nicest part of that is always knowing why something must be done.' Although Henrique receives designs for food mixers, he rambles along with the workers who interviewed him, into completely different fields of machinery or services until they find a better and more efficient design. Putting all this together is only possible when there are no limitations imposed on your work.

Once a shop floor worker wanted to know why a piece of equipment was constructed without a filter and a waste pipe. His question compelled Henrique to re-examine the assembly plans.

'It took us a few hours but in the end it helped everyone to understand why he or she wouldn't be including an important part of the equipment at that particular time,' says Henrique, who regularly works from home but never after hours. 'We had already specified the answer on the plans, but we forgot to say why.'

We want our people to dive, enjoy the scenery and then tell us about it. Wallowing on the boat, or watching full tanks on the wall reminds us of how much there is still to see underneath the surface.

CHAPTER 3

It's Not About The Money

MY BOARD RECENTLY told me to take a hike. I'd settled next to a junior marketing assistant on this particular day. Semco's board has nine seats, two of which are always open for the employees who sign up on a first-come, first-served basis. On this lazy Monday afternoon, I introduced myself to them.

The newcomers fell into the patter and joking that takes place at these board meetings, which belie the fury with which members defend their points of view. For a first-timer, these meetings are a heady and confusing mix of personal camaraderie and conceptual battles. One minute someone would be up in arms against our CFO, José Violi, about corporate expense allocations and in the next, fighting alongside him to reduce investments in a start-up. People and issues are almost never confused, so it is amusing to see individuals raising their voices at each other, and then pouring coffee for one another. The young marketer on my right, Danilo (no relation to our other Danilo but constantly having his leg pulled about it) probably felt like a spectator at the Wimbledon games, with his head swinging back and forth in anticipation of the winner of each argument.

That's when I raised my concern over too much growth. We had just seen a graph showing that the company was set to grow yet another 42 percent – after years of some 35 percent expansion per year. I told the others I was nostalgic for some of the sense of security and levity that accompanied our cruising altitude years. And that I felt perturbed at the idea that we now have thousands of employees.

Certainly it strokes my ego to employ that many people at Semco. It also vindicates my conviction that our model of democracy and freedom in the workplace will lend itself to bigger companies. But growth *per se* is scary. We don't fear losing control, because we've come to grips with that one. But I worry that our culture is diluting too quickly, that we have two or three new employees for every old timer who has been with us five years or more.

The board members reassured me to a degree. They believe that our growth is not internally induced – that we do nothing to push the company past its organic size. The growth we're experiencing is a result of growing markets or market share – both of which should be sustainable.

Danilo and our boys at Semco Ventures are determined to make Semco a $1 billion company in five years. They made the usual comments about growth being necessary for clout, scale economy, geographical and human resource distribution, career perspectives and competitor comparisons.

I wasn't too impressed because – as always – a couple of sequential whys would reduce many of these arguments to rationalizations.

Their final argument, however, was an interesting one: To act on my reservations, wouldn't Semco have to artificially cap the growth of its business units? Wouldn't we have to exert control, and wouldn't that fly in the face of the democracy and freedom we so flamboyantly advocate? How do we explain that ole Dickie (my nickname at Semco, in the very diminutive form) is getting goose bumps over our growth rate?

Well, I concede that a shareholder obstructing his company's growth is not standard fare for board meetings, but I still felt myself turning red at the smiles and guffaws.

Head for your mountain ranch and watch the grass grow during your long hikes, one of the board members half-joked. I got the message (in fact, I began a botanical garden that is scheduled to be ready in 2017 – my concerns assuaged by slow-growing Sequoias that will mature in time for my great grandchild's wedding).

Our meeting left critical questions unanswered: What is success, and what does it have to do with money or growth? Why are we so obsessed about it? Why is success a natural culmination of talent and calling if it is measured in numbers?

Success begs for a definition, to understand what we strive for. It's a deceptively easy word to toss about, but a very difficult concept to comprehend. In a business context, most people define success as growth, profit, product acceptance, and quality. But if we apply this to personal life, do those definitions hold up?

If growth is necessary to success, how do we guarantee that it continues? What grows indefinitely? In nature, growth is only temporary. The tallest trees are the first to get struck by lightning. Or another example: When I asked once at a medical conference if anyone knew of an organism that enjoyed perpetual growth, someone answered, cancer – and remembered that it eventually kills its host.

So has business invented the only organism – the company – that grows endlessly?

What is the value in endless growth? Is an evergreen tree superior to a tree ablaze with bright yellow leaves in the fall? Is McDonald's better than the Five Flies restaurant in Amsterdam, which has remained the same size and has been owned by the same family for hundreds of years?

I once took a physics course, at the end of which the professor had only one question: How far can you go into a forest? The correct answer was, midway. Beyond that and you're leaving the forest. I think of this when I consider my company's growth. There's no such thing as perpetual growth. Yet that's what traditional business people crave.

But what is growth meant to achieve? If Oxford University is so successful, then why isn't there a branch in Washington D.C.? If a symphony is successful with 120 musicians, why not even more so with 600?

The minute I hear conventional explanations for business practices – like the idea that companies are required to grow, that profit is paramount – I know I'm hearing nothing more than crystallized – or even calcified – thinking. Any time that happens, I immediately want to ask why? Why greater wealth? So that we can make even more money, and then be obliged to earn more beyond that? Why is growth necessary beyond the minimum that comes with the natural expansion of the market being served? Why do we have to make more money every quarter or face demotion by analysts on Wall Street? Because Wall Street needs to guarantee income to pension funds, which in turn finance ever-increasing numbers of retired people. Because it must compensate for one too many bad bets on upstarts, dot.coms and even mature players. Because it has hired too many MBAs who make too much money and drive costs ever higher.

None of these are good reasons for more growth.

And why does growth create a competitive advantage? Crystallized thinking would point to strategic positioning, mass, global deployment. Why isn't remaining similar in size and getting better at what we do more advantageous than hiring new people that we do not know, opening new plants that will have a long learning curve, and losing sight of what we've already learned to do best?

Are there not – every year – hundreds of telcos like Global Crossing, auditors like Arthur Andersen, retailers like K-Mart, or car companies like Volvo and Rover, who over-extend themselves and lose control over their businesses (and end up broke or sold to competitors)?

Profit (beyond the minimum) is not essential for survival. In any event, an organization doesn't really need profit over and beyond what is vital for working capital and the small growth that is essential for keeping up with the customers and competition. Excess profit only creates another imbalance. To be sure, it enables the owner or CEO to commission a yacht. But then employees will wonder why they should work so the owner can buy a boat.

And ploughing profits back into the company is akin to saying: The army has extra food, so it's time to enlist more soldiers. Or there are extra violins, so let's find some more violinists for the orchestra. Ultimately, balance is thrown out of whack.

Upsetting the seesaw causes problems of its own. A deficit can be deadly; but a surplus can create a monster, too. Someone will start spending that surplus, and it'll probably lead a company to build more factories than it can sustain, lease a new headquarters that isn't necessary, or acquire a company that wasn't in the cards.

An organization can remain small and focused for centuries. Witness Bologna University, the Vienna Philharmonic, Orthodox churches, Dutch schools or Scandinavian paper companies – all of which are many hundreds of years old.

Another argument says that in a constantly growing company, all boats rise with the tide. Everyone will do better if the company does, right? Wrong. With a few exceptions among the higher ranks, it is absolutely untrue that workers make more over the years as the company grows. One of the rarely debated policies of large companies is the one that exploits turnover to substitute expensive employees with cheaper ones. In the case of global companies, this can be brutally simple: A plant in Texas is moved to cheaper Ireland, then moved again to India, and finally, shut down in India to open up in Vietnam. Are employees in this growing company better off, now that the average hourly rate has dropped from $22 in the US to 21 cents in South East Asia?

At Semco we've concentrated instead on finding the right organic size for each of our markets. Growth and profit are rarely an issue. We concentrate on the process – and look only for growth that can endure. Recently we were approached to sell real estate management software to a Brazilian national fund that has 5,400 sites. The sale was sewn up, but then Zeca stepped into the fray. He fired off an e-mail that questioned whether there was an ethical conflict in our software sale to the national fund. He'd discovered that even though our customer was making a *bona fide* purchase from us, it was integrating our software into a sale to the fund that was based on a kickback commission. The customer had been selected to supply the fund because of corruption, and we were within the scope of their supply. No one was asking us for any money, or to carry out any incorrect procedures. But Zeca had discovered that the ultimate sale was corrupt.

Three hours after Zeca's e-mail went out, a dozen replies poured in. They were unanimous. We should withdraw our bid, even if we were at arms-length from the dubious part of the transaction.

Although this says a lot about the culture that has formed at Semco in terms of ethical conduct, it also reinforces the notion that growing completely within the law is more onerous than simply seizing every opportunity. Some superficial calculations have indicated that we would be almost three times the size we are if we had agreed to play the dubious ethics game. But this is merely growth for the sake of it.

Recently we ran into another situation that brought the issue of credos to the surface. We'd entered a joint effort with a giant US multinational to sell a safety-training package to a leading national oil company. The American company did the selling, and we came along as a preferred partner. After almost a dozen presentations, our consortium was awarded the $30 million contract. About $6 million was ours.

Much to our surprise, when our people went to settle details with the US multinational, we were told that the sale had involved a kickback to one of the client's directors! Our people were shocked and a chill went down their spines. Not only did they not know about it, but were surprised that this American company had agreed – they are a Fortune 500 giant. But mostly they were upset that the American firm didn't know that Semco was famous throughout Brazil for its vocal anti-corruption position, and thus wasn't the right party for such business practices. We had already provided evidence that led to prosecutions and convictions for extortion and bribery on several occasions. We weren't about to take part in a kickback scheme now.

The multinational's directors were adamant – they were sticking to the deal. They encouraged our people to accept the circumstances as a given. These were just the facts of life, they said. E-mails flew back and forth. One executive of the US company, who had spent hundreds of hours on the project, and who knew what it meant to the year's budget, asked pointedly: Is this the reply that Semco will give in the future to all such situations? He knew that our market would be severely limited if we stuck to the straight and narrow path. Huge business opportunities were emerging in the very large, very corrupt, oil companies.

Danilo Saicali and José Violi, our CFO, answered simultaneously, their e-mails crossing; Danilo said that there is no issue of past, present or future, that this was the way Semco acted, end of story. Violi, although well aware of the cash that would stream into that business unit, was curt: 'Return the order.'

The US multinational in question has a credo and mission statement that is beautiful to read, and may bring tears to the eyes of most. We write nothing down. When push comes to shove we write our own history as we go.

Perhaps this sounds corny or self-aggrandizing. But we think that the trip through life – personal or corporate – adds up snapshots and memories of moments which, in the end, tell us how happy we were, and how true to ourselves. We think we have a minimum common denominator with those taking the trip with us, and we need to feel good about how we have travelled.

Even though we could be much bigger, we're convinced that rejecting opportunities such as these strengthens our management practices and earns us respect. That makes it easier to attract the talent that we need – at any level – and then, finally, to generate better business (even size and profit).

So it's not about being virgins in a brothel. It's that ethical issues can actually generate good business.

For those who want growth at any price, there are mergers and acquisitions – just another form of keeping score on the big board. Legions of lawyers, consultants and auditors have made fortunes from mergers and acquisitions. No words ring as musically in their ears as 'due diligence,' the process of digging (I like the recent fad for 'drilling down') into the depths of a company's psyche and ancient filing cabinets, searching for lies, risk and other fodder for the negotiation table. Where does all this frenzy for joining two as one, taking over and buying out originate? What does it say about growth?

Why would two companies decide they'd be better off as one? The crystallized, conventional answer is that it increases clout and competitiveness, while reducing duplication. Theoretically, then, it would be even better for three, four or five companies to join forces.

Under this assumption, the ideal business community would have two or three companies or groups of companies in each business niche. No more. They'd achieve the maximum possible scale economies, clout and technological capacity. If so, why do these dreamed-of gains, so convincingly exhorted at merger announcements by two CEOs, rarely if ever see the light of day? Why is it hell to work in a recently merged company? And why do these merged entities then have to re-merge and further merge, until the Big Eight are Four, or the Seven Sisters are Three? Are we saying that peace on earth and happiness on the board will occur only when the Big Four have become the Big Two, and the Seven Sisters have turned into twins?

Mergers are about growth and profit. But many times they are also a solution for bad management. Companies with mistakes to cover up are the first ones in search of a merger. Companies that are doing beautifully are usually only interested in acquisitions.

Semco has been down the acquisition road (five times, in fact).

My first trip was to obtain a subsidiary of the Reliance Corporation, itself a division of Exxon (it made large machinery).

The summit of our negotiations was to occur at the Citicorp Center in New York City, on 53rd Street. It was set for 5p.m., and I uncharacteristically arrived on the dot – but then needed a quarter of an hour to get up to the meeting room. The reason: The marvellous building was emptying its contents at that precise time. Thousands of cattle-people were abandoning the building as if a fire alarm had sounded. Secretaries in dresses and sneakers, office assistants in suits and Nikes were simply fleeing – getting the heck out of there. It was impossible to enter the building because the revolving doors were whirling madly in the direction of the street, pirouetting and spitting out batch after batch of weary office dwellers, every last one of them eager to get home as soon as possible. I remember thinking of what would happen if one of them missed a step or tripped – surely the person would be duly scraped off the revolving door and thrown in a recycle bin by a security guard, whilst the flow resumed.

I later realized that my attempt to swim against that tide was a metaphor for our dealings with Reliance Corp. We mistook greed for synergy, and overlooked what was really going on – we were trying to do better on our growth scorecard.

This attempt at an acquisition was thwarted by an innocent question. After hours of debate at a board meeting, in which we addressed the intricacies of scale economies and market integration gains, Clovis Bojikian said: 'Excuse me, I know we've looked at all the angles, and that we will grow by three times with this acquisition, but just indulge me with one response: Why is it really that we are doing this?' A two-hour discussion ensued, and the raging soul-searching that accompanied it resulted in a landmark decision for Semco: Looking for growth just for the sake of being bigger is no strategy.

We dutifully informed Citibank and Reliance that we respectfully declined to pursue the acquisition. They'd toiled endless months on this deal, so for their part they dutifully recommended that our board engage in group therapy – four times a week . . .

Corporations go through cycles of growth and retrenching – what I call corporate yo-yo dieting. Companies that expand continually are companies that grow fat. Then they're forced to diet (downsizing in 'corp' speak) until they can grow again and reengineer (a new body in 90 days!), merge and acquire other companies (weightlifting and muscle training) until the cycle starts anew and they're forced to reduce again (lose 20 pounds in 6 weeks!). No wonder people who work in these places are perplexed, weary and soft.

We know that's unhealthy. Especially when companies expand but do not grow 'taller,' or find new markets. Yet so many business leaders believe that no growth is equally disastrous.

In the last 8 years, none of our businesses grew less than 22 percent per year. One grew an average of 44 percent every year. But rather than rejoicing in healthy expansion, so much growth alarms me.

At Semco RGIS, for example, we are constantly between a rock and a hard place. Growing quickly is strategic, because we have fast become the market leaders in this business. National stature, which means launching in five to seven new cities every year, is critical to servicing large global retailers like Wal-Mart or JC Penney. On the other hand, hiring in a hurry, shoring up the back office, finding experienced front line supervisors and setting aside the huge amounts of capital that growth consumes is a challenging proposition.

RGIS, under Marcio Batoni, has experienced phenomenal growth – 50 to 80 percent every year. The rest of us are constantly trying to hold Marcio back because we think a slower rate of growth will ensure quality – not to mention our sanity. But Marcio is convinced that a Semco presence in every major South American city is the only guarantee against encroaching competitors.

So it's common for his people to ship thigh-top computers to a small town overnight, complete an inventory, and then ship them back on the first plane the next morning.

On one particularly bizarre occasion, a supervisor took a bus 1300 miles, from southern Brazil to Brasilia, to deliver 80 computers for that night's inventory. The Brasilia manager, Izak Santos, came to the bus station to help unload the equipment – only to find that the computers weren't on the bus. The supervisor had forgotten to pack them!

'I still can't believe that happened,' Izak says, completely befuddled. 'The guy was so dizzy from consecutive inventories, that he couldn't, and cannot to this day, explain what happened.'

Today, when we are growing 'only' 40 percent a year, we consistently earn a 98 percent satisfaction rate for quality. For that performance, Marcio Batoni won an award for 'exceptional results' at the annual RGIS convention in Las Vegas. But growth consumes a lot of cash. It dilutes company culture, requires hiring a lot of new people, and forces us to defend higher ground. The faster the growth, the less defensible or sustainable the company feels. We are number one in six out of eight markets, and are constantly under siege from the other players. In our property management business the two international giants that compete with us are determined to target and ferret out our people. Luckily, only one out of 17 headhunting expeditions (that we know of) has been successful.

If size and market share were definitive measures of success, surely the automotive companies would be good examples. They're huge and have existed for nearly 100 years. Yet only a handful of people have profited enormously. Has it been worthwhile for everyone involved with them? Have employees, suppliers and customers all felt gratified to have worked with one of the giant carmakers? My impression is that the answer will mostly be 'no' or 'not really'.

It's a balancing act – size shouldn't alienate the people working in a company. Just because Semco RGIS aspires to open in every major South American city doesn't mean we should ignore the minimum size of feasible groups of workers. Organizations must respect the natural, atomic structure that most benefit social animals – us. Take another example: the pyramids. People gape in awe a full 5,000 years after they were built. Engineers speculate about the precision of the stone work, logistics experts wonder at the amount of dragging that went on, architects ponder the geometry.

With such a marvel, wouldn't the construction be labelled a success, whomever you asked? But what if you asked the slaves who dragged the stones (I'm ignoring the archaeologists who believe they may not have been slaves after all)? Would they agree the toil was worthwhile? That building the House of the Thereafter for the mummies of their rulers was a gratifying way to lead their lives? They probably would not be as radiant as the monarchs.

Most executives would say that it doesn't matter what the slaves thought or wanted – without them, the monumental pyramids would not exist and the world would be poorer for it. Henry Ford's family might say the same. But is this the only way to achieve greatness? Would the world consider palaces built by prisoners in Gulags or concentration camps as marvellous successes of humankind?

Success is more than just physical, intellectual or economic performance. Or endurance. It also requires some sense of whether the activity behind and around it was worthwhile for the participants, and for those served by it.

At Semco, 20 years of success has taught us that ignoring growth, avoiding long-range business plans (we don't have one), and downplaying profits (I'm not sure of the actual figure) are why we thrive. We focus instead on whether the people who work for us are able to balance their aspirations with Semco's purpose. I know from two decades' experience that once the balance is achieved and self-interest kicks in, new business, growth, and profit inevitably follow.

Take Jorge Lima. After years with Semco Johnson Controls and then Cushman & Wakefield Semco, he was tapped by us to begin a new van-based operation. This is a business to provide mobile services such as maintenance, cleaning and security to an area (town, city, or neighbourhood) through a specially qualified engineer travelling in a van. This person, called a Super Joe (man or woman!) is maintenance engineer, electrician, air conditioning repairman, sales person and help desk administrator all rolled into one. He or she has an assistant who rides along and does some of the tasks, to ensure productivity.

These vans, equipped with notebook computers, tool kits and wireless devices and gadgets, roam from customer to customer (like FleetBoston, Nextel, ATT and Carrefour supermarkets in a given geographical location). This enables the engineer and his assistant to drastically reduce their mileage, turn around on a dime, perform scheduled tasks, and supervise operations such as cleaning, security and maintenance. Complex software and computers control the best possible moment for changing a light bulb, a compressor or toilet paper. Then it's a question of coordinating the sub-contractors who carry out the service, and acting as a liaison with the client. *Voilà!*

Easier said than done. We'd been trying to put this together for six years. But at two meetings, Semco employees repeatedly rejected the business plan, despite my vociferous opposition. I believed the van business had great business potential, and I didn't want it shelved.

Then Jorge Lima began to believe in the business. As luck would have it, two of our major competitors contacted Jorge through head-hunters and offered him deals that were vastly superior to his terms at Semco. (One of our global arch-enemies, Jones Lang LaSalle, was intent on prying our people from us – out of 17 headhunting targets they managed to snag only our Rio de Janeiro Branch Manager for Real Estate Transactions – by offering him 240 percent over his current package.)

Jorge rejected the competing job offers in favour of 'the Semco way,' or job satisfaction through challenge and not higher salary or title inflation. He wanted to stretch his limits, so with a nod here and there from the board (unofficially, since it was obvious that a formal approval wouldn't be forthcoming), he started the van-based business. He pursued local retailers, bank branches, gas stations and cellular antenna operators. In the first two months he picked up 200 sites to manage. Within another month, he had 400 sites, and was up to five percent of the entire market estimate. The business plan had predicted reaching five percent by the second year.

And then Jorge was diagnosed with leukaemia. The first days were awful. He grew very depressed. He came to see Clovis, Danilo and others in tears, asking them to look after his family. Everyone was shocked beyond words. Jorge needed Gleevec, a medicine that helps control blood cell levels, but he could neither find nor afford it. At $3,000 a pop, Gleevec would cost him his house in a year, and he might need the drug for five or 10 years. Needless to say, the health insurance plan that Jorge had chosen was based on his feeling immortal (he is a 38-year-old charging bull, a paradigm of fitness who plays night football), and it didn't cover this type of medication.

People sprang in all directions to help. Semco paid for the medicine. After the terrible first two weeks, Jorge became an encyclopaedia on the disease, and a control patient in local clinical trials with leukaemia sufferers. He began to take various medicines, and started chemotherapy. Some days he would arrive at work ashen, and soon his gray pallor became standard. By the third week, however, Jorge began fighting the disease head on. He was determined not to die. He vowed to return to work, full blast. And blast full he did. By the seventh month, the van-based business had signed up 2,100 sites, making it the biggest player in the field. In its first full year, it looked like a $10 million business and one that would become a $30 million unit in a few more years. And Jorge had spent no more than $50,000, mostly in unauthorized start-up expenses (in keeping with our adage that it is better to beg forgiveness than permission).

Now he was on a roll. Visiting three to five cities per week, and spending 16-hour days on aeroplanes and in vans, Jorge's leukaemia began to recede. He had strict doctor's orders not to get upset or work for more than a few hours, but he would just laugh them away. At night he promised his wife that each phone call after 11 p.m. was his last.

Jorge started to look better, and his blood work came back much improved. Finally, his disease stabilized, but his astounded doctors had no clinical explanations – they just know that his recovery stems from his strong will.

Sure, Jorge could have opted for spending all of his time with his family. But he found a fundamental purpose in work. Establishing the van business is a big goal, surely, but leaving his mark on the world is more important to Jorge.

'At Semco I've found the place where my fullest potential can be developed,' he said recently in an e-mail to several directors. 'There is freedom to act, to err, and to fulfil life's purpose. I don't intend to die anytime soon, and have surprised the doctors regularly. I'll continue doing so until the leukaemia goes back where it came from. I still have much to do and live for.'

Jorge is a fine example of the re-definition of success and growth. We're not against the face value of either, but there's got to be balance, too. A business like Jorge's must be big and pervasive to succeed, but that is only part of the challenge. To be big and unwieldy, or ultimately unsustainable, is a pyrrhic victory. Success is three-dimensional. It's not enough to tackle it from one angle only. The van business worked because Jorge found in it a purpose, his identity, and his reason for getting up in the morning.

You could say that Eugenio Singer re-defines success, too. He's successful, all right – a multi-millionaire, and money like that certainly spells success to most people. But it took nearly ten years of disastrous losses to get there. Any other company would surely have shut him down after a couple of years. Certainly there were times when our board wanted to. But Eugenio had a gut feeling about his business idea, and we had a gut feeling about him.

Bright-eyed and humorous, Eugenio impresses everyone who meets him. The son of Israeli parents, an environmentalist at heart, he enjoyed a long academic career, earning degrees in engineering, biology and ecology, and teaching at one of Brazil's leading universities. He was always a visionary, as well. After many years at Alcoa, the aluminium behemoth (where he rose to run the environmental department) he decided to strike out and formed his own company, RAL (Environmental Resources, Inc., in portuguese). This might easily have been a mistake.

He gave up security, and a guaranteed income, on a hunch. The hunch was right, but it would take ten years to find out. In the meantime, Eugenio almost lost everything. His company, a seven-person outfit, barely made enough to keep heads above water. Eugenio's partner, Ricardo, was the salesman, and several of his university students filled out his technical staff.

Eugenio's income plummeted, but he was in RAL for the long term. In 1995, a few years after RAL started, several of us read a newspaper piece on an upcoming boom in environmental services. Rogerio Ottolia, who then worked in Semco's brainstorming unit called NIT (Nucleus of Technical Innovation), 'discovered' Eugenio, much as a scout finds movie stars.

A negotiation ensued, and soon Semco owned 70 percent of RAL. It didn't take us long to fall out with Eugenio's partner, whose business views were incompatible with ours. He left, and that's when we discovered the salesman in Eugenio. But the environmental business in Brazil was far from ripe. And our focus was far from clear. Eugenio tried to run the company single-handed – he bounced back and forth between sales and engineering, from biologists to the bank. We began having all sorts of quality control problems, and no one was paying proper attention to details in the complex reports that we sent to our customers.

For five years we made no money at all. As a matter of fact, we lost so much that every quarter there was uproar in the boardroom over demands to close down RAL. Some of us cajoled endlessly for another chance. The board decided to allow a maximum monthly loss of $10,000, a sum hard to justify, and hard to live with, considering that RAL had long been racking up losses and its outlook was bleak. But it was the maximum the board could stand to throw out of the window.

Eugenio gave up a chunk of his salary – and he was already taking home a pittance. He tried to make do with no more than $1,500 a month. At Alcoa he would have made 10 times as much. He continued to spend, however, and as a consequence, his personal debts multiplied.

One memorable afternoon in the late 1990s, José Violi, our CFO, called me.

'We received notice that Eugenio is about to default on a loan to the Italian bank, Sudameris,' José said in a hushed, apprehensive voice. 'He owes them about $80,000.'

I spoke to Eugenio. It was worse than either Violi or I knew.

'I haven't paid for my kid's school in months, either, and I'm late on rent and car payments,' Eugenio admitted. We hadn't known – and Eugenio hadn't told us – that he was spending as if his eternal optimism was money in the bank. He overlooked his mounting debt, hoping that business would turn up at any moment and save him.

Under extreme pressure from all sides, Eugenio resigned. We then spent several hours at my house, hollering at each other about responsibility, irresponsibility and our unerring belief that he was the right person to lead the company. But how?

'Isn't it obvious that I cannot work like this?' he screamed.

I was irritated, too, at the thought that we'd come to this. Three times, with Peter's denials to Jesus on his mind, he resigned. Three times I yelled that he couldn't resign just because he had made a mess of things, that we would have fired him long ago if we thought he couldn't do the job. Kafka should have been there.

In the end, we rehired him, Semco covered his loan at the bank and increased his salary, and we added a chief operating officer to remove the day-to-day strain from Eugenio so that he could concentrate on what he did best: think, strategize, sell.

Looking the board in the eye, however, was more difficult. To our US partners, the developments with Eugenio were ominous. Their director came to Brazil to actively participate in the shouting match – and we then spent hours at a castle hotel in the British city of Bath, selling to the ERM Group directors the same concept we were pushing to the board in Brazil: Let's make the losses bigger, in order to make the losses smaller. Right.

Eventually the grand plan was approved. We hired Yanko Guimarães as our new COO (chief operations officer). Yanko's deep set green eyes turned out to be our lifebuoy. In his determined, quiet manner, he was the organizer, the calm in the eye of the storm that we needed. After all, freewheeling with creativity requires solid backing. We frequently pair visionaries like Eugenio with practical managers who can hold the fort, like Yanko. It has always led to great success. One without the other makes for a band of poets, or a stodgy, boring outfit. Together, they teach each other something everyday.

Just two years later, Semco ERM (with RAL folded into it) became one of the most profitable companies in the world-wide ERM group. All it took was Eugenio's knack for enchanting customers combined with Yanko's talent for delivering what he sold. Yanko eliminated our quality control problems, and sharpened our complex customer reports. He also managed the precarious cash flow that ensued from Eugenio's lack of interest in finance. With that we could require advance payments, hire better people, deal on a win-win basis with speciality consultants, and obtain from the customer the time to do the job. In just three years, the unit grew from $2 to $10 million in revenue, and became Brazil's premier environmental consulting company.

Eugenio went from taking home a piddling salary to earning a few hundred thousand dollars a year. Semco forgave him the shares that he had put up as collateral for the loans we paid off, and restored his 20 percent stake in the company. He invested in real estate and became a mini-millionaire. ERM Group, about to go public on the London Stock Exchange, offered him over a million dollars for shares that were, four years earlier, worth $50,000. Eugenio followed his heart, and growth and profit followed him.

CHAPTER 4

The Fortunate 500

IF MONEY IS NOT the barometer of success, then how does a company know when it's doing well? What if all the classic measurements we use today are faulty?

What, if not growth or profits, constitutes success? A balanced mix where all do well. Where stockholders, employees, clients, suppliers and community are all canvassed for their opinions, and where this three-dimensional exercise results in a complete picture. We are working on such a scorecard, one that will enable us to compare progress, anticipate trouble and tweak our priorities.

After all, we want to be able to exchange revenue-based evaluations for something much more complex. By evaluating success from everyone's different point of view, we believe we'll land on the new list of companies that unite sustainability with all-round gratification. Let's call this list the Fortunate 500.

After all, over the years, we've all been dismayed to see companies that appeared healthy falter and even implode – IBM in the 1990s, Ford in 2002, Apple or Netscape in their early days, Enron, Arthur Andersen, and WorldCom just recently.

Why aren't a balance sheet, a stock market price, and customer satisfaction ratings enough to indicate how a company is doing? If public businesses are so mysterious, what's to be said of NGOs, libraries and hospitals?

We need a new format, a new way of evaluating companies – a 360-degree, comprehensive measurement gauge of how well an organization is doing.

The numbers are a useful place to start. It's vital to know how much companies sell, spend on marketing, or earn as profit. We need to know their debt levels and ratings, as well. All of these are an important part of what I call the barometer.

99

But the debacle of companies that were touted as successes only to topple shortly thereafter prove that numbers are not everything. Organizations agree that responses from customers are important – they just don't know how to ask the right questions, or get the client interested in answering them.

It's not surprising that auto makers and airlines have changed so little in the last hundred years – and find it so awfully hard to make money consistently (none of the big car companies or airlines have ever enjoyed consecutive profits). Just look at the questions they ask their end users: Is this year's model better than last year's, is the car dealer's service satisfactory, was an airfare better than that of the competitors, does the company fly through the right hubs.

These are the same status quo questions that the US Mail service asked its constituency in the 1980s, before UPS and FedEx came along. Or GTE asked its telephone users before Nokia appeared. Or Philips asked its portable radio users before the Walkman was invented. Wrong questions will generate wrong answers, followed by wrong directions and a mistaken idea of how well an organization is doing. Questions bordering on the absurd are more useful.

- What would you like your car to run on? Solar energy, electricity, gas, helium, but not fossil fuels.
- How would you like to change a flat tire? In no more than four minutes, without dirtying my hands and running risks in shady neighbourhoods.
- What would you like as food in an aeroplane? Something that I can select from a pre-sent menu (that includes pizza and burgers), and is cooked to order.
- When would you like a big parcel delivered? Next day, guaranteed.
- How would you like to use a phone? While I jog (old answer, laughable at the time), without having to dial, carry equipment or use batteries (new answer, laughable now).
- How would you like your cassette tape player to work? While I walk in the park (ridiculous at the time), or by downloading music while walking in the park, without cables or batteries, just by saying what I want (absurd, now).

Asking the right questions, even if you are not prepared for the answers, is fundamental to our barometer.

100

One of first times I answered such a questionnaire was at the behest of a cashier at a hotel who slid one under my nose, suggesting that I answer it in two minutes, while he printed out my bill. Easy, timely, effortless and meaningful – to both sides.

Marcio Batoni has put together a customer survey that is close to what we need. It's open-ended, and conducted with the client immediately after an inventory and is offered at the end of the service, when the interest and action are simultaneous. It asks users to describe their ideal service, to say how quickly they need inventory results in hand, to state how many of our people they would like to see in their stores. We've had requests that would have been absurd just a few years ago, including downloading data every two minutes (which we do) or taking inventory in a supermarket full of shopping customers (which we also do).

We are also initiating a system that makes these comments useful. It's too easy for managers to ignore the results, or to shrug away the most negative comments (of course, it was filled out 'during the hot season', or 'after a strike', or 'just before our newest product came out.').

Another angle of this puzzle is employees.

If we have a moral code, it's our insistence on trust. We want Semco employees to have faith in their company. We measure that with a survey asking our employees to tell us anonymously once a year what they think of the company, its management, its future. We circulate questionnaires and ask them whether they feel like coming to work on Monday morning, whether they trust their leaders, and whether they believe everything we say in our internal and external communications. Since 1996, between 85 and 94 percent of replies have been in the top brackets – good and great. And those percentages have increased almost every year, indicating that leaders take the responses seriously.

Integrity, after all, is only tested when push comes to shove – when people who are left to their own devices show that they are willing to celebrate dissent.

The ratings that result from these questionnaires give us an invaluable picture of year-to-year trends. How many companies want to hear the answers, though? Much less publish them. But that's just what we plan to do at Semco. In the hopes of convincing people and markets that transparency pays, we are planning to begin publishing survey findings (our barometer) together with our financial reports. Once we start, we'll have reached a new level of accountability, one that will surely benefit us as well – after all, minority shareholders, customers, employees and suppliers will all prefer to be close to a company that is above-board and willing to learn.

Suppliers, consultants, independent contractors and third parties are rarely queried, either. Once a year we convene dozens, show them around Semco, and ask them pointed questions. Since most depend on us, they can't be expected to talk truthfully or openly about being squeezed too hard by us, or to tell us that we're slipping behind our competitors (which many will deal with, naturally). We then ask them to take pencil in hand, and fill out an anonymous questionnaire. We instantly tally the results so we can discuss them on the spot. The result of these evaluations will also be published in our barometer.

Organizations must be accountable to the public, and they should comply with realistic regulations. So scrutiny should also focus on the world beyond business – environmentalists, legal protection agencies, government, and all sorts of NGOs. Today NGOs can protest outside G-8 Summits (and see their supporters or opponents get dragged off to jail), and present reports to the public. But even though NGOs have little influence over powerful, international corporations, they cannot be ignored entirely. They must be taken into account, even if it's only in a small way. It is a bit more difficult to affect the corporate world. Certainly, companies pay increasing lip service to social responsibility – to the extent that it has become a cliché. Social Balance Sheets are becoming so common that they all look alike: They describe environmental compliance, parks and rivers a company has cleaned up, schools for the poor that a corporation has financed, and the thousands of hours of training in social responsibility furnished to their employees. Soon, you won't be able to tell one Social Balance Sheet from the other, just as has happened to credos and mission statements.

By adding this dimension to the barometer, we are adding a vital link to accountability. Sustainable practices in companies are closely related to the laws and social issues that NGOs, government agencies and the general public are concerned with. If no company is an island, dealing at close quarters with groups who see companies in the light of the greater good is vital to success.

We're creating our barometer as a definition of success. By combining numbers and people, customers and suppliers, and government agencies and NGOs, we hope to produce a well-rounded evaluation of the word 'success'. If we can find sustainability and gratification for all these groups, we'll have an all-encompassing success. And that'll make Semco one of the Fortunate 500.

And what barometer do we use to determine success or happiness for individuals? Even the richest of them? I once spoke to a billionaire's group at the Ritz Hotel in Paris. I faced the one hundred highest net worth customers of the (then) Chase Manhattan Bank. These men, royalty of the coin, came together to ponder, meditate on their condition and, as two of them confessed, to monitor their wives' shopping (I'm not responsible for the sexist division of activities!). What interested me, as I surveyed them from the podium, was the motivation that took them to the office on Monday morning. I asked them to tell me why they were in business. The laconic reply reverberated in waves: To make money. The more politically correct among them parlayed this as 'enhancing shareholder wealth'.

So I asked the group what their goal had been when they started out. Mostly self-made men, they had set numerical targets, such as $10 million, $100 million and even $1 billion. (Why is it that no one sets targets of $83 million? And what if they set $100 million goal but achieve only $83 million? Do they become disillusioned, thwarted, frustrated? What is it that a magical number does to people's self-esteem? The most wonderful part, however, is that wherever in the world I heard this, people always wanted to achieve a hundred million somethings – dinars, pounds sterling or yens – no matter how divergent such values were. Which went on to prove that these were tribal, ego-related sums – never business necessities.) To a tee, these men had all grandly exceeded their goals. So what took them to the office after that, once their targets had been achieved?

The reply was the same I found at a program I had attended at Harvard. Fully one-third of that class had made their riches and then sold out – but of these, no less than 88 percent had eventually purchased another business. In essence, these people were in business to dip into their 'reservoirs of talent', that pool of inherent interests and skills that is unique to all of us. They dip to make themselves feel alive, to provide purpose and identity, to satisfy their egos with the trappings of status, to feel that their lives were worth living. Never for the money.

That's why any discussion of happiness brings us to wealth – somehow our tribe puts these two together, even when its members realize it ain't so. I have a theory about wealth. My friends just sigh when they hear this . . . my theory is that the maximum personal wealth is $12 million. And I've done some calculations with economists to bear out this cabalistic, and admittedly provocative, number. Not a cent over $12 million. After that, all millionaires are the same.

It's really Leonardo da Vinci's fault. He worried about proportions between man, space and the divine. The rules that Leonardo identified as he drew, painted and invented are the ones that hold people to $12 million. I call it the Da Vinci Constraint.

Da Vinci's friend Paccioli made the point in 1509 with his book, *Da Divina Proportione*. Da Vinci illustrated this book with many drawings, one of which everyone knows – the one with the bearded man with two pairs of arms outstretched, squaring the circle. What I call the Da Vinci Constraint, therefore, is a way of applying that theory to wealth. It has to respect proportion to be useful.

Humanity is limited in how much it can indulge – how many times a person can eat, how many toys a child can play with, how much horsepower a car can generate before it becomes a plane. A neighbour of mine in São Paulo built a house that reminds me of a South American dictator's compound. He may have spent his entire allotment of $12 million on the house. But now his problem is Leonardo, who points out that a human cannot possibly feel at ease in such a disproportionate house. Certainly my neighbour can live there, open it to photographers from design magazines, and be admired from afar. But in winter he'll huddle in the tiny TV room on the second floor, withdrawing from the cavernous rooms to seek a more human scale.

That's what the $12 million does. It gives you the access to a large city house or apartment, a beach house, a mountain cottage, three of your dream cars, and even renting a helicopter – if you absolutely must. Three meals a day, a personal trainer to do away with their side effects, clubs, spas, elegant European travel. Seven or eight servants, dandy schools for the kids, much opera, season tickets galore, and accounts at Donna Karan. That's what Leonardo da Vinci will let you have. And that's why all millionaires are the same after that sum.

Collecting money is like amassing any other item. By definition, no collector can ever be happy. There will always be a piece, a unit, a set that can't be had. On a trip to Bangkok, I met a man who had made his fortune in tomatoes, import and export, and steel. He was proud that the flight over his tomato fields took 40 minutes.

We went to dinner. A chain smoker, my host was said to light one match a day when he got out of bed. With every cigarette he would light the next. Throughout dinner he did not once put out a cigarette, eating with one hand and smoking with the other. As we left the restaurant, his driver appeared out of nowhere in a World War II era Mercedes stretch limo. What a relic, I exclaimed, as he explained offhand that he owned a vertical collection of Mercedes. I knew from wine collecting that vertical meant an example from every production year.

As we parted he mentioned that he liked to fly the same airline I was taking to London. But how did he manage a 14-hour flight without smoking, I asked.

'Oh, I buy first class,' he explained. But so did I, and I still couldn't smoke, I retorted.

'No, sir,' he smiled wanly between puffs. 'You fly first class. I buy first class.' He regularly booked all 16 seats in First Class so that he could close the section and smoke to his heart's content. So much for $12 million and Da Vinci – after all, $12 million doesn't last long when it costs $150,000 just to fly from one place to another.

Many people are like that in small eccentricities, and so are many organizations. That is why we so often stand in awe in atrium headquarters, gaping at the cathedral ceilings and all the attributes that pass for solidity, comfort and making a statement.

The men at the Ritz sat at the pinnacle of Abraham Maslow's Pyramid, the one built from the theory that motivation climbs a ladder of needs. At the conference, I asked them what they did with the extra money that had rolled in through the cashier's window. They spoke of the need to return it to society, to be sensitive to the human environment, to help cure disease, make the landscape greener and the library more voluminous. Surely, I said, if these were their needs, it was something that they did in silence, for inner relief. How many of them had once dedicated a hospital or museum wing named 'The Anonymous Wing?' Surprisingly the reply was . . . none. Then perhaps their grants are nothing but ego trips? Would they have donated if their name wasn't on the opera seat, the brochure or the zoo gate? Self-aggrandizement and the lure of social status are hard to resist.

We've been know to suffer from those also, albeit unwittingly. On a one-day trip to São Paulo with my fine partner, Cushman & Wakefield CEO Arthur Mirante II, we needed a helicopter to squeeze all our appointments into 10 hours. We choppered around all day, until, as we were leaving JP Morgan's high-rise headquarters, we realized that we hadn't eaten lunch. Our chopper was hovering over the building, unable to land until the passengers were standing by. We looked at each other, shrugged and took the elevator down to the lobby, crossed the street, and went into McDonald's. As we quietly munched cheeseburgers, everyone around us craned their necks, trying to guess whose helicopter was kept circling for so long.

But how else could we have visited six bank presidents in one day in a traffic-jammed city of 17 million? Surely not without the chopper. But no one delved deeply into the question of what would have happened had we seen two presidents fewer. If we had stopped to question everything we do, we might have had a more nutritious lunch, and more time to think together.

Part of the justification for jets, limos, and titles has little to do with productivity, and much to do with mystique or self-image, or the need to impress people. Since that frequently includes bankers, investment funds or customers, it is seen as a valid business tool. Until these possessions take on their own life, supplanting reality and making work the purpose of living and not a part of the balance.

So it is that organizations, as well as individuals, need to find the real key to success. The easy replies about money are fraudulent; it all has very little to do with cash. A list highlighting the Happiest would have no names in common with one listing the Wealthiest (even if People Magazine were doing the work behind it).

The same is true for companies – cash, revenue and profits are wonderful indeed, but say precious little if taken on their own. A reservoir of talent that is tapped, a calling that is heard, an organization that honours a well-rounded definition of success lets people know they've arrived at the end of a journey where money is just fuel. Organizations and people need other measurements for how well they're doing. It might create a sense of relief for individuals, and push companies to compete for a slot on the Fortunate 500.

Part Three

Management By (O)mission

'Wu wei er zhi' – 'Do nothing in order to govern.'
Chinese Emperor Hang Jing Di, 157-141 BC

1. Why do we tell our employees that we trust them, then audit and search them when they go home?

2. Why does our customized and carefully crafted credo look like everyone else's?

3. Why do we demand and go to war for democracy as nations, yet accept with docility that no one has the right to choose their own boss?

CHAPTER 1

Order Of The Day: Give Up Control, Sir!

IMAGINE A GENERAL convincing his superiors that he has a glut of provisions and therefore needs to enlist more soldiers. Profit is highly important to us at Semco, and we're as avid about it as a general is about his supplies. If provisions run out, his soldiers will die. If a company ceases to make money, it too will die. But armies are not raised to create a place to feed soldiers, just as employees should not be expected to work just to generate profit. Food fuels the soldiers, keeps them going. But they have to have a higher purpose – a reason for going through boot camp and charging the enemy in battle. Like workers or millionaires, they must answer a higher calling.

For companies, this calling is named 'mission'. And it is wed to its brother-in-arms, 'credo'. Why are we here, where are we going, what do we believe? Beautiful. And mostly useless. Because all of this can be replaced with What We Stand For.

If values are going to be organic, and a part of the larger whole, they must come from the ground up. Giving up control creates these values, because they grow in organizations like moss on rocks. Then they're integral to a company – no one can tell who decided what, who determined which way the company would do things.

Generals make an easy comparison if you want to understand why grassroots values are successful. Officers maintain that if soldiers don't know which enemy to attack, the troops will charge in the wrong direction, right? Of course not. Does that mean that they don't know why they are fighting the war – are they protecting their homeland, eradicating communism, or deposing a particularly hideous dictator? If they're not sure, does that mean they won't be able to fight? Gibberish.

111

What army fails to grasp that it's protecting the homeland? Isn't that the obvious mission? It's easy to enlist farm boys to kill Vietcong fighters on the basis of loose threats of global McCarthyism. What few religious or territorial issues are necessary for Arabs and Jews, Hutus and Tutsis, Turks and Kurds to prolong ancestral feuds? How much marketing does it take for an army to annihilate an entire (and already devastated) country like Afghanistan, in the search for one terrorist?

Missions and credos are easy to configure and sell to the general public. So it is with companies, who copy the military model for their constituents – employees, customers, partners and the public. They consider their mission and credos unique, fundamental and all-inspiring.

I once conducted a workshop for 56 CEOs of Fortune 500 companies. I asked the participants to use a pencil to write in capital letters their company beliefs statement, the values that went into it, the credo that resulted. When they went out for a coffee break, I shuffled the cards on which they'd written their answers. Then I laid out the cards at random on their tables. When they returned, most of the participants agreed that if not for small features of the handwriting, they wouldn't have been able to differentiate among the credo statements.

No one can avoid platitudes when formulating a mission statement – 'to provide the best service from the happiest employees at the most competitive price to satisfied customers, while enchanting shareholders.' It's as if every time I meet someone new, I said: 'Hi, I'm Ricardo Semler. I strive for the best in the world and I want you to be utterly happy to meet me.'

What is left, then, if mission and credo are gibberish? What we stand for. The way we do things. The facts on the ground. The way we are perceived, and the satisfaction and success of those involved. Imagine an organization established to save seals. Isn't their mission to save water borne creatures who cannot save themselves? What happens the day they discover a pod of whales in jeopardy? Do they check their mission statement first, and adapt it? Or do they do what comes naturally? By that token, their purpose could also include villagers victimized by floods in Bangladesh.

Moving an organization or business ahead by virtue of what its people stand for means removing obstacles like official policies, procedural constraints and relentless milestones, all of which are set up in the pursuit of quarterly or otherwise temporary success. It means giving up control, and allowing employees to manage themselves. It means trusting workers implicitly, sharing power and information, encouraging dissent, and celebrating true democracy.

Few things are harder for managers, executives, shareholders and owners to embrace.

Nowhere are those procedural constraints and official milestones more obvious than in corporate mission statements and credos. They're nothing more than a feeble attempt to force workers to look in one direction. They dictate to employees – here's why you should get up in the morning and go to work. Here's your purpose, and it had better fit perfectly with our company goals. It's like telling soldiers why they need to destroy a country – and not giving them latitude to think about it for too long. Pound any independent thought out of their heads at boot camps, wear them out and pack them onto aircraft carriers or into the bellies of B-52s, otherwise they'll start to wonder whether they're really doing the right thing.

Yet at a company, profit, growth and quality will happen only once employees feel it's worthwhile to get up for work. That's not going to happen if their outlook on the world is already shaped and restricted by a company mission. They have much more time to think about what they're doing than a soldier in a war does.

I once met the grandson of a man who manufactured tram cars in Boston. The grandfather knew what his mission was – the best tram cars on the planet. So enamoured was he of his product that he determined that every cent of profit was to be reinvested by a trust fund – into tram cars. His descendants thus lost everything, because their attorneys could not break his ironclad will. While he was alive, he was the prescient general – after he was gone, he became a dispirited Napoleon Bonaparte. His Waterloo was the Boston Commons.

A few years ago, it was popular for business gurus to equate companies with armies, and a barrage of military paradigms such as marketing warfare, flank attack, Sun Tzu's war strategies, Von Clausewitz's strong-arm tactics and endless ballistic comparisons became all the rage. Now the same gurus equate a good company to a symphony orchestra. An orchestra brings together individuals with initiative, discipline and love of their art. These musicians join forces to create something that cannot occur without cooperation and participation. They're professionals of the highest standard, who achieve those moments in life when the heart soars and a rush of adrenaline produces a natural 'high'. These emotionally charged moments spark intense feelings of being alive, and are powerful reminders of our potential. Orchestra musicians, who make a living through such an expression of inner self, through permeating their music with emotion, and through seeking perfection with every move, must feel those moments of happiness constantly.

On the other hand, there are countless hours of self-discipline, difficult passages that must be played over and over, autocratic maestros to deal with, and the usual amount of bickering, back-stabbing and quibbling over money.

The other advantage of an orchestra is that a single person can direct 120 musicians, as opposed to the five-to-15, manager-to-employee ratio in most organizations. Why? Because in a symphony, everyone knows what they're doing and they play a common score. *Voilà* – business gurus fell in love with that metaphor. The mission would be the score.

But why? Isn't the mission the goal? And isn't an orchestra's goal to make music for an audience while also seeking personal growth and gratification as musicians? Can you keep a first-rate violinist in an orchestra that plays the same piece over and over like a cruise ship band?

A company's reason for existing is no different than that of an orchestra. For one it's the product, for the other, the sheet music. Believe it or not, manufacturing a bus is similar to playing Mozart in the park – both have a purpose, a system, and people who take the product to a waiting public.

But the mission varies. At times the mission of an orchestra is to take classical music to the widest audience possible. Witness the Three Tenors – three overweight gentlemen making fools of themselves in kitsch concerts backed by overlarge orchestras and a program of cantina songs. Is this a good way to serve a mission? If your mission is to make opera popular, definitely yes. After all, that is how opera started.

The same is true for Shakespeare in the park, or chefs parading their culinary skills on cable TV, or vintners producing 'second wines' to popularize the beverage. At other times, the mission of the orchestra is to stretch their limits. To make life interesting for the musicians. Or to indulge in a conductor's fantasy. Or to introduce new composers at world premières. Or to study a piece to death, either as a showcase for its members' virtuosity, or to offer something new to the public.

So it should be with companies. Organizations must help workers indulge their interests and talents by seeking the same professional growth and satisfaction as musicians.

Now most people might be wary about working for a company that doesn't define itself, has no mission statement, no plan. But at Semco we have neither a mission statement, nor a credo. We do have a *Survival Manual* – and it tells employees to customize Semco to their wishes. If asked why Semco exists those of us at the company will fall back on the same answer we'd give about ourselves: We're not entirely sure, but it has to do with collective gratification and a reason to live and work.

Oswaldo Guimaraes tested this reason many times. An engineer and draftsman at Semco's machinery company, Oswaldo is always full of new ideas. An emotional person, he sometimes expresses his values and convictions in dramatic ways. In the 1980s he ran into trouble when at a company convention he sketched a cartoon of our then-financial director drawing blood from innocent engineers with his budget cuts.

But Oswaldo knew how to show that missions are really designed on the ground, in day-to-day operations, and not in lofty statements on paper. His unit was doing badly in the mid-1990s. Oswaldo was always up in arms about the lack of a can-do attitude, and he was sick of the constant griping about the dearth of business. One hot afternoon he walked into the sales floor, where the entire force of sales engineers sat their desks. His blood rose, and he clambered up on one of their desks.

'How the heck are we going to sell if all of you have your butts planted in the head office?' he shouted. 'How, how, how?'

The embarrassed and stricken salespeople looked up at him incredulously. He stormed off, and office lore says that slowly, discreetly, the sales engineers started packing up and heading for the exits. Without written statements of credos or conduct, any one can – and sometimes somebody has to – get up on tables to scream. Screaming from on high may not be recommended practice, but in this case, Oswaldo's frustration inspired many of those same sales people to hit the streets and redouble their efforts. We'll never know if it led directly to improved sales, but we like to think it shook up the hen house.

115

With nothing but intuitive values in place, trust becomes a fundamental part of our process. Some business practices make this difficult, however. Telling people that the company trusts them and then auditing them makes it impossible for them to feel secure. They know they're under some suspicion, that they've been subjected to a sort of Napoleonic code declaring everyone guilty until proven innocent.

At Semco, we don't require expense accounts because of what they say about character. They're insulting for two reasons – they imply a worker did not really take a taxi for the company, and if she did, that we question her judgement about it.

We've learned that peer control is as effective as reporting and auditing. If people know there is no auditing, no official policing, they're more aware of how they behave and what goes on around them. They'll know that trust is in jeopardy if accounting is fraudulent or sloppy; they'll watch for thieves because they know there is no security department filling that role.

We massage our truth index all the time, creating an environment where documents, memos, and reports to customers or clients are honest and representative. Many times I've watched as people drafting reports and memos sent them back with a note: Don't forget to add this or that, in an effort to cultivate truth.

We once had an employee who was in the habit of telling customers he couldn't make a meeting because he was calling from the States. He'd say this on the phone in front of colleagues, so he thought of it as normal and acceptable. But it bothered many people, and countless of them mentioned it to me. This kind of mistrust is the bacteria that creates office politics. Semco has a low level of rumour, gossip, and politicking because our system doesn't lend itself to it, and the germs of mistrust don't proliferate as they would somewhere else.

On the other hand, offering complete trust can also backfire. It's a chance you have to take when military control is chucked out the window.

When Semco launched its RGIS unit, we brought in managers from the US and Mexico. One was a real dynamo, a man with two decades of experience in the inventory business. He was doing a bang-up job when suddenly an unusual American Express bill arrived at our offices. Apparently this manager had been powerless to stop his wife from regularly overdrawing his company credit card. He'd left her back home in his native country and had taken up with a Brazilian woman. His angry wife had taken her revenge with the American Express card, until the manager faced a debt worth nearly two years' salary. It all happened very fast, but another company with stricter controls would probably have discovered the problem sooner. Sceptics could argue that this is a definite drawback to our open system. But we still haven't added oversight. Even in cases of fraud, we shun audits or policing procedures because we feel that responsibility and peer interest are stronger than any internal controls, (and that was before the collapse of Arthur Andersen, the king of audits and controls!)

In the case of the manager, we had a difficult decision to make – we needed his talents, and he'd been a stalwart executive. On the other hand, he'd known his wife was using his corporate card and he hadn't told anyone. He'd hoped to cover the debt by selling property at home, but it didn't happen. Clovis suggested turning the debt into a long-term loan, but others worried that we'd set a precedent with that. Our honour system had to be preserved. So we arranged for the manager to go home, paid his moving expenses and wrote off the debt. We felt it was the best we could do.

It's rare for a company to reject internal audits. But audits are designed to seek out breaches of trust. (Almost all big companies have external auditors who inspect the books and review procedures to guarantee to shareholders that an independent entity has verified business claims. But the main activity is an inspection designed to ensure that everyone is following the rules.)

Auditing is also used to ensure uniformity; inspecting is a tool for control. It's a lose-lose situation: If you are inspecting to ensure uniformity, then you are using it for control. If it is because you believe people will do wrong, then it is mistrust.

At Semco, any company that is 100 percent owned by us is not audited at all, internally or externally. Further, about half of our joint venture partners, all of which have strict auditing rules at their headquarters, have accepted our philosophy and don't audit our units, either.

Trust extends beyond company walls, too. Take certification requirements. Precious little binds a company's true interest in quality to its certification requirements. I know that as a consultant to companies that want to adhere to ISO standards, and as a customer of dozens of certified suppliers.

117

When the ISO fad started, Semco was delivering marine pumps via a shipyard to the Shell Company. At a memorable meeting at their Rio de Janeiro headquarters, they asked us to include ISO certification in the bid we were about to win. They knew we would need several months to attain this, at best. So they were willing to let us deliver the first of three ships without the ISO certificates. We asked to think about it. We made a few calls to São Paulo, determined what the basic ISO 9000 parameters were, and calculated what it would cost us.

After 40 minutes we told the Shell representatives that we would be glad to comply. And that we'd learned that we'd be delivering eight tons of pumps and two tons of paper. And that Shell should add 6 percent to the price of the pumps for the cost of the paperwork that they now needed, and reduce the warranty period from our standard five years to the ISO standard of 12 months. They gulped. They asked for time to think about it. When they came back, they announced they'd pass on the ISO.

We never supplied them with certification. They trusted our old way of doing things.

ISO and other forms of certification sound wonderful on paper and seem to add healthy discipline to a company's procedures. On the surface, it looks like more order – creating repetitive and certifiable ways of conducting business guarantees predictability. If you document, record and trace every step of a procedure, then you can learn from your mistakes. Wunderbar!

But in reality it adds even more distrust than mere auditing of accounts. The catch is that people are less valued in such a process. Intuition, creativity and ad hoc decision-making are actually discouraged. How many times have we all been thwarted and utterly frustrated by employees who state: 'There are rules around here. There is nothing I can do.'

No one person or group at Semco sets our common denominator or philosophies. No one (least of all me) has ever said, 'Our common denominators will be honesty, trust, integrity.'

So where does the essence of Semco originate?

From an organization that exposes workers to all its different aspects, and guarantees them a degree of mobility among the parts, so they will find a niche and not feel the need to look for a better life elsewhere.

We have your new life here, somewhere; it's in the job you were hired for, or the project you stumbled across, or in another unit in another building.

The day may arrive when that employee has spent 15 or 20 years with Semco, and he's lived through seven different corporate lives, and has become an enormous asset. He's seen us do things seven different ways, and helped us be successful five times and fail twice.

Now I ask him to sit next to a 21-year-old recent hire, because he has something to teach him. And they both learn. And I learn. And I'm left with people and lessons that the merger mania, re-engineering and turnover have cost other businesses – a shared culture. A shared set of minimum common denominators. 'Minimum' is a critical part of the phrase. Even the smallest common denominator says that we're all here for the same reason. Employees may have their own agenda, their own careers to consider, but the common denominator anchors all of us to the company. So now, whatever the company may do, I have the seeds of sustainability. I have something that will endure through turnover, cannibalizing, and time. And it's not a set of mission statements, credos or values that I have decreed from a mountaintop. It's the philosophy that working together for years has left people with.

This naturally evolving, shared culture bonds people at a company, and it's founded on trust. You cannot have integrity, dissent, respect, or open communication without trust. You must believe those features are constructive, even when they are sometimes painful. That only works if people trust each other, and trust the company. (And working 'trust' into the mission statement won't cut it.)

A company that lacks integrity will eventually lose its best employees. Some will quit, others will stay and be dumbed down. Anyone who stays will disengage emotionally, and soon will be a candidate for motivational seminars. But a company can't expect integrity from its employees until they see it in the organization. People need to have faith and feel pride in what a company promises to its customers, includes in contracts, or touts in its advertising. If they know there are falsehoods or deceptions involved, their willingness to associate with the company diminishes. Soon they'll be working there just for the paycheque, and be embarrassed to tell anyone.

I'm often asked: How do you control a system like this?

I don't. I let the system work for itself.

I am sure that if somebody in the company decided that the only way to compete in a business is by paying a 10 percent kickback, the Semco system would choke the idea before it emerged. That's always been the case. I don't know who would object or call a meeting to discuss it, I don't know how they would stop it, but I can be absolutely sure that people would stand up and ask if this is now how we do business. A debate would ensue, and I am confident it would end in a unanimous rejection of the idea. No money will ever be bundled into a briefcase and handed to the buyer. Integrity is part of our minimum common denominator.

As they did with the deals involving the Brazilian national fund or the US multinational, I imagine that protectors of the crown will jump out of the woodwork, that Oswaldos will leap onto tables to scream and shout. Outsiders will argue that I can't know this for certain – or that it's possible that people will vote to pay the money in different circumstances. So let's accept that it could happen. I am equally certain that the reaction would be long and bitter, and intense enough that some people would threaten to quit and operations would be disrupted. Is it worth it? What's more valuable? Paying a 10 percent kickback to win business or protecting the core of this company?

In 1997, an ATM at a bank managed by Semco was robbed. It was Carnival time, and the thief got away with $36,000. The branch manager immediately expected us to cover the loss, because we were responsible for managing the ATM network. But security was run by a third company, and we knew we needed time to investigate the theft with that company. We didn't argue with the bank manager, however; we just sent him a cheque. After looking into the crime, we found flaws in the security system, and six months later, the security company paid the bank for the loss. Happily, we got our money back, though we'd never been sure we would. We chalked up the experience to an investment in integrity.

For me, the best part is that the owner of the company won't even be a part of the debate. Integrity will develop without me, because of the minimum common denominator that we share at Semco. I'm not required to pen some lofty set of values that any idiot can write. Shared values are those that evolve naturally over the years until one day you realize you're living by them.

By then, no one remembers whether they were written down, or where. At a Semco convention in 2001, Jorge Lima, one of our CEOs, confessed that he had never seen our *Survival Manual*, a cartoon-illustrated handbook of our guiding ideals. In our effort to legislate as little as possible, the grand total of our philosophies and policies is contained in this one small book. It focuses on respect, trust, communication, and freedom. There are no codes – no dress codes, no behavioural regulations. The manual has no credo, but rather is a declaration of our values and our culture. We add to it or re-write it whenever our employees want it to change – but since we feel that even after 20 years we still haven't perfected democracy in the workplace, our workers haven't felt the need to change the manual. We're not there yet.

Jorge Lima didn't know what it said. Three other executives then admitted they didn't either. Clovis wanted to reissue the manual, but that wasn't the point. If Jorge could lead hundreds of subordinates for 12 years without ever having read our only written philosophies, it's because of two possibilities: One, Semco values permeate our air and water so they're obvious to anyone who works with us, or two, managers have the freedom and latitude to operate as they wish, as long as they find willing subordinates.

Either answer is flattering.

Sometimes our own people are at odds about directions to take, and meetings of the mind don't occur. We're not advocating endless paralysis by analysis, nor striving to make a Woodstock hippie compound out of our management team. Many times leadership or initiative make the day. And sometimes they create muddled outcomes, because encouraging people to act freely can lead to trouble – especially when there are no written or official guidelines.

Like the instance in which Vicente Gomes, our technical assistance engineer, was constantly telling his boss that the pumps we had delivered to the Belgian caustic soda giant, Carbocloro, weren't going to work. His colleague, a new engineer called Valdomiro Costa, a bright and voracious careerist, was anxious to make a name for himself. Valdomiro was sure that the pumps only needed some further tightening of their gaskets, the rubber rings that are attached to both ends of the pump.

The boss and Vicente insisted that this was not the solution, but Valdomiro wouldn't hear of it. He had experience and schooling, the others didn't. He was so insistent that the three took off to the Carbocloro plant after a few days of technical disagreement.

Now, we were already famous at that particular plant because

121

Rolney Magalhães, our sharply dressed sales manager, had walked through the emergency showers without knowing that they would turn on as soon as someone pressed a switch with his foot. The workers all hid behind pumps and generators, racked with laughter at the sight of this 'suit' in his drenched clothes.

Engineer Valdomiro and the other two showed up to solve the faulty pump problem. Valdomiro, feigning mechanical experience, grabbed a wrench and stepped up to the pump. Vicente, some bosses and several workers all backed up swiftly. Valdomiro looked behind his shoulder, snorted and proceeded to wield the wrench. As soon as he tightened the gasket the pump emitted a long groan and exploded. Caustic soda covered the area, workers fled in all directions, and in an instant everything was covered with white foam, as if in a new fallen snow.

In a company with set procedures this would never have happened (the very reason Carbocloro employees didn't dare manoeuvre the pump). At Semco, our mission is clear (make the customer's pumps work). All avenues are open, even if they lead to dismal failure in front of the customer. We can only do this if we accept that control (over employees and how they do their jobs) will hinder our business. Once we let go, the net effect is that companies like Carbocloro remain steadfast customers, even after (or maybe because of) the shows we've put on at their plant.

Giving up control also means relinquishing exclusive rights to information. Privileged information is a dangerous source of power in any organization. Information that one person has that others lack can be terribly important, and can give them the upper hand.

To annihilate information hoarding and illegitimate power, information must be shared. The argument that competitors might latch onto sensitive information if it is widely known is not convincing enough to stop the free flow of information.

Business information should be as useful and immediate as possible. Any good company will be a moving target anyway. During the dot.com craze, everyone ran around with carefully constructed NDAs – non-disclosure agreements. Whereby you could end up in jail for talking in your sleep when your wife could hear you.

Certainly someone could conceivably draw conclusions about our strategy for products from our balance sheet, ads in the paper, and headhunting forays. So what? What can they do with that? Even if they received a copy of a highly confidential presentation on strategy, what can they glean from that? As I said, we start every new meeting as if the one before hadn't happened, and constantly re-examine everything. A two-week old presentation may as well be last month's newspaper.

At any rate, all our plans are limited to six months into the future. We deliberately give it only a half year because of the assumptions people make, that information is right, so the plan must be right. But factors in the business world change so frequently that any plan is in jeopardy. That makes it ludicrous to have a five-year plan. We don't want to follow a structure that might become nonsense in six months. So we brainstorm three, five or ten years into the future, but we only write down the next six months. We need the freedom this process guarantees. (Besides, every one-year plan that I've seen has all the good things happening in the second half.) We'd rather look ahead just six months – whatever looks bad on that horizon needs immediate action, not rhetoric. That way we combine freedom with strong business sense – and they are not incompatible.

Yet openness, truth and exposure upset people at Semco as much as anywhere else. I discovered that when I sent some very public e-mails about individual salaries. At Semco we've always been open about salaries. They're posted and widely known. But this time, people got angry.

We don't use blind e-mail copies when we circulate information. If a sender copies his e-mail to others, everyone will see who the recipients are. Sometimes, people inadvertently copy an e-mail that contains a string of messages with upsetting comments. But if all communication is open, then it shouldn't be possible to 'inadvertently' share information, right? Still, some topics are more sensitive than others are. Like salary talks.

This time, I sent everyone at Semco copies of an e-mail that contained details of particular salary negotiations. José Alignani, the CEO of our Cushman & Wakefield business, was infuriated – I should be more delicate with this kind of communication, he insisted. E-mails containing salary discussions can create all sorts of problems for unit managers, José told me. They're too direct, too easily misunderstood, and too hurtful. Some people are not ready for such open communication, he cautioned. People need time to adjust, and sometimes they have to adjust more than once.

But open communication is important enough that it should be tested, even if there is a price to pay. It's at the heart of shared culture. The only source of power in an organization is information, and withholding, filtering or retaining information only serves those who want to accumulate power through hoarding. Once an e-mail is not circulated, or if it is edited, then illegitimate pockets of power are created. Some people are privy to information that others don't have. Remove those pockets, and a company removes a source of dissatisfaction, bickering, and political feuding.

Open communication and truth are not only factors when dealing with employees. They're equally important with clients.

It often takes a customer time to get used to Semco's way of doing business. Many of them are wary of our reputation for democracy, dissent and flexibility. Those things just mean chaos to people who don't know any better. Customers are not expected to adopt our philosophies when they hire us, but we make it clear that we'll continue to practice them, and that has caused some unexpected culture clashes.

There's a premium everywhere on appearance in the work place, but in Brazil it can be quite overt. Any tourist coming through our airports, hotels and restaurants will notice they're staffed by attractive young people. At Semco RGIS, we made a point of saying we don't take appearance into account when hiring. On our customer satisfaction survey, a question about overall appearance is meant to monitor sloppy dressing, two-day old stubble, slovenly behaviour.

We quickly learned that many of our retail customers were quite concerned about this element: After all, many inventories are taken while the stores are open to the public.

When one of our Rio de Janeiro customers rated us a 2 out of 5 for appearance, Izak Santos investigated. As district manager, he was naturally concerned. His team had gone to work in perfectly starched uniforms, and he hadn't noticed a single loose thread. But the store's manager was adamant: 'All the women who came to do the inventory were plain or ugly,' he said, 'whereas your brochure displayed a beautiful blonde counting stock!'

Izak laughed heartily, only to realize a second later that the man was dead serious. There was nothing to be done but diplomatically explain that we did not intentionally send ugly people, and wouldn't intentionally send pretty ones, either, because looks are not criteria for hiring.

Others have argued that they should be. We've been told repeatedly that a pretty girl working on the help desk in our Concierge service would attract more business. Executives would want to talk to her! The counter argument is that a skilled concierge would do more for the customer in the long run. Sceptics say we'll never know, because they won't stop by in the first place. Does that mean we have to give up appearance for smarts? I don't think so – there are plenty of people with both. But in any case, competence alone is always enough for us. We just have to communicate that clearly to our customers and suppliers.

'We often have to educate our clients in our philosophies,' explains Rogerio De Mattos Gonzalez, who works at Cushman & Wakefield Semco. 'They don't always understand, and don't always want us to teach them. They don't accept us very easily.'

But if we don't make ourselves clear, then we run the risk of being misunderstood.

'Sometimes it's not good to tell clients right away,' said Rogerio Ottolia. 'They can think we're not organized enough, or that we just don't work, or that we'll charge unnecessarily high prices.'

So sometimes it's easier just to show them.

This is why my people have often been flabbergasted at my admission of guilt or product deficiencies during customer presentations. Dismayed, they would see our case going down the drain. More often than not, however, the customer would be taken aback by my frankness, and believe in the rest of what we had to say.

In one famous incident, we'd been battling with Anglo-American Mines over who was at fault in a mishap with gold mixing equipment. I went to see them, and confessed that we had found drawings that definitively proved that the fault was ours. Though the drawings had been found some time before, I had only just learned about them.

Our people were shaken. The $450,000 cost of redoing the equipment was a lot to us at the time. But Anglo-American reacted as I had hoped. They thanked us for our honesty, and ordered two more mixing machines. We used the money to fund the replacement of the older machines. They're avid customers of ours to this day.

Nevertheless, José Alignani and his people at Cushman & Wakefield Semco have learned to tell me as little as possible, and to take me to the customer infrequently.

On another occasion, at a presentation to a bank, I shared our findings about their engineering department with the directors seated around me. I said we should be hired because they had an incompetent engineering concept in place, and because their contracts were inflated, both of which indicated corruption to me. Everyone blanched. Alignani glowered at me in the elevator down to the garage, as the rest of our group meditated on the format and type of numbers used in the cabin by the elevator company. Turns out we got the contract, but Alignani and his people still spent the next two years explaining that I had not read the report carefully, and that I am a bit unpredictable. But after the purchasing manager got fired for corruption in the second year, things improved.

My people never know how I'm going to use internal information in front of a client – but then neither do I. In the beginning, they didn't see the merit of being totally frank with the customer. Over time, they realized that this path is much more productive, but they are still afraid of where the conversation can go when they're not conducting it carefully.

On several occasions I have taken our internal profit calculations out of one of the director's briefcases and given the customer a copy. Here is what we plan to make as a profit, I've said. Do you think it's too much? What do you suggest? What should we do? Many times this is the first occasion in which a customer has seen a profit calculation, and he'll pinch himself. But this strategy almost always turns out well.

This occurred for the first time when I pitched a Semco Johnson Controls facility management contract to Fiat, the car company. We offered to take over technical cleaning, maintenance and security at their main plant in Betim, Brazil. As I sat with the president I realized that they usually dealt with suppliers in a head-on, confrontational manner. They're in a very competitive, tough industry. We were suspect even before we presented our price.

As the meeting went on, it became clear that they were going to press us for a price reduction, regardless of our margins. Further, I was certain that the Fiat people had never negotiated for such a contract before, and were surely imagining that we'd pull any manner of tricks to profit from their ignorance. After all, we could vary the number of engineering site visits, cleaning teams shifts and surveillance areas, and their automotive engineers would never know the difference. So when the time came to talk price, I pulled out our cost calculation and put it on the table. The president's eyes bulged, and everyone leaned forward. 'This is what we make and how we calculate it,' I said in a mellow tone. 'Look at it, re-calculate it any way you want, take out people, shifts, cameras – anything you feel you know something about.'

We then proposed a system whereby they could adjust our staff and equipment over time, reimburse us for those costs, and then pay us 50 percent of the net gains we generated for them in the first three years. With the numbers laid out on the table, they had our fixed management fee and our possible profit right in front of them. It was easy for them to make a decision – and thus we landed our first big contract.

Sometimes the issue is not profit or contracts. On one memorable occasion I went to see the director of a bank whose building we had just begun to manage. The property manager there had been known to sexually harass the cleaning women.

This man was close to some of the bank managers, and they protected him. I asked the director what he'd think if I brought him a newspaper clipping with the headline: 'Bank Manager Harasses Women – Board Aware and Silent.' He looked stunned, and our directors, not knowing that I was going to bring this up, looked at the ceiling, out the window, at their shoes.

After a brief pause, the bank director answered with two words: 'Fire him.' Since then, that bank has asked for our help with delicate issues that require meeting the truth head on.

At Semco, we practice truth with a simple formula: Free sharing of information. We are so committed to it that we don't just tell people they have a right to information. We actively present it to them in e-mails and at democratic meetings. We also encourage people to learn how to use the information at their fingertips. It started because two decades ago Semco was run via a series of management meetings. I put the system in place, along with Clovis and a handful of top managers – a group of us who came to be called the Musketeers. Every week the CEOs of each business unit would meet, and any interested party could attend.

In addition, once a month the top directors would meet. This monthly meeting centralized power in the directors' hands and was often the decisive moment for company plans. This closed group of directors became known as the Friends of the King. (We're not sure who made up the term – it might have been us, it might have been good-humoured or cynical employees. But there it was.)

The CEOs (five at that time) had their own monthly meeting with their managers, and that gathering came to be called the Friends of the Prince. Every week, a third type of meeting took place that was open to all employees and came to be called Little Guys' Meeting.

Of course we also held quarterly board meetings with shareholders, and once a month an open meeting for all employees of each unit. The intention was to openly examine and debate Semco's numbers. Shop-floor workers, machinists, clerks and cleaning people were invited to the open meeting.

The advantage of this system was that within a few days, information flowed to all levels, down to the humblest janitor. It was correct and honest information – not rumours or doctored reports and memos. Conversely, all the workers' concerns and suggestions flowed right back up.

In the mid-1980s and again in the early-1990s, a series of economic crises rocked Brazil. One arose from the huge foreign debts that burdened Latin America and brought business to a standstill. People still describe the 1980s as the lost decade for Brazil's GNP. Another crisis was sparked by President Fernando Collor's senseless plan to curb inflation in Brazil by freezing all bank accounts. Perhaps Collor read Von Clausewitz, because this warrior attack on inflation merely brought the economy to a screeching halt, and set off endless feuds among companies and individuals over who was due what money. But Collor – who eventually was impeached – succeeded in stopping inflation. A profound recession ensued instead.

Few companies in developed nations have experienced such disastrous times. Semco's system of two-way communication made all the difference. We shared our director's concerns with employees at the Little Guy's Meeting. They saw all the numbers and forecasts. They heard our worries. More often than not, the groups would break up to work together on solutions – which in those dark days involved lay-offs. Ideas would flow upwards, we'd receive new input, make suggestions, reach disagreements, renew pressure, and then start again. This always seems a drawn-out process to outsiders, and that creates the impression that crises generate terror and prolonged suffering. But we never forget that we are dealing with adults who are responsible and well informed, at that. They quickly offered solutions that were more clever and realistic than those first suggested by management. They also imagined radically different implementation. Once everyone had a chance to air their concerns, look at the figures and share the pain of difficult decisions, the atmosphere became one of trust and transparency. The dull rage that comes from lay-offs or cost cutting was directed at the economy, or particular management, but not at the company as a whole.

This probably explains why we never had negative press during the crises, never suffered collective lawsuits from employees, and never faced a strike in more than 15 years of adjusting to the difficult Brazilian economy. This is certainly not the story that our industry peers have to tell. They've all been plagued by huge lawsuits from ex-employees, obstruction by Brazil's strong unions, and incessant press investigation.

Naturally, no matter how much we grow or how well we do, we still make mistakes in direction, confront unexpected losses of contracts to competitors, and deal with sudden downturns in the economy. It's vital that we have a system that adjusts organically to these ups and downs.

Given all that, we quickly realized that opening our books to employees meant they had to read them – and this required quite a bit of training. The complicated accounting procedures didn't make a lot of sense to the common man.

Take the profit and loss statement, for example. It takes the revenue, and then separately subtracts variable and fixed costs. As such, you are unable to identify the payroll, for example. Payroll is divided up into various line items, such as selling and general administrative costs, manufacturing overhead or services provided, and then further broken up between nominal salaries and benefits, social security, and so forth. It doesn't exist as a separate expense.

Confusing.

To our straight-arrow shop floor workers, these convoluted reports just clouded the issues. They were right. We needed a clearer method of presenting our accounts. We realized there were only a half dozen numbers that really mattered at any of our businesses. (A fact I've found to be true of all businesses I've encountered in the last twenty years.)

Once we created a new, simpler accounting system, we needed to validate it. So we turned to the one organization that could establish its credibility. After all, factory workers tend to see David Copperfield when they look at accountants. We didn't want them believing we'd simplified our numbers to the extent that they didn't add up, or

129

contradicted our more complex accounts. Who could validate this new process for the workers?

The union. We met with Walter Barelli, an economist who is now Brazil's secretary of labour. At the time he led the Inter-union department for the study of economics and statistics, making him the all-powerful czar of a socialist worker's view of capital.

Mr Barelli and his staff were stunned to hear that any business person wanted to open company books to workers, not to mention to a Socialist union. So, pinching themselves periodically, they sat with us for long hours over many weeks to design a simple but truthful profit and loss statement. They also accepted our invitation to come to the company regularly and teach workers how to read balance sheets. Their lessons led to a Semco instruction guide illustrated with cartoon drawings, in keeping with our tradition of taking things lightly. The drawings equated a company to a supermarket, with workers on both sides of the counter, buying and serving. It moved from there into the revenue stream, how the payroll is made up, and so forth. Using the booklet, the union held many classes and our people filled the meeting rooms to learn. Only a few stayed away. Soon after, the monthly meetings to report on and debate our accounts became very lively indeed.

We tried to emulate the best practices of worker cooperatives, and even brought in some salutary Socialist concepts. We were convinced that employees who knew the whole truth could be counted on to stay longer, better understand the vagaries of economics, improve their work life, and thus enrich our financial performance. After all, they had an important profit sharing program to make them part of the gains.

Sharing accounting information with workers has benefited them. The information enables them to make better decisions about their own salaries and financial planning. Angelo d'Ariano is one who uses this information nearly every day. Angelo is a quality inspector at Semco Processes, and a quarter of his annual income can come from profit sharing. As a result, he knows his unit numbers better than I do. He follows company results closely. He understands exactly how variable remuneration works, and knows what must happen for him to earn the equivalent of three extra paycheques each year – 45 percent of his success depends on the earnings of the unit, 35 percent on the cash flow results and other 20 percent on goals he sets for himself, like validating processes or qualifying suppliers.

When communication is open, Angelo and others like him understand our books and pay close attention to them. They're not just improving their own chances of making more money – they're improving Semco's as well.

This is why the culture that arises from daily acts takes the place of corporate policies. Instead of writing ourselves down in a set of rules, we evolve slowly based on what we do.

But sometimes evolution can be quite painful.

I once adamantly believed that more than one of our manufacturing plants had to be closed down. Our business was becoming increasingly global, and when I looked down the road, I saw imports devastating a local manufacturing industry that concentrated on producing everything in Brazil. I believed we could outsource much more than we did, thus removing the burden of our existing legacy. It would make us lighter on our feet, and freer to move into new formats. I called a meeting, and most of the executives came. I laid out my concerns and a plan, and they were shocked. No way, they exclaimed, you cannot be right. We decided on further study. Over the next few weeks I called several meetings. A few people showed up out of pity for me, and the rest refused to spend time on such an absurd assumption. Eventually it became clear that no one would show up at these meetings anymore, so I gave up.

Almost a full year later these same executives (José Alignani, Clovis Bojikian, Marcio Batoni, João Vendramim and José Violi) reconvened to debate the plan. Some of them had let the idea mature, and finally thought there was some merit in it, even though they didn't believe in my particular proposal. More meetings ensued, and they showed up for these – eventually putting into place a plan that bore some resemblance to my theory.

You will say that the company would have been better off if I had insisted on my way and saved Semco 12 months of expenses by closing the plants. But the plan was refined greatly in everyone's mind during that one year, and the end solution was better than mine. Also, by now a lot of people were confident of the direction that we needed to take, so they were infinitely more convincing when dealing with the employees, clients and unions.

In the end, it's an exchange that works; out go mission statements, credos and the control they imbue, and in come self-interest, conviction arising from practice, and a developing set of values. As control wanes, creativity and shared values bloom. An army that fights for what it believes in arises from this harvest of ideas, varied practices, and close contact with the real world. Missions take a back seat in the army jeep, and Generals can relax while the soldiers and lieutenants draw the map themselves.

CHAPTER 2

Do It Your Way – See If I Care

GOING AWOL IS sometimes necessary. So are court-martials. At Semco, dissent starts with me – when the security guards don't let me into the Semco building. For years, Semco has declined to issue company identification cards to every employee. We have a fence around our property, and a front gate with a guard who checks all our employees and visitors. He's trained to ask for some sort of ID. I don't agree with this practice, and since I frequently leave the house without my wallet, I have been known to arrive at the Semco front gates without identification. One Saturday the guards phoned our administrative supervisor, Paula Regina, to let her know that someone calling himself Dickie had shown up at the front gate without any ID, and they'd turned him away.

For a week Paula waited to see what the fallout would be, and when nothing happened, she went to speak to the guards herself. They could only say that a man they'd never seen before had approached the gate with no ID, they'd turned him away, and he'd complimented their professionalism as he got back in his car and then drove off.

Of course, when I arrived home that day I had to phone the people waiting inside Semco for me and tell them why I'd missed the meeting. I believe IDs are just a bland panacea for security, but when confronted with the rules, the tiny Thoreau in me practices civil disobedience by not arguing with the powers that be.

A lot of Semco people do the same.

To traditionalists, let alone militarists, this makes it impossible for the company to hone in on one objective or a single way of doing things. But ironically it is organizations that have implemented relentless, orchestrated missions that rarely sustain themselves.

The heirs of Sam Walton, the tenacious founder of Wal-Mart, would do well to remember Sears, Macy's and Woolworth's. They were once similar retail powerhouses. Marks & Spencer was a star of the sales-per-square-foot crowd, and Harrod's a shining temple of commercial expertise. K-Mart invented the hypermarket concept. Yet all of those famous chains have either faltered or been sold since their heyday. Their success couldn't be sustained with rigid structures, slogans or mission statements. Building Wal-Mart required a relentless commercial instinct and a penchant for penny-saving tactics. There's no blueprint.

Success in retail owes much to tenacity, yet we are quick to credit values, mission statements and credos for the winners. No one argues with success. But then the company-wide 'brainwashing' begins, which is followed by the 'this is the reason for our success – this is how we've always done it' syndrome. That's the biggest mistake successful people and companies make – believing that their success immortalizes their way of doing things. Questioning that syndrome is viewed as sticking a thorn in the side of success. Any dissent is usually cut away like an unwanted cactus tip.

To be sure, organizations like Semco that welcome – or better, invite – dissent are more complex to manage. Without direct instructions, managers and employees end up engaging in a lot of back-and-forth. Traditional managers will argue that this slows the company down, and is therefore a competitive no-no.

Let's take the time Semco's military heritage shone through, despite our best efforts to quash it. Our CEOs gather for an annual hoopla so they and their spouses can debate 'the Semco way'. Naturally we argued about the insistence from some quarters on introducing badges for Semco people and visitors. We had grown too much, added hundreds of new employees in a few years, and augmented them with enormous numbers of third parties, independent contractors and vendors. The ensuing flood of new faces was creating some insecurity across the company.

The CEOs were not – save a few exceptions – convinced that badges were necessary, even for visitors. But a raging debate arose. To this day we still kid each other by putting 'Badges' on every agenda for the annual meeting. In the end, we concluded that dissent was more important than knowing who was right or wrong. The dissent, in fact, had gone beyond words, and several offices in our buildings across Brazil had already introduced badges. We just shrugged after exhausting our arguments at the retreat and via e-mail, and let the dissenters have their way. Two months later badges for employees were eliminated because nobody liked them, too many people left them at home, and many people began to complain about 'excessive control'. To my knowledge (how would I know?) badges are still used for visitors.

What traditional executives don't consider is that decisions arising from debate are implemented much more quickly because explanations, alternatives, objections and uncertainties have already been aired. Because of democracy, employees have had their say, and projects or ideas have been analyzed from every point of view. Even the badges were implemented in less than a week, compared with a huge campaign to explain and set up the regulations that a traditional company would require.

Dissent and democracy go hand in hand. Semco recently decided it needed a new logo. We'd had the same 'visual communication' for 20 years, and our signs, our brand and our identity seemed outdated to many at the company. A lot of us felt the logo no longer represented the company, since we'd added so many new businesses in recent years.

The last time around, when I led a change in logos around 1980, the rationale was the same. But the process was a bit different. At that time, we did what practically all companies do. The board or owner makes a decision, a small committee is formed, and someone is given the task of coordinating a proposal. Leading graphics or marketing companies are briefed, then begin the complex process of learning about the company, interviewing its chief officers, collecting all of the printed and advertising material, and so on. It becomes a multi-pronged, multi-person, multi-months project, and large companies can spend months or even years, and millions of dollars, to pick a new logo.

As with any art form, opinions and concepts are wide-ranging and subjective, so that no idea, no matter how good, receives universal acclaim. Even the chairman's wife can have veto power. This is why many design and communication companies try to show only one version of a proposed new logo or brand to a customer. But with a shortage of Renaissance men or women in the top tiers of most companies, new ideas are often met with a blunt rejection: 'Forget it, buster, we'll look at what you did and tell you what you need to change.'

The end result is few groundbreaking logos. Most companies follow the example of their industry brethren, so logos are largely repetitive. Maybe it's because the logo industry is saturated, and the sheer numbers have exhausted the creative possibilities. Or perhaps the big marketing and graphics companies are successful precisely because they are conservative and predictable.

Name three logos that are distinctive and brilliant, but (most importantly) tell you inherently what product is represented. It's not easy. Take the Coca Cola logo, or that of Nike or McDonald's. They're recognizable anywhere in the world. But do they tell you what the product is? They're worth billions only because people already know what's inside the can, the shoebox or under the arches. The logo's recognition factor is not a result of creative concepts, but rather of the money spent to memorialize it. Any logo can be rendered just as famous and meaningful if a company has millions of dollars to promote it and create a globally successful product.

I wanted our new logo to stand on its merits. After some debate, we hired an independent graphic designer with years of experience. He'd brought new ideas to Levi's and dozens of other old-line firms, and was a respected professor. He was a loner, an artist, and also disillusioned by the commercial path taken by a lot of his colleagues. He came to work for us full-time, dedicating all his effort to our new identity.

Many months passed, peppered with open meetings to discuss the process step-by-step. Every one who came to a meeting had a voice, and could direct the logo development. People who didn't show up lost their chance to influence the outcome.

I didn't go to any of them.

I had an opinion, of course, but I knew that in the end, the designer would create three new logos and we'd choose one in a company-wide referendum. I'd be able to express my opinion then. Though I cared very much about the new logo, I trusted that employees would decide in Semco's best interest.

I cast my vote during the first ballot, and my choice was defeated. Many people were also disappointed. They wanted another chance to vote on colour and typeface. So a second vote was held, and the winning logo changed slightly. The new version was still quite a departure from our 20-year-old logo. It was more modern, and the artist depicted our dedication to going the extra mile by stretching the letters of our name upward. Overall, it was an improvement, but whether this would be obvious to the public was another question.

I then proposed that we have dozens of logos. People yawned, looked up at the ceiling. Yes, I went on excitedly, that way our people could send out the logo that they thought most represented that deal, or proposal, or how we were all thinking at the time. More yawns. People resisted the obvious urge to explain to me why it is important that a logo be fixed in people's minds, that it represent something secure, ongoing, blah, blah, blah. I'm glad they resisted. So much for mobile logos.

In a sense, it's like looking at any art. If you go to the Tate Modern or Guggenheim Bilbao with an expert, you will suddenly see all kinds of hidden meanings – most of them genuine, as you oooh and aaah softly in the quiet gallery. A logo is similar – if only you had a guide who would explain the lofty meanings of each part to the customer who receives your letter, or to the big-bellied fella who sits on the sofa with a beer in his hand watching your TV commercial.

In the end, virtually all our employees voted for the more conservative of the new logo possibilities. I was rooting for a new, golden yellow version. Most people wanted to keep our old blue.

So how can change be enacted in a democracy? What would have happened to all great inventions if they'd required a vote of approval from lab assistants? Invention surely requires solitude. But look at it another way. How happy would you be if the president or prime minister of your country headed a small committee to change the flag and the national anthem, and then informed you on a Monday morning of the result? Smacks of Uganda's Idi Amin Dada, doesn't it? Even Fidel Castro probably wouldn't have the guts.

We're still working out the final design of our new logo. One variation would place the newly chosen logo (blue) on a small folded triangle, at the upper right hand corner of the page, or calling card. That's because in Brazil there was a custom among gentlemen of folding the upper tip of a business or calling card when hand delivered to demonstrate a personal touch. We're toying with the idea of placing our new logo on such a folded triangle in visiting cards, letterhead or even e-mail. And folding business cards at the printers seems easy enough – but how do you fold the corner of an e-mail? The idea is to convey that Semco is the embodiment of an old art of care and personalization, merged with a modern, technological face.

See?

Maybe not . . . it's like my moveable feast of logos, it gets knocked down by too much democracy (how I'd love to be an unbridled South American dictator at Semco for just two weeks).

Clovis and I don't think that we've yet managed to make democracy a reality at Semco. We feel that we've still got a way to go. Conditioning remains strong. We still make more decisions from on high than we'd like (and see them ratified at the base), and we decide more than we should from behind closed doors with a troika of our intelligentsia. We continually excuse ourselves, feel remorse, hoping that at least we've increased our chances of meeting St Peter at the Pearly Gates.

Sometimes our policies lead to surprising ends. Paulo Valle helped fire the man who hired him, for example. Sergio Ofina interviewed Paulo for a position at ERM, and when he won the job, Paulo knew he owed the offer to Sergio. But it soon became clear that Sergio's management style wasn't suited to ERM. The unit was faltering, and job cuts were necessary. Sergio had to let three people go, something that happens rarely at Semco and was very difficult for others in the unit to witness. Unfortunately, many of them thought Sergio was callous about the lay-offs. He let one person go when the man was out of town, by calling him on the phone and telling him he was out of a job. A few minutes later, he was cheerfully laughing at jokes shared in the office. His insensitivity made ERM's remaining workers fear for their jobs. They were scared and angry. Finally, a meeting was called to discuss the discomfort, and 30 people showed up.

The unit was ripe for mutiny. We had a board meeting scheduled for the same day, and the international director of ERM was on his way. When Arnon Garonzik arrived he was met with news that a group of employees had gathered upstairs to voice their unhappiness over the layoff. All work had ceased.

Arnon's immediate reaction was typically corporate: A mutiny must not be allowed! This was paramount to a strike. We needed to re-establish authority. How could we lead employees who thought we didn't have any backbone? What kind of wimps would allow employees to review decisions and vote on whether to work or stage a rebellion? They wouldn't respect us, and worse, they'd question every little thing from hereon out.

I personally assured Arnon that at Semco we were comfortable with the mutinous attitude. Watch, I said – we'll learn a lot from this incident. Fortunately, Arnon had always been a quick learner, and was eager to do the right thing – even if it didn't sound right at the moment. I asked for the benefit of the doubt, playing on Semco's past successes when facing unlikely policies.

Arnon headed off for two days of travel around Brazil, wondering as he left whether that would be enough time to calm the sailors or chain them up and throw them in the brig. I assured him that the mariners would make HMS Semco proud.

Off he went. We immediately took rigid action by doing ... nothing. Meetings went on all afternoon and evening. HR people were called in, declarations made. More people got involved, including the CEO. A lot of dirty laundry was hung on the line.

By the third day, the workers were able to persuade CEO Eugenio Singer to see things their way. Originally he'd been incensed by any hint that his management was at fault, that leaders were chosen with the wrong criteria, and that the workers had been excluded from several recent hires. This last complaint was true – Sergio had come from Alcoa, where he'd worked with Eugenio, and was recruited in confidence.

The day Arnon returned from his travels, Eugenio and the employees struck a deal: To remove Sergio and transfer him to a more technical job, reinstate the fired person, and choose a completely different person as the manager of that area. Arnon was a bit wary of the precedent the deal might set – but he was willing to wait and see.

Sergio left Semco on his own two months later. Paulo Valle works for us to this day.

José Alignani, the CEO of Cushman & Wakefield Semco, wants 'all of my managers to be part of the human resources strategy.

'We don't want a human resources department to be the mother and father of everyone in the company,' Alignani explains. 'Before we got rid of it, nearly everything that happened to employees at Semco went through that department.

'They had lots of power, but they weren't taking care of the directors or managers, or the hierarchy, because they knew they were better at dealing with the employee than the untrained leader. So when someone had a complaint, they would go straight to human resources, without even thinking of talking to their direct bosses. That's a problem, and this was corrected when HR disappeared and these issues went back to where they really belong.'

The same principle motivated our machine operators to take over cleaning and maintenance of their machinery. A separate team had always taken care of it, but it made more sense for those with intimate knowledge of the machines to step in. It's the same with people. Sending them to another department for their personnel needs is counter-productive. It reminds me of Henry Ford's sociology department.

We also expect our accountants to follow up on billing customers. Why should a salesman spend his time chasing payments when he could be cultivating new customers? The person who created the account should see it through to the end. We want each account handled correctly by the person who best understands it, in one complete business cycle, without the red tape of territorial procedures in different departments.

On another occasion of open dissent, an employee named Marly dos Reis Leite was dismissed from one job only to move into another on the same floor. She complained constantly about her new situation, and quickly got into personal fights with her director of operations at Semco Johnson Controls. He could have simply fired her, but he was wary of the consequences. For one, other employees would have wondered whether he'd been bullying her. He'd have a lot of explaining to do. He tried to be careful, knowing that he was negatively disposed to her anyway (the feeling was mutual). Firing her wouldn't be fair.

Marly believed she'd been relegated to Johnson Controls because she'd complained about her previous job, even though she was convinced that her gripes were legitimate.

Marly thought she was given harder work than anyone else, in an effort to manipulate her into resigning. She couldn't prove anything, of course – such manoeuvring is inherently subtle. She increased the volume of her complaints, expecting others to join in the fray, or protect her somehow. After all, she'd been with the company a long time, and had helped to start up the Semco Foundation, which strives to implement Semco practices in educational institutions. But the brass on her floor was also close to her boss, and did nothing out of respect for letting the process play out.

Finally, even her colleagues began to find her disruptive. Whenever an article featuring our commitment to transparency or the development of our people appeared in a newspaper or magazine, Marly snorted loudly. When our sales proposals described our contented workforce, she laughed sarcastically. She seized every opportunity to slam Semco and sow scepticism. Considering her past connection with the non-profit Semco Foundation (which relies on trust, integrity and truth for its credibility), it's not hard to imagine what a pain in the neck it was to hear constantly of Marly's rampages against our reputation.

Several directors were in favour of firing her immediately; others thought we should phase her out. Many were indignant that such a person was left unchecked by top management; some supported her dissent but thought she was defeating her own point by voicing her insults on the office floor instead of to the targets of her ire.

There was pressure for a formal Semco reaction, but Clovis, José Violi and I could only respond one way: If she wants to quit, that's up to her, but we can't fire her for dissent. We've always said dissent was important to us, and now we're being tested on that. Our integrity is at stake now, too. All the expletives from Marly are less damaging to morale than firing her for dissent would be. And later, when someone else has complaints, they will know they have a voice. In the meantime, Marly's experience will teach others to be more diplomatic.

So we did what we always do when there is dissent: nothing. We believe blindly in the virtues of dissent. We don't want a crowd of brainwashed workers. We don't want them to sing company songs, memorize company mission statements, and learn to speak only when spoken to.

Sure, we get plenty irritated by being blasted daily at 90 decibels, but it is up to the people who work around that person to find a balance, and either believe her or ignore her. It's up to them to resolve the issues behind the complaints. The people at Semco are responsible and sensitive adults, who would know how to judge such outbursts. And if she's right, we'll all learn something and change.

Another business unit could have hired Marly. After all, a person can be right for one job and a disaster in another. But then her boss chose to lobby for her transfer to another unit. She went to Cushman & Wakefield Semco, but that didn't improve her low opinion of the company directors, whom she continued to debase openly. By this time, it was obvious that years of secretarial work had taken its toll on Marly, who thought she deserved a more challenging position. A mix of Peter's Principle, (whereby people rise to the level of their incompetence) and what may have been a perfectly legitimate aspiration – who could know?

141

This happened in 1999. Marly is still with us, at Cushman & Wakefield Semco, and has settled down. Her griping eventually subsided and then stopped. She now handles relatively complex tasks with the help of assistants; it seems to be a working compromise. It's still hard to say how happy she is, but she smiles a lot more. Some years ago she recommended Semco to her 23-year-old daughter, Valeria, who now works for ERM. To date, I don't know what changed in her. Could I have found out, by requesting information or talking to her in the corridor? Maybe. But could I have done that and not have gotten involved? Process is king, I believe, and so these things have to play themselves out – there's no right answer. Sure, it takes some organizational cold blood. And it might leave the reader, as with many Semco employees, miffed or unconvinced. That, however, is the essence of giving up policies, procedures, missions and credos. As with long term analysis, it does no good to want to know, up front, what the real problem is, and where the solution lies. It can take years to find out. Perhaps when Marly retires from Semco in a few years time, we still won't know what really went on. As unnerving as it may be, the only question that occurs to me is: Why do you want to know?

João Vendramim, our jack-of-all-trades director, recently told a reporter about another case of dissent at Semco. It revolved around an accounting issue: Depending on how we classified an investment we had made, we would show a small profit, or a small loss.

The loss meant an income tax rebate, and in fact that had been discussed openly. Everyone at Semco knew we would be showing a small loss, and understood the reasons behind it.

But I saw no sense in choosing that route. Unnecessarily showing a small loss for a small gain in taxes was not sensible. Investors wouldn't understand, or see things in context. Also, the press had its spotlight trained on us. A loss, no matter how insignificant, would put us in the 'poorly performing' category.

I was in favour of showing the small profit and losing the tiny tax gain. The other directors heard me out, and decided to take the issue back to the board and some key employees. I waited, and crossed my fingers. Ultimately, the board members decided that our internal and external credibility depended on leaving the numbers exactly as they had fallen and respecting the way they'd been presented at numerous employee meetings.

So it stood. I was unhappy, but my intuitive feelings about the accounting method could not outweigh the board and Semco's employees. We haven't had a loss in any quarter since, so we haven't re-visited this specific issue. It was clear, however, that the democracy in place at Semco functioned even when sensitive issues were involved.

Sometimes dissent is not as antagonistic. Fabiana Kahn, a building manager for Cushman & Wakefield Semco, started a contest to rival the more traditional 'Employee of the Month' that most companies indulge in. Hers was called 'Jerk of the Month'. She issued yellow and red cards and told everyone to write up anyone they wished for 'being a jerk'. The fault could be described on the card, and the subject would be able to read it and sign off. The winner would be the person with the most points (yellow earned one point, red got two). Fabiana even held a little ceremony – and discovered that she was the first place runner up!

CHAPTER 3

Undressing Chairman Mao

JOÃO VENDRAMIM HATES plastic cups. João, one of our long-time chieftains, and our Resident Corporate Shaman, longs for the day when we'll have only ordinary glasses in our cafeteria. He once came to work early for an employee breakfast, and when he went for coffee, he noticed several cleaning ladies choosing plastic cups over coffee mugs. He politely asked whether they preferred the plastic cups. Their answer startled him: The glass cups, they said, were only for office workers.

In that moment, the only thing João could think was that all our efforts to create democracy and total integration had utterly failed. Twenty years of work meant nothing if people didn't believe everyone had the same rights. Of course when he recovered from his surprise he realized our efforts are not a total failure, it's just that even we still have room for improvement. What matters most now is consistency. If we consistently reinforce democracy and freedom, we can change the way those cleaning women perceive their place at Semco.

People can't be commanded to accept a democratic workplace. It's ironic, but democracy goes against the workplace grain. Workers are so conditioned by society to accept a paternalistic hierarchy that at first glance, democracy looks like chaos. But declaring that we're all going to be democratic from now on isn't necessary anyway. If left alone, democracy will evolve. Organizations can nurture freedom by declaring it to be an abiding principle and then stepping back to let it flourish. But democracy cries out for diversity and diversity requires treating all people alike, and that is the hard part for most managers.

For years, Márcia Fração worked as a secretary at Semco. Then we got rid of secretaries. Márcia had long wanted to change direction

144

anyway. But she felt held back by artificial barriers.

'When Semco decided to no longer have secretaries I became a sales assistant, but most of the managers were still treating me like a secretary, asking me to photocopy and place phone calls,' she remembers. 'But I had new activities that had to be done. I had to impose myself in order to be respected.'

She struggled to prove that her interest in marketing was worth more than her limited experience. Still, she had a calling. She finally found an opportunity when she volunteered to help Rogerio Ottolia organize Semco's booth at a commercial fair called Technoplus. At first she simply helped Rogerio; by 2001 she was running the whole program. Now Márcia has other ambitions – she's taking an english class that Semco subsidizes – and says, 'I've grown addicted to the challenge of doing more than I know how to do. Five years from now, I want to be responsible for the whole marketing department.'

That kind of distinction is why cleaning ladies who come to work at Semco bring with them the idea that coffee mugs are only for white-collar workers. That distinction erodes any confidence people should have about their role in the workplace. Uncertain or insecure people will never speak up for themselves, much less with an innovative idea or a criticism.

Only self-confidence makes freedom and dissent possible. An organization that insists that there's only one way to do something, brainwashes workers to think alike, and freezes a company culture to eliminate risk, will only breed complacency and make itself unappealing to anyone who might inject some oxygen into it. Consider this: How long would it take an anthropologist to identify the tribes that co-exist in the typical work place? Station an anthropologist in the parking lot to watch how people dress and listen to them talk, and I wager that within two hours she can map all the big tribes in a company.

Once upon a time, it was easy to caricature the idiosyncrasies of the 'tribes' in the manufacturing industry. People lived up to the clichés – the engineers went around with plastic shirt pocket protectors for their coloured pens. The marketing people wore loud yellow shirts and piped music into their section, while the controllers favoured thick glasses and carried oversized brief cases. The owner drove a Mercedes but the janitors owned old Ford Galaxys. And the salesmen sported worn shoes and cars, and looked as if they'd just gotten back from a Willy Loman conference.

Like talent, anthropology in the workplace often goes unnoticed. This may be because tribalism now looks a bit different on its surface – plastic pen protectors are out of style and on Casual Days everyone looks similar in the parking lot.

But tribes often speak a language that outsiders can't understand. Try talking shop with tax attorneys or information technology types. You won't understand them any more than if they were teenage hip-hop rappers.

Tribalism satisfies the human need to belong. Tribes have all sorts of rituals designed to exclude outsiders, approve of members, test loyalty and reinforce belonging. We can enhance this integration by mixing people of different backgrounds, experiences and ages in working groups and office set-ups. We've done that at Semco with our offices – our employees work at a different desk every day, sitting next to a different person who might be younger or older and who may have a wildly different background than the person who sat there the day before.

We've done it with our garden meetings, where blue- and white-collar workers rub elbows in the same outdoor space. And we've done it with programs that encourage workers to move around the company, seek new challenges and test the limits of their interests and abilities.

As people begin to realize that job rotation is about exploring new worlds, and fighting repetition and boredom, the concept catches on quickly. Once tribe members begin to circulate, any departmental mind-set is quickly undermined, and uniformity is left behind. People don't have to look alike or work alike. Pretty soon, units will include workers who can speak for or defend another unit because they've visited or worked in that other place themselves – and they understand it, even if they are not similar to the others.

I often begin workshops of mine by asking people to explain some of the things they do every day. For example: 'Why are you all dressed in suits and ties?' Most people reply with something like: 'Because we're a group, or because we look alike this way.'

So then I ask a second question: 'Why do you want to look alike?' People then shift in their seats and begin to look uncomfortable. Some smile. A few might reply that uniformity makes for a comfortable shared standard, others might say that it projects an image of seriousness and prestige.

Each of these replies begs a third why? Why are people comfortable looking like someone else? Or, why do companies want their people to feel comfortable when comfort leads to complacency, or further, why do we need to look serious so that people will believe we truly are?

I then ask them about their conventions, and strategy or brain storming sessions, and I learn that on these occasions, they're asked to come in casual dress. So they can be themselves, and think freely. So what are they supposed to be doing the rest of the year?

People shift uncomfortably in their seats as I repeatedly ask why, but gradually they begin to understand the true answer. To coin a phrase – it's a control issue. Uniformity makes it easier to tame people, their ideas and expectations. Anyone who wants control will prescribe conformity. And outward appearance is a fine place to start. School children are a great example. Some are obliged to wear uniforms, and those identical jumpers and suit coats are defended by parents who worry about discrimination over clothes and by teachers who think that it's easier to control kids who believe they're equal. Mao Tse Tung understood this and dressed millions of Chinese in dull-coloured, plain suits. Any drill sergeant sees the advantage, too.

With schools, religious institutions, government and the mass media promoting conformity, it's no wonder it's second nature by the time most people apply for a job at a company like Semco. By that time, their thinking has crystallized. They've endured a typical upbringing, which includes years of schooling in boring classes and lectures on subjects they don't identify with. They've learned how to say 'yes, ma'am,' to please, to appear cooperative, and to make the issue at hand go away.

Then, at 17, they're expected to decide what they want to be in life. How can they know? Yet most people have been asked since they were 10-years-old what they want to be when they grow up.

But the majority of college people haven't pinpointed their calling in life. Yet they're presented with a list of choices: medicine or law, art or engineering? They're asked to choose whether they want to spend the next 50 years examining toes or livers, divorcing couples or prosecuting criminals, photographing or painting, building bridges or calculating impellers for pumps.

Alas, by the time they finish college and come to work at places like Semco, GE or Amazon.com, they've been trained to ask why only when solicited, and then only in the strictest sense. They've lost the capacity to question everything from scratch, because they've learned the first and most important lesson in getting along in the system: 'Don't rock the boat.' We wear suits and ties because that's what we do.

At Semco, there's a motorbike aficionado who has worked as a messenger for several years. Toninho is 37, athletic, and his entire body is covered in tattoos. You can't miss them, but just to be sure the tattoos are appreciated, Toninho always wears sleeveless T-shirts to better display them. Several of our customers have complained about his appearance, calling his tattoos unpleasant, unprofessional and even menacing. An insurance broker even rang to demand we send a different messenger with his deliveries.

But Semco doesn't have a dress code. We don't need a uniform approach to feel comfortable and secure. On the contrary, we don't want to feel secure. So we don't say a word about how employees dress or what they look like. When Lucia Kobayashi joined Semco during our dot.com expansion phase, she arrived with blue hair. One of Lucia's colleagues, Sheilla Alvares, decided to pierce her tongue. She only hesitated because her parents warned her that she would lose her job if she turned up one day with a stud in her mouth. But when Sheilla saw Lucia's blue hair, she realized that appearance had nothing to do with her position at Semco. She went ahead with the piercing, and on the same day dyed her hair pink.

When Alex Guedes was hired at RGIS as a team supervisor, he was told he'd need a car. On the day of his first inventory, his manager went outside to help him pack the computers and other high-tech equipment. The manager was shocked to find Alex standing by a broken down Volkswagen Beetle, a rusting hulk that had seen better days 20 years before. For a fleeting moment he thought about cancelling the inventory. But then he remembered that a car is a car, and there were no rules about what it had to look like. Alex had done his part by bringing a vehicle. The manager looked at him.

'Is this a car, or only a means of locomotion?' Alex just shrugged. They packed the car, and rumbled off to the inventory.

And Toninho, our messenger, is one of the most efficient, reliable and speedy messengers we have. In a city plagued with congested traffic like São Paulo, that's invaluable.

When I speak about Semco to an audience, at the end of my talk there's always someone who tells me that only a very special employee could work for a company like ours. I always answer that I've never found that to be the case.

But outsiders rarely believe me right away. In fact, everyone at Semco is bound by the doubters we encounter. Rosalie Kovacs, a Japanese-Brazilian with long black hair and an easy smile, laughs when she thinks about how long she's worked at Semco.

'I was born here!' she says, adding that she started with the company 18 years ago when she was just 17.

'I first noticed the difference between other companies and Semco because of my husband,' Rosalie says. 'He didn't believe in Semco's transparency, in the philosophy of the workers helping run the company, because he thinks people should just punch their cards, do their job and go, because companies hide information from the people. He said "this company won't last three years."

'He still doesn't believe in it because he works in a very traditional company, so he still doubts whether Semco really works or not,' she added. 'But because I've been here 17 years, and we talk about work, he knows at least that Semco isn't typical. Now he says, "it might work there but it won't work elsewhere!"'

'Nobody believes it!' Claudia Veloz agreed.

'I run into that all the time,' added Nilton Moraias, a purchasing manager for 19 years at Semco. 'Whenever I go outside the company, people ask many questions but they don't believe the answers. Everyone thinks we're biased. I just spent a month in San Francisco, and all my time went into explaining Semco.'

The same sceptics grill John Mills, one of our export managers.

'I'm in sales, and I go out and say "Semco", and then I have to spend the first half an hour talking about it. Two weeks ago I had an Italian company here about a possible partnership. When I explained to them about Semco, the president couldn't believe it. He called in his general manager, and they were really taken aback. We then signed the partnership.'

'There are so few companies that do this,' said Edi Lima, an administrative assistant who started with my father 20 years ago. Everyone has his or her own ideas to explain this.

'Multinationals aren't interested in informality.'

'Laws are handed down from the corporate office.'

'Family companies are not open to new markets.'

'It's difficult for other companies to implement because there are no rules to it, no regulations. You don't learn it, you conquer it.'

'It's not enough for a businessman to want to change processes,' Nilton offered as a final word. 'Convincing employees is the most

149

difficult part. They don't believe in the boss. They think the boss wants to take their skin off.'

Ironically, I've learned that any adult welcomes freedom, flexibility and responsibility if it increases the gratification he gets from what he does for a living. The easiest thing may be finding people who slip into the Semco rhythm. And although many people have left Semco over the years because they couldn't condone the 'excessive' freedom and lack of control, it's telling that most of them were managers.

But the mix of people who remain, requires us to view talent in a new light. Culture is like a long-simmering stew, even at a business. And talent is a delicate ingredient. It must be added smoothly. Too much, and the stew gets salty, not enough and it has no flavour.

An avid cook and music buff, I've learned that stew (say a *boeuf bourguignon*) parallels Ravel's Bolero. They both seem so easy to do. Stew apparently just has to sit long enough for the meat to tenderize. And Bolero seems like an unending succession of the same simple notes. Like a company culture, they both belie the complexity, timing and fragile combination that contribute to success. If you add too much salt too early in the stew, or make the flame too high, nothing will save you in a few hours time. Conductors, also, die ugly deaths by playing Bolero in front of sophisticated audiences. One mistake in the intensity or timing, and the piece climaxes too soon – and the ending is an overplayed mess. As with the *bourguignon*, one has to rush in in the last few minutes.

Culture in an organization is like that. Too many MBAs and it tastes salty. The uniformity with which our educational system produces MBAs is actually a threat to organizations. It guarantees the past. It guarantees uniformity. It's scary to observe that MBAs are the same the world over. Their uniformity virtually assures that change will not occur.

Companies respect conformity and uniformity, but fail to see how limiting they are. Without change and innovation, companies cannot adapt. At one time, Singer was one of the biggest companies in the US. Today, we're not using Singer cell phones, because the company was unable to adapt.

When young people or seasoned managers come to us from completely different worlds, we try to value the differences they bring. Of course growth dilutes culture. The trick is to find merit and charm in the new ingredients.

Jonathan Graicar is a good example. A blonde specimen of city smarts, he always wears designer clothes and is at ease in any cappuccino bar or techno disco. He is fast with numbers and anxious to make a million or two (after all, he's already 19). We sometimes call him 'the Clone' because he is one of several similar-looking and similar-aged whiz kids at Semco. He comes from a wealthy family and cannot possibly imagine doing the same thing for two consecutive weeks, much less 30 years. Jonathan is the secretary of a group that set itself up to 'detonate' what they view as Semco's complacent culture! They became known as the Taliban Group, and they meet every two weeks to think up ways of injecting new life into Semco's products and services. They're the ones who – for reasons unknown to us simpletons – think that Semco will only be a success when we become a $1 billion company. The rest of us shrug and avoid their meetings. One of the few who regularly went to the Taliban meetings was Danilo Saicali.

Most of the time, Jonathan sits near João Vendramim, who at age 61 has been with us for 20 years and is our in-house philosopher. João uses computers, but likes to prop a pencil behind his ear. He figures he needs to explain to Jonathan what a pencil is for. Once, a group of them went to lunch together, and Danilo and João were commenting on the new bus routes. They took to reminiscing on the years of bus riding they did to and from their first jobs. The Clone's eyes glazed over, and the others decided to ask him whether he had ever gotten on to a bus in his life – and the answer, with a sheepish grin, was no.

Cultural integration, and mixing backgrounds is in the grain of what we do at Semco. Often that's easier said than done because even at Semco, people tend to explain 'the way things are done around here'. But when they start with our *Survival Manual*, the cartoon-filled collection of generic exhortations (such as: 'Question everything around you, take nothing for granted.'), newcomers are reminded that we welcome new influences and want to change with the times.

But preserving the culture that evolves in an organization is just as dangerous as ignoring it – witness communities like the Amish or Orthodox Jewish sects. Only certain people can live under such severe rules and with such limited options. When tribes co-exist in a workplace, they infuse one another with new concepts and different experiences. They form their flavour slowly, like a good stew.

Now, after almost two decades of working together, Clovis and I both think we are farther from our original ideal that we were some years ago. The unexpected growth has led to a lot of new influences, and we've lost some control over the culture of the company. The dilution has generated a culture that we don't understand completely, and has done away with certain *modus operandi* that we valued and understood, such as highly participative planning, endless meetings of the mind on philosophical issues, or high levels of close-knit solidarity.

On the other hand, we may be waxing nostalgic. These times of e-mail overload, multi-headquarters and driven young types has catapulted us into a new era, and we may never – and maybe should never – return to the mould that we knew so well.

Sometimes we feel a bit out of touch with real life, or wish we made time to talk more and e-mail less, but the Clone and the Taliban make sure we don't rest too easy.

Diversity can throw together leaders and followers whose styles are almost incompatible. Felipe Knudsen, a manager of our Bidcom unit (otherwise known as the *Kursk* project) discovered this himself. Knudsen had a rather high opinion of himself, one that might befit a manager at another company but that grated on some nerves at Semco. He wielded his power too overtly for a democratic environment, riding roughshod over minority opinions, and leaving himself only the more important tasks. He also had a penchant for yellow ties. It happened that the bathroom doors near his office were adorned with a Barbie doll and a Bob the Builder doll instead of signs indicating which gender should enter. Some of Knudsen's employees took it upon themselves to put together another doll – a Bob wearing Barbie clothes and a yellow tie. They hung the doll exactly between the two bathroom doors. Their message was plain: The high and mighty manager could pick and choose whichever bathroom he wanted, and the other men and women would just make way. Knudsen saw the humour in the stunt, and 'Bob with the Yellow Tie' hung on the wall for months. His fellow *Kursk* project workers think it helped him slip into the Semco rhythm – it put management into perspective for Knudsen, and after Bob went up he was more modest about his role. Knudsen's style still differs from other Bidcom workers, but it didn't matter after they made it clear that this kind of diversity was a plus – not something to be flattened by a top-heavy tractor.

Most people find it easy to adapt to the latitude we encourage. Jorge Pitol and Rogerio Ottolia worked in the same area, in machinery design. Whenever they were mulling over a new product – and sometimes when they were just bored – they'd pull out a bag of golf clubs. The two men had rearranged desks in their area to expose the in-floor AC plugs. These plugs were tailor-made for golf, since a ball would plunk perfectly into them. They'd play a round or two of mini-golf, forcing other salesmen, messengers and various staff to scoot around the greens or suffer the consequences.

During one round, their boss, Marcio Batoni, happened into the room. He frowned at the golf game, declined an offer to join, and left. Pitol turned to the onlookers and said: 'Don't executives arrange to play golf with each other on Wednesday afternoons, under the assumption that big deals are struck on the golf course? We invent great solutions while we play, and it doesn't even cost the company greens fees!'

Sure, a minority doesn't adapt to Semco because they need more direction, because they feel better when everyone arrives at the same time and abides by the same rules. There are also a lot of people who are not impressed or in any other way moved by the Semco system because for them, a job is nothing but a job. Participation imposes a weight they'd rather not carry. We'll always have a place for those people because of Semco's voluntary culture.

Fabiana Kahn is a good example of how far Semco people go to respect the tribal culture of clients. She runs an unorthodox building – or to be more precise, a very orthodox building – the São Luiz office tower in São Paulo. Owned by Benedictine fathers, it is paradoxically one of the city's most modern buildings, and houses the headquarters of several multinationals. Fabiana manages the building for Cushman & Wakefield Semco, and she devotes long hours and exceptional attention to detail to her work, well beyond the call of duty. But Fabiana also practices the empathy with the customer (as well as with different tribes that we encounter) that every good property manager learns. In 2001, the two Trane refrigeration compressors responsible for the St Louis' 600 ton system burned out. One right after the other, within two weeks. Trane accepted responsibility and vowed to install new compressors. But the delay left the building with a weak air conditioning system for over two months.

During that time, Father Roberto, the Benedictine cleric, asked

Fabiana to be as discrete as possible, to avoid alarming the tenants – after all, summer was near.

The situation grew tense, there were endless delays, it became unbearable. Finally, Trane showed up with the new compressors. Given that two out of two had failed, and considering the long delay in substituting the parts, Fabiana refused to take any chances. Since there wasn't much she could do in technical terms, so she resorted to the available tribal talent.

When the Trane engineers came to start up the new machines, she immediately announced that Father Roberto was going to bless them! Trading amused glances, the Trane mechanics held off until the cleric was ready.

Father Roberto walked into the boiler room, elaborately enrobed as if for Mass and not a little agitated. He was wearing a red stole on top of his Benedictine dress, and had a vial of water with an aspersorium in his hand. Fabiana and her assistant, Nelia, were in smart business dresses. Father Roberto instructed them all to hold hands and gather around the compressor. The puzzled, slightly concerned mechanics joined in – after all, the customer is always right.

The priest sprayed holy water on Fabiana and Nelia, and asked whether the engineers also wanted to be blessed. They promptly declined – God knows what hidden sins will come to the surface, they probably thought. Next, Father Roberto solemnly blessed the compressors, sprayed some water on them, and authorized a technician to start up the machines.

The correct button was pressed, the machines purred into action, and they've worked magnificently to this day.

At other times, our internal tribes clash. And there is no one and no system to restore order after the collision. A few years ago, Eugenio Singer, then CEO of our environmental consulting unit, questioned what we did with paint waste at our machinery plant. Essentially, paint residue was allowed to run off into a waste water system behind the factory.

This was ironic, since the machinery plant and our environmental remediation unit exist side-by-side at Semco. Biologists at Semco ERM (the unit Eugenio heads) knew that visitors from large chemical companies had seen the paint run off and had criticized the practice. He wanted the machinery unit to immediately spend $50,000 to divert the paint residue away from the waste water system.

The machinery plant wasn't breaking any laws. Rogerio Ottolia, the CEO of Industrial Machinery, agreed with Eugenio that the paint residue should be dealt with differently, but also pointed out that his unit was in compliance with regulations. Eugenio countered that the regulations were flawed, and would soon be updated. And besides, he said, we knew that our paint installation was damaging the waste treatment system. We didn't need a rulebook to tell us that.

But Rogerio had no budget for diverting the paint waste system, and in fact, had more urgent priorities. He needed a new computer system that permitted salespeople to put together engineered on-line proposals in front of the customer. He didn't have $50,000 to spare for the paint residue problem.

A heated debate ensued, and others joined the fray. Someone suggested moving the painting off site. Ethical versus legal concepts were extensively argued. Many people sided with Rogerio, agreeing that he couldn't afford the luxury of investing above and beyond the law when he had competitors hot on his heels.

Some joked that Rogerio might earn a Congressional medal for environmental citizenship on the same day his creditors sealed his front door in a bankruptcy procedure.

Eugenio didn't give up. He offered Rogerio free environmental consulting services, at a street value of about $30,000. Rogerio accepted only about 20 hours of consulting to evaluate the situation and his options. The conflict continued for months, accented by a series of angry e-mails over dragging feet and mistaken priorities. Along the way, Eugenio and others appealed to me and to Clovis Bojikian. They assumed that if two business units were at odds, the corporate office should intervene. Both Clovis and I believed that the company should stop allowing the paint residue to run off. But there was no mechanism for us to intervene, and we weren't about to create one.

We would remain energetically committed to one of Semco's time-honoured practices: doing nothing.

Eventually, the environmental unit gave up.

Months passed, then a year. And one sunny day auditors from the Environmental Protection Agency arrived at the plant. They inspected extensively in search of anything that could lead to a penalty. Naturally they found the paint installations. In fact, they also discovered that paint containers were being stacked in a different place than indicated in our building plans. The regulations had been updated, as Eugenio predicted. Rogerio's people had not been organized or interested enough to keep track of the law and react to the changes. So the EPA fined us. Rogerio then had to hire special attorneys at a cost of $30,000. Some of ERM's staff walked around with 'I-told-you-so' on their faces, but most stepped in to help the company obey the regulations.

Now the machine plant is compliant, but whether or not we learned a lesson is still up for debate. If a similar situation arose, we would never say 'remember last time, and take heed: Correct the problem early.' That's too obvious – and it's the calcified answer. Try following that statement with a why (or two, or three). Very quickly it would be clear that for the same solution to be the right one, both the circumstances and the probable results would have to be identical. And that's virtually impossible. So next time we face a similar problem, we'll do just what we did before: nothing.

I call this kind of management 'active omission,' and I preach it constantly to my people. It allows the process be the supreme mover. And no two processes are alike.

In India, managers and employees at a company called Addon Engineering learned the value of 'doing nothing'. Dilip Patel, one of the company's senior managers, wrote to me about the time several employees used Addon's phones to repeatedly call a horoscope hotline. Someone speaking the local Bangalore dialect answered the phone, so none of the workers suspected they were making long-distance calls. In fact, the calls were international, and the phone bill skyrocketed by 60 percent. When management found out, the workers stepped forward, pleaded ignorance, apologized, and waited for the axe to fall. Dilip and the other managers decided to . . . do nothing.

The workers paid for the phone bill in instalments, but no one was reprimanded or demoted, and the company didn't lock up the phones. Dilip wouldn't have said Addon was following the Semco model, but after he read my first book he realized 'it reinforced many of the values lying dormant' at Addon. But his company's partners 'had apprehensions in rushing towards making Addon a transparent, participative organization.' There was no problem with Addon's workers or managers, though, because 'the trust we had built . . . through the likes of the telephone incident years ago was alive and working.' In the end, Addon did more than nothing. It also gave up control after gaining courage from the Semco stories – something most people wouldn't expect in a traditional society like India.

'We have removed the supervisors and inspectors from some of the production shops,' Dilip told me, and started teaching workers 'how to read the balance sheets so we could share this information with our employees on a continuous basis.'

Management by omission is meant to create room for a company culture to breed. To do that, tribes must find their place, discover their values, and solidify their way of dealing with the other groups, inside and outside the company. That can sometimes take time. Doing nothing seems counter-intuitive. But allow me to repeat – process is the supreme mover. And that takes some cold blood.

That brings up the question of how we hire – or add new people to our tribe. We do this by respecting tribal rites of passage, such as sizing up potential new members.

That priority was foremost in the Spring of 2001, when we decided to hire a finance controller for the corporate staff, and for one of our real estate management units. The business was expanding rapidly and we needed a strong liaison with our American partners like Cushman & Wakefield.

We placed open advertisements with Semco's name at the top, and asked for résumés via e-mail. Four hundred people applied. Over 80 percent were currently employed, and some 30 percent held more senior jobs. CFOs are in great demand in Brazil, so none of these people would have been unemployed for long. It was unusual to get so many applications in such a tight job market.

We usually divide the vetting of applications for any senior executive position. Under normal circumstances, our human resources point man, Clovis Bojikian, would share the task with the CEO directly involved, and with various other volunteers. In this case, there were simply too many résumés. Since I was interested in the process, I joined the effort. We recruited several other people, including someone who no longer worked at Semco but who Clovis thought could help. We divided several hundred résumés into random piles for each to review. Anywhere else, the human resources department would have handled this process.

We followed no rules for narrowing down the résumés. We didn't want a list of requirements to limit our options. We wanted the process to be highly intuitive – to follow our gut reaction to the résumés. We didn't need paradigms to guide us. I liken the process to the approach of a chess Grand Master who uses intuition and analytical skills to see a board. Bearing in mind that (as Clovis says) a person's *curriculum vitae* is advertising – and therefore rarely includes honest assessments of shortcomings. We promptly made a lot of mistakes about whom to call for an interview. Great candidates surely slipped through our fingers, and we'll never know. Many early applicants would have.

We winnowed the pile down to 20 candidates that each of us classified A+. (I also set aside seven résumés that I thought were from good candidates for other positions at Semco. They had nothing to do with the controller's job. With active, senior executives vetting the résumés, we could keep our eyes open for other opportunities.)

The 20 candidates were asked to participate in a collective interview, which we sometimes use as a rodeo of sorts – there, the candidates have an opportunity to see the other pretenders. We mix it up with many Semco people, and this brings collective behaviour into play. Four at a time would come to a meeting with about 15 Semco employees. The Semco employees would collectively interview all 20 candidates. And the candidates would understand how important interaction and novel situations are at Semco.

Our interview and selection process was not unlike the way we hire at any level. We rely heavily on the shock value of intensive mutual exposure. The candidates can decline, of course, and there's no penalty. They continue a more private interview process. But we believe that only by spending a lot of time with the greatest number of employees will a candidate get any real sense of Semco. At the same time, Semco employees get to voice an opinion about the people who might be joining their team.

We address compatibility head on with this overwhelming, and admittedly scary, exposure.

First, we create a template for the job. This is a draft list of the qualities we are looking for, and the weights that should be attached to each of these. Employees help design the template. They can log onto the company Intranet and suggest what we should seek in financial controller candidates, and then the scoring value to assign to each subject. Basic qualifications, like an international experience or schooling, fluent english, and a firm command of financial technique are not a part of the template.

These are either irrelevant, or they're a prerequisite covered by testing. For example, if english is vital, as it was in this case, the finalists will take a test called Test of English as a Foreign Language – Business Version. It tests the candidate's ability to communicate well for business purposes. An intricate test of financial knowledge gives the candidates two hours to put together a balance sheet, comment on profit and loss statements, and answer questions about tax laws and current issues in finance.

As basic abilities, therefore, english or finance skills shouldn't have any weight attached to them. Which meant that an MBA from Wharton would do nothing for an applicant's grading.

This is important because it prevents placing undue value on experience and schooling. The fact that a candidate has an MBA is worthless to the template. Those skills may open the door for a candidate, but they add little to his qualifications. So we don't review or grade those basic abilities. It may have got him in the door, but it doesn't give him any better chance of landing the job – even though MBAs would be highly suited to what we're looking for in a controller.

That sounds counterproductive. But in fact, it's not. If we included an MBA credential in the template, we'd end up with a raft of MBA candidates. And that leads us straight to uniformity.

The qualities that were listed on the template for this job included a quick analytical mind, the capacity to integrate easily, an attitude of teamwork, transparency/openness, a lack of a yes-man (yes-person?) attitude, a career of deliberate and solid growth and a sense of humour.

Interviewers can rate candidates on a scale of one to 10. Of the 10 possible points, two went to the interviewer's 'feeling as to whether this was the right person'.

On the controller template, the subjects were integrity, personal presence, the candidate's handling of issues. It also included the english test, the financial and technical test, and an assessment of how the candidate might put together a budget. It happened that in this case, people wanted to be confident of the candidate's technical competence.

After the template is designed, two or three interested Semco workers volunteer to coordinate the interview process. Someone has to call all the candidates and ask them if they'll come. The date of the collective interview is posted so any employee who is interested can participate. For the first round of controller interviews, 37 Semco employees responded. That high interest was a reflection of the importance of this new position.

By the same token, if no one had shown up for the collective interview, then we'd have gotten rid of the controller's position before it was even filled. No-shows would have meant that no one at the company cared about it.

The 20 candidates were reduced to nine. Then, the 37 Semco employees who had expressed interest were handed a copy of the template showing which candidate attributes we were interested in, and the score value assigned to each. They could come to the next rounds of interviews, ask whatever questions they wanted, in whatever language, in search of answers for the template.

Each candidate made three to five trips to Semco, each time spending an hour or two with different groups. Each met more Semco people than they could remember. A dozen Semco employees showed up for the final round of interviews with the three best candidates.

These sessions were intense but light-hearted because everyone tried to make the process easy on the candidate (we're ganging up on them, after all).

One finalist was particularly self-confident, spoke many languages fluently and talked laudably of himself. One Semco interviewer could not restrain himself and inquired, in a gentle and non-confrontational manner: 'Did anyone ever tell you that you are very arrogant?'

The candidate answered that yes, he was known as pigeon-breast to some – that he seemed that way at first sight, but that we were free to speak to people who had worked with and for him, who would tell us that this impression disappeared over time. His reply earned him many supporters, although others saw this as a studied response to a substantial fault.

The three finalists were seen one after the other on the same day. Some of the dozen or so Semco employees who showed up had seen them before, but most had not. Each Semco participant then filled out his template response sheet. The resulting scores would define the winner. Their rankings would be unknown to the CFO of Cushman & Wakefield, who would also interview each of the three. If the results differed, the Semco group would reconvene to hear the Cushman & Wakefield CFO's arguments. They could change or stand by their ratings. Whatever they decided, it would overrule Cushman & Wakefield's CFO.

Incidentally, my vote was subordinate to the Semco employees' choice, too. My opinion would carry as much weight as that of the CFO of Cushman & Wakefield, but no more.

As it turned out, the candidate who got the job was chosen by virtual consensus. Ivan Maluf scored highly on the english and technical tests, though he's not a native english speaker (whereas several others were, including Pigeon-Breast, who was British). Ivan's mother, who spoke no english, arranged private lessons for him when he was a boy.

Very tall, lanky and timid, Ivan seduced Semco by being both a careful listener and full of firm opinions. He has neither an MBA nor a finance background, but he'd been CFO for Philips and a GE Capital company, and he did extremely well on our technical test, which had sparked controversy among some candidates. After sweating through the test for half an hour, the CFO of a large US multinational stormed out of the building, cursing it as unreasonable and protesting that someone in his position did not have to know those things. Several other candidates complained heavily about the difficulty of the technical test. At one point our CFO, Violi, became concerned that maybe two hours was not enough, since candidates were regularly returning unfinished tests. Violi then asked Zeca, our resident young Turk, to try the test. He finished in 38 minutes and earned an almost perfect score. So we continued to use it.

Ivan also did wonderfully. I participated in one interview with him, and I asked him why he was unemployed. All the other finalists had jobs.

He'd left the GE Capital company four months before when they decided to pull out of Brazil. He had turned off the lights. He'd been paid a bonus, and received several offers to move to other GE companies. Instead, he used the bonus to search carefully for a job. He had refused three final offers from other companies.

But he wasn't just job hunting. He filled his time with his other interest: storytelling. Of Arab descent, he was volunteering for a Jewish congregation in a program that sent people to shantytowns to tell stories to poor children. He'd even taken courses to develop this ability. While he told stories and looked for work, his wife's income as a head-hunter and his bonus from GE kept his household together.

Several months after he started, we began receiving e-mails full of praise for Ivan. Fran Clerkin, CFO of Cushman & Wakefield International, lauded Ivan as beyond everyone's wildest dreams.

As unusual as our hiring practices sound, it's actually traditional corporations that rely on loony recruiting methods. They're using a 100-year-old system to choose their people, while we respect a time-honoured, thousand-year-old method of admitting members to the tribe. Cavemen and fellows in medieval artisan guilds worked no differently. They all based a decision on how well a group accepts a newcomer.

Our collective interview allows candidates to see that 37 people are interested in the job they might fill. They can hear their concerns, their preferences, even their complaints. Some applicants run screaming for the hills. But isn't it better for both sides to know that? When would he have run for the hills at another company? Six months after he started? At Semco, we don't want to spend six months trying to integrate a new hire only to discover there is no chance of compatibility.

And how many companies misrepresent themselves in interviews? A human resources specialist will present his company as the perfect work environment. With 37 interviewers, there's an informal, unplanned and uncontrolled element to the meeting. The chance that one of those people will say something real and revealing, either in jest or between the lines, is very high. Candidates can form impressions from side comments or attitudes. They can glean a lot of information from 37 people sharing their opinions.

On the one hand, we're unmasking the inscrutable face of the company. But on the other, we create something of a free-for-all that leaves us vulnerable. It's the 'scare off' meeting magnified 37 times, and that can be highly effective at scaring off candidates.

But it's also a dialogue. There are four rounds of collective interviews, each with fewer candidates as we narrow the field. By the end, candidates should have a strong sense of their compatibility and of whether there is adequate balance between their personal goals and ours. Ivan came back six times, and when he finally started, he knew several people by name that I myself had never met. So when the successful candidate shows up for his first day of work, there'll be a large number of people on hand who are already familiar, with whom he feels solidarity, and who are invested in absorbing him and supporting his success. The benefits of our hiring process thus outlive the interview and selection period. It may take longer to start, but productivity and sustainability make up grandly for the 'lost' time.

But we also need to make these tribal sniffing sessions sustainable.

And that occurs when we let members of one group check out the jobs of another.

When we ran our very first tribe integration program many years ago, we put a small group of finance executives together with salespeople.

At the time, the debate of the day was over whether the salesmen were too eager to sell at any cost, thereby eating up the company's working capital with over-generous payment terms. The debate raged but never went anywhere. When we proposed that a finance specialist and one salesman change places, many people were flabbergasted. We couldn't do that, they insisted. Salesmen and accountants don't mix, they said, they're not interchangeable! They warned that the salesman's customers would be dismayed and hostile, and we'd lose business.

And then there were all the errors and mix-ups that the salesman was sure to commit in the finance office. We did it anyway, and new worlds opened up. And the experience went further than that.

From finance we chose a short, stout, hardheaded cost accountant named Antonio Carlos Iotti. He wore extra thick glasses with a definite greenish sheen. He smirked a lot, making it impossible to know when he was being humorous or smug. He habitually nodded as you spoke, so you believed he agreed whole-heartedly with you. As soon as you finished, he'd nod again, and then declare: 'I disagree entirely.' And off you'd go on another round of convince-me-if-you-can.

He belonged to the tribe of long lost eccentric accounting savages. Of which José Violi was one at the time. There were five, and in good tribal form they'd joined Semco at around the same time, like cannibals closing in on their prey during the night.

They had all worked for an offbeat Italian entrepreneur who made industrial sewing machines, and where business was often conducted at the top of the Italian's lungs. At Semco, Iotti rose to plant controller. He was known for his passionate attention to detail and his immense work capacity. He was tough, and directly challenged any operational assumptions. Many days he left work at midnight, after finishing off a calculation in his small, exact handwriting, his face glued to the paper and his tiny, swollen hands pressing on a pencil. He was wary of computers. But the man could calculate like there was no tomorrow, and no one ever caught him making a mistake. Most of all, he was suspicious of salesmen.

So we put him in charge of sales. For a year he went out to see the real world. A typical desk man, he even had a hard time finding the addresses he was now obliged to travel to. Very quickly he revised his concepts of how easy it should be to sell on better credit terms. Slowly, he began to take a different view of the wide world that he was discovering. Soon he became the CEO of that manufacturing unit.

Iotti was the third person from finance to go into sales and then become CEO of a business unit. Before him Alipio Camargo, another accountant, had moved over and risen to sales director before running a unit, and after him Violi became CEO of another of our manufacturing companies.

The most direct result of all this was that the finance people never again confronted the sales group with simplistic requests for shorter payment terms. The two tribes can empathize with each other now, and they're more careful about the plans they make that involve the other.

Today, due to the immense re-shuffling that goes on within the Semco tribes, it is no longer enough for an anthropologist to sit in the parking lot. When the BBC came to do their special TV program on Semco, they were totally confounded by what they saw. They had imagined that they could simply follow the corner offices, the secretaries, or the assembly line rationale, and identify who's who. They discovered that this is impossible at Semco.

Sure, anthropological connections among people are still naturally preserved. Some strife among different groups will always occur. Companies must open themselves to this diversity. But it requires an acceptance of divergent attitudes, And very few workplaces are open to that.

But cliques, sects and clubs that reinforce tribal affiliations in organizations can be softened when employees manage themselves. In an open organization like Semco, people come into the office less often and have more time to themselves. Their need to belong to a tribe can be satisfied with their hobbies or personal communities. It doesn't have to be met in the office.

There is an assumption that the workplace is where most waking hours are spent, and therefore that tribal connections have to be made there. But this wouldn't be true if people were free to mingle work and personal time in a looser way.

The lines between groups softens, and this difference can be seen in the immense respect found at Semco. Deprecating comments about another group or departmental biases are practically non-existent. And when anthropological issues are subdued, the real reason for working comes to the fore.

And now we can add the dot.com tribe to our efforts, as we try to find new homes for those boom-bust orphans. In the high-tech 1990s, conventional business rules were thrown out the window. When the dot.com gold rush was over, the world economy was littered with human detritus. Hundreds of thousands lost jobs in industries with any connection to the high-tech sector, from hip webmasters running avant-garde start-ups in Soho to middle-aged engineers making staid computer chips in Tokyo. The dot bomb was a great equalizer for these disparate people, turning all of them into high-tech orphans.

When the shoe dropped, 65,000 people who worked for Internet-related companies in the US were laid off between December 1999 and early 2001. The same companies that only a year before touted philosophies of freedom, hard work and big reward buckled under pressure from shareholders or venture capitalists and slashed employees with abandon. Everyone knows how mercilessly cruel teenagers can be to one another. The dot.com sector was juvenile in its downsizing, too. Misleading company statements circulated, people were laid off en masse, and pink slips made the newspapers before workers were told.

One company near Seattle sent an e-mail to 20 percent of its employees telling them to go to a hotel for a meeting in 15 minutes. Once there, they were laid off, and then told the office was locked and they'd need an appointment to retrieve their belongings. In another nearby company, 60 people in a conference room listened as 40 names of those being laid off were read aloud. At a third business, employees at a meeting were informed there would be lay-offs, and then were told to check their e-mail to see who'd gotten the axe. At other companies, new hires reported for a first day of work to find they'd been laid off already.

The painful process of going bust is much more violent among the kids. Such bungling wouldn't happen at Nestlé, or General Motors. Yet outside Seattle, off Mission Street in San Francisco, or around the Revolutionary War towns near Boston, all the commitment to independence and bucking the status quo dissolved into a bloodletting because those ideals failed to help the company make it from adolescence to adulthood and longevity. The kids couldn't survive the jungle. They never made it to sustainability.

What would have become of the dot.com adolescent if he'd been left to his own devices? Would he have survived?

No. In the jungle, adolescents are not fit for survival. Most will struggle, wither away, and finally die. A few may survive, but they're hardly worth crowing about when in the midst of the high death rate. If a handful survive, they represent a system that overall is a complete failure.

Now, where do they go? At 30, they're not fit to work at GM. How can they ever turn to GM once they've had an office with a bean bag and could bring their dogs to work?

But in the organization of the future, there has to be a place for the talents of these kids, plus the thousands who come into the job market at 22 (or even 18, since most of the world's teenagers never attend college).

Traditional organizations must be structured with them in mind, so the new views and start-up skills they brought to their own businesses can be utilized. At that point, the mature veterans can step in. Without recognizing this, many traditional companies will face the same fate as some of the industrial giants of the 20th Century like Singer Sewing Machines, International Harvester, Westinghouse, RCA, Woolworth & Co. In the middle of the 20th century, these companies were indomitable. No one could imagine a time when they wouldn't exist as a huge part of the economy. Now they're mere shadows of their former selves, if they exist at all. Traditional companies today face the same dilemma – they may look good for a time, and convince Wall Street that the current quarter is glowing, but without new ideas, new approaches, new blood, they won't last either.

A sustainable company will put a 57-year-old GM alumni in an office with a dot.com kid. They both have significant talents to offer. The office may even have a dot.com kid environment. It will design a workplace that allows the 57-year-old to sit, side-by-side, with dot.com and net generation kids, and where each has equal freedom to pursue their passions. It will not subordinate the 25-year-old kid directly to the 57-year-old's rules, but rather to his wisdom or experience. In exchange, the elder worker cannot use his maturity to restrain the dot.com kid. If he does that, what's the point of having an entrepreneur in your midst? Everyone recognizes that attracting and investing in talent are touchstones of organizations. But what people consider sufficient effort and enough investment is what separates the men from the boys, the women from the girls.

Often in Semco's history we've put talent in place before a business existed – the cart before the horse, so to speak. In 2000 and 2001, we had several other senior executives like Danilo Saicali who were overqualified for the job we had for them at that moment. We invested $120,000 per month in half a dozen executives who were to build the next phase of Semco on opportunities that our business units were pointing out. At the time, however, we didn't know whether they were feasible. Thus, without business plans or the firm intent to enter these businesses, we invested in the people whose experience and intuition could put us in those markets. It might have ended in nothing at all, and then we would have lost the investment.

Notker Raschle was such a case. He was irritated when our head-hunters approached him about becoming a CEO for our Semco Johnson Controls unit. He'd been with Asea Brown Boveri, the huge Swiss-Swedish capital goods conglomerate, for 26 years. He wasn't about to entertain head-hunters. He even told them that he'd stop using their services at ABB if they insisted. Hmmm . . .

We liked that. So we set out to hunt him down. I invited him to lunch at my home, where we spoke of nothing in particular. Certainly not about a job. There followed an invitation for Notker to participate in a Semco Johnson Controls board meeting. And then, for months, the odd contact. And then an invitation to meet up with me at the mountain ranch. There the two of us spent many hours on the veranda, and sitting around the kitchen island while I cooked from what was in the pantry.

After a few more encounters, we spoke about a job. By then Notker had a good idea of what it would be like to work at Semco. The challenge was to leave a solid career (he was president of ABB Services, an enormous and successful part of ABB's business) to become an entrepreneur. We were offering him a 10 percent stake in the Semco Johnson Controls business – in line with our philosophy of having a CEO who owns a chunk of the business. And he'd have the opportunity to work with other Semco start-ups.

Notker's wife thought he was just joking around, that he couldn't be serious. After all, a stern and reserved Swiss, with a brilliantly planned career, endless benefits and nine years from comfortable retirement would not make a risky move. Or would he? I spotted a gleam in his eye, an itch for independence, the thrill of starting anew. There were signs. Notker had a 3-year-old son, a second family after his first round of kids had grown up. He had the energy to refuse the easy road, and to take on our challenge.

Our other executives, who had met him at a Semco convention we had invited Notker to, were unanimous: He would never come. If he did, two of them said, he'd surely miss all the structure, the backup, the formality and power that he'd learned to appreciate at ABB. Well . . .

Notker finally joined us, after 7 months of chase. Like Danilo, he heard the 'scare-off' warnings, but did not heed them. To everyone's surprise, he fitted right in. His first day was spent in the Semco integration session, along with two trainees. There he watched a video on Semco, received our *Survival Manual* of cartoons, and debated human resource issues that he'd never even heard about at ABB. He then looked for a place to put his notebook, went out to smoke, and began to ponder what his new life would be like.

His wife had already agreed to her own sacrifice: There would be no more company secretary to take care of her worries and errands. A new world was opening up for them.

A while later Notker began to sit next to a teenager. Rafael Tinoco, an 18-year-old physics student who'd started hacking computer systems at age 13. He'd already been invited to participate in a selection process for the largest telecom operator, in Rio de Janeiro. They asked several of the candidates to prove their abilities. This youngster decided to do so by hacking into their website. It took him less than six minutes, and he left his name and phone number with an invitation to the telecom to contact him for further interviews.

Rafael came to my attention after a profile in one of Brazil's main magazines described him as one of the country's foremost hackers. The telecom company had offered him a job with a $130,000 starting salary. I thought we needed that kid, and a conversation with Zeca, our 23-year-old whiz, settled it. Zeca was a grandfather by Rafael's standards, and he'd look after the youngster.

To do what? Ah, that we didn't know. We called Rafael and offered him the opportunity to come work for us. What he would do, how much he'd make, all that would come later. For now all he had to do was give up the other offer, and come work for us free of charge, of direction, of job description, of future. Yummy, huh?

Well, after a day scouting around Semco, Rafael accepted and entered our *Lost In Space* program. Three days after starting, he asked our computer specialists why Semco employees couldn't work from home as if they were inside the Semco Intranet, thus avoiding the dial-up into the system through the worldwide web. Our people patiently explained that this required a big investment, and went on to describe the change in server, firewall, and on and on. The onlookers pitied the boy Rafael, who sat there desolately looking at his shoes. The meeting ended.

Two days later Rafael came back with a solution that involved UNIX and some free software. It wouldn't cost the company a cent, he declared. Companies know very little about free software. But hackers understand it completely. There are no legal or rights issues involved, just a question of knowing where to look and what software to combine. This time, our IT people looked down at their shoes.

Rafael also devised a company that provides remote anti-hacking security. Not the actual service, but the intelligence. We would come up with the strategy, hire companies to do the monitoring, and be responsible for keeping huge sites free of hackers. Software that Rafael put together diverts the hacker to a live game of speed digital chess. The hacker is moved to a harmless computer, anytime of the day or night.

We intend to start a series of companies with Rafael. Lord knows where we'll end up.

Rafael became friendly with Notker because they smoke together. These two mingle in the non-territorial offices where everyone sits in different places every day. Notker had no office, no secretary, and so he is open, for the first time in his life, to interact with an 18-year-old hacker. Hiring people such as Rafael is not the trick – any telephone company can do it by waving enough money in front of someone like him. But attracting, and especially, retaining him, is another issue. Money won't do it.

At Semco, Clovis Bojikian, our HR chieftain often works closely with Zeca, who joined Semco after managing Internet, manufacturing and entertainment ventures for one of the most important and aggressive investment banks in Brazil. His uncle introduced us, and when I met him, I instantly took a liking to him. He has a passion for putting his intellect to use and truly enjoys work, even though he refuses to take it completely seriously.

We shared the same goals for a new business called Semco Ventures that would scout out high-tech prospects. When he left the investment bank, his bosses there took it personally. They couldn't understand why a smart young entrepreneur would leave such a formidable organization, forsaking huge bonuses and a bright future.

Zeca left because he wanted something more than money and a conventional career punctuated by periodic promotions and raises. He followed his calling. He wanted a job better suited to his 'reservoir of talent' (though he didn't call it that).

Certainly some of that was because of his age. Youth goes a long way toward insulating us from life's little details – salary, savings, retirement, what job we'll be doing in 10 years. Zeca could still make choices without factoring in how he was going to support a couple of kids, for example. Youth makes it easy to be selfish and spontaneous. But youth also means Zeca is part of a generation accustomed to living by new rules, including the assumption that risk and change are good for business, and that organizations should take a more open, flexible approach to management, communication and planning. And, mostly, they want the freedom to be themselves.

And they live with technology the way the rest of us live with our cars.

When Zeca met Clovis, he met a man who had once sworn that he would retire without ever learning to type, much less operate a computer. Now, at 67, Clovis sits in our non-territorial offices and fires away at his screen. But Clovis' 60 years of writing skills dominate his two years of computer skills. As such, he starts many of his mails with apologies for starting what will be such a long memo. His are precise, careful, and there is never a grammatical mistake. When memos go to Clovis for vetting, they come back with detailed corrections of grammar, as well as incisive comments on essence. But Clovis is a meticulous man who knows no other way to communicate.

That makes it entertaining to watch e-mails batted between Clovis and Zeca. Zeca is adept at the Internet-age slang: monosyllabic messages, dismissive comments, rude language, and a complete lack of niceties. The F-word is his main tool. Clovis might send a long e-mail, describing the many reasons we should look carefully at terminating a relationship. Zeca's entire reply might be: 'Fuck the guy, fire him.'

Or Clovis might argue for looking again at a business opportunity we'd discarded. Danilo Saicali and many of the old-timers would come back with short but careful responses, mostly supporting Clovis' desire to re-open the issue. They'd show enormous respect and a real concern about hurting feelings or making a rash judgement that would inhibit future initiatives. Zeca's reply is more likely to be: 'That business is fucked, forget it.'

Now e-mail has made it possible to merge these old and new styles. There is no right or wrong. We don't want to teach Zeca to be Clovis, or vice versa. They learn from each other, and we learn from both. Recently an issue was bouncing around on our internal net, not going anywhere. Zeca suggested a fitting end for the debate, and Clovis responded with the first expletive I've seen in 20 years: 'Fucking good,' he wrote. Now the playing field is level.

As tribes mix, a constantly evolving culture emerges. It becomes evident that a profound respect for differences, idiosyncrasies and democratic ideals will gel into a new kind of organization. One where people know there's a place for self-management, self-propulsion, self-discipline. With those, workers can repeatedly dive into their reservoirs of talent. Loosening up (rejecting the military model) unleashes productivity. I believe this, and our numbers also back it up – all of Semco's business units consistently perform above published parameters of productivity per employee.

It's easy to talk about respecting diversity, tribal characteristics and dissent. But when action is required, anyone who has tried to lead in a democratic manner knows how frustrating, slow and cumbersome it is. That is why business leaders take the short route; command and execute methods, tainted with a little show of concern for how employees feel and what customers think. The short route is a path to nowhere. It doesn't lead to the productivity gains that occur when people find it worthwhile – even inspiring – to get up in the morning for work.

Coq au Vin cannot be compared to Chicken McNuggets – even if both are merely cooked fowl. Taking the long way – or simmering a slow stew of culture, tribalism and democracy – serves up a more savoury dish.

Part Four

A Long Line Of Pied Pipers

1. Why do we have a flock mentality and follow rams that turn out to be wolves?

2. Why do we think we are equipped to choose schools, doctors and mayors, but don't trust our capacity to lead ourselves at work?

3. Why do we continuously look for saviours and heroes to lead us?

CHAPTER 1

Let The Followers Lead

SOME YEARS AGO, a group of Semco factory workers commissioned one of Brazil's foremost artists, Tomie Ohtake, to paint an entire plant as if it were a canvas. She designed the ceiling to invoke the sky, wanted to paint the machines light blue and draw huge, abstract blue stains across them. The plans irked the safety engineers and other more regulatory souls. They couldn't imagine an industrial plant without gray and green machinery, black and yellow safety lines, or red fire exits.

Ohtake's flight of fancy didn't go far. Many workers instead favoured choosing their own colours for their machines, nearby columns and walls. This exercise in self-management ended with wildly coloured factories, a trend that lasted at Semco for over five years. Today, there are still coloured machines, and much greenery between the machine tools, but Tomie's sky was never executed. The workers couldn't agree on the exact colour and form.

No management works quite like self-management. And working at Semco means self-managing as much as possible. It isn't nearly as frightening as it sounds. In the end, it's self-interest at work. It requires conceding that managers don't – and can't – know the best way to do everything. People who are motivated by self-interest will find solutions that no one else can envision. They see the world in their own unique way – one that others often overlook.

By letting people off the hook of grand policies, procedures and rules, we release them to be accountable only to themselves.

I once lectured before a group of General Motors vice-presidents in Detroit. At lunch, the head of one division told me that his biggest problem was a lack of people. He had 112,000 employees. Yes, I cooed in sympathy, you immediately need to hire another 2,000 pairs of hands.

I've heard the same argument in pharmacies employing six people, schools with two hundred teachers and boat crews of eight. I'm sure every football team agrees that if they had one more person, for a total of twelve, they would be able to perform wonders.

Organizations always suffer from the conviction that productivity is never high enough.

What else can happen if workers are waiting for someone to tell them what to do, or they're following a formal plan, or confining themselves to the dictates of their job description? They're not taking initiative to increase productivity, or asking themselves three times, why? Why do we do things this way? Why can't we do better?

At Semco, self-organized groups discover that they have extra productivity just floating unnoticed in their midst. If nothing else, they can harness it by eliminating the immense daily waste of time lost to unclear goals, adolescent-style rules, in-fighting and gossip – even traffic jams.

It works in our inventory business. Every time our teams are about to begin a new inventory, they spend half an hour bantering about the best way to do their job. They've done many inventories using the newest computer equipment, and there's an established system to it. But they still ask: Why?

Marcio Batoni dreaded the possibility that Brazil might make it to the 2002 World Cup football final. Not that he wasn't a fan of Ronaldo and his team of magicians. Rather, he was worried about an enormous inventory scheduled for a new customer on the same day. Carrefour, the largest supermarket chain in Brazil, had recently hired Semco RGIS, and as luck would have it, had chosen the worst possible day to take inventory at 42 hypermarkets in more than 20 cities. They'd scheduled it for June 30, the day of the World Cup finals.

On a typical day, Semco RGIS would have a five to 10 percent absentee rate – mostly because people had difficulty reaching some of the inventory sites. Marcio knew that between 30 and 40 percent of his staff wouldn't show up for work if Brazil won the World Cup and the country took to the streets to celebrate. In most countries, it's just the team that plays in a championship. In Brazil, the entire nation takes to the field.

Of course, Brazil won and Sunday turned into an all day celebration. Sheer havoc reigned in every city. Even a 'command and execute' organization would have had a hard time convincing Brazilians to show up for work that day. We needed more than 1,000 workers at once – even Semco RGIS didn't have that many people. We'd been counting on a worker's cooperative and several independent contractors to pull off this complex logistical nightmare.

In the end, self-management won the day. People all over the country understood what this Carrefour account meant to Semco RGIS. As usual, the numbers were on the table and our plans had been openly discussed. It was no longer management's nightmare.

In a military model, Batoni would have unleashed a reign of terror to coerce workers to show up – they'd have been threatened with dishonourable discharge, court-martials, prison. Instead, our open books and policy of self-management made it clear that this was a collective effort.

Managers and employees throughout the country asked workers to give their word they'd turn up for the inventory, regardless of how the Cup turned out. That Sunday, each unit managed itself. That included deciding how to work around the Cup. Some people decided to begin their inventory early, and take a two-hour break for the game. Others jumped in their cars within 15 minutes of the game ending. In the end, we counted stock at 41 stores. We missed one franchise because the customer messed up. Our profit margin was a negligible 1.2 percent below budget, which meant that our unit leaders hadn't used bonuses or overtime as incentive to show up. Self-management prevailed at a time when a traditional carrot-and-stick approach would have surely meant poorer results. In fact, the second largest supermarket chain in Brazil asked us to step in and replace our major competitor only a week after the World Cup – because our competitor failed to put together enough people to count inventory at 60 smaller stores.

The Semco engineers who make industrial pharmaceutical mixers are also self-managers. When the order comes in, they assemble as a group to discuss the mixer they are about to build, what drugs it will be used to mix, how it will function, what the customer expects to receive. They do the same for other mixers, as well – like the bubble gum mixer built for General Foods.

Several months after the gum mixer was installed, its large stainless steel arm snapped. The General Foods engineering department concluded that we designed the arm poorly. Under normal circumstances, an investigation by a manufacturer's technical and production departments would have led to bitter denunciations, denials and finally, a $300,000 replacement arm.

Yet again, self-management changed the ending of this story. The Semco team had brainstormed the project together from the start, understood the specific uses of this particular mixer, and had gone to the General Foods site in the interior of the State of São Paulo to examine the mixer's future home. That was pretty unusual for any manufacturer, but the Semco team decided they needed to make the trip. Now we were faced with culpability for that $300,000 arm. But our team had some insight, and wanted to return to the General Foods factory. They were convinced that the mixer's dimensions were correct, and refused to believe the arm would break in normal mixing. They wanted to visit the night shift of the factory. They talked to workers on the processing line, and discovered that sugar had been sporadically added to the mixer. The system had been calibrated so that an automatic feeding machine would signal a request for sugar every 23 minutes. A worker was supposed to add the sweet stuff. But overnight supervision was scant, so the mixer operator had decided to ignore the signal so he could sleep through a few cycles. He'd made up for it by adding two to three times as much sugar to the mixer the next time he was awake. The gum base mixture was extremely dense, and ultimately broke the mixing arm.

Obviously, the mixer operator was self-managing, too – but for a very different reason than Semco's workers employed. With their initiative – from the beginning of the project through the detective work after the arm broke – they self-managed us out of a potentially huge mess. Sure, they had a stake in the outcome because they participate in profit sharing. But they also take tremendous pride in the mixers they build. Evidently, the General Foods people couldn't say the same.

We've learned that if people don't have a good idea of their role, if they don't grasp the purpose of a process, then the group will use only 70 or 80 percent of its talent and expertise. It will squander the amount that's locked up until people dip into their reservoir of talent. But they'll dip only in an environment that prompts them to.

Does that conjure up images of 'empowerment?' Certainly that word has been overused to describe self-management techniques. It's become a facile cliché, one that few companies can resist. Sure, we could find cute words and slogans to prove that 'empowerment' means bestowing power on those who've lost it – and call the method 're-powering'. Or say that it's an insult to declare that people don't have power – that they need to be freed from obstacles – and call this 'co-powering'. And so on, and so forth. Each of these could possibly spark a fast-selling business book.

All very nifty, but senseless. The true question is: Can an organization let people do what they want, when they want and how they want? Can it let them participate actively in the direction we're taking? Can it live with active dissent? Can it let them participate to the extent that they have the power to vote down company decisions?

Our first experience with self-management came in the 1980s, when we needed to move into a bigger factory. On several different days, nearly all of Semco's employees filed into buses to visit and choose among different locations. They chose the site that upper management liked least – in the eye of a union hurricane. But we stuck to our commitment to democracy and self-management, and went along with their choice.

Since then, we have had innumerable experiences like that, from small things such as employees choosing to spend year-end money on company parties, or presents for kids or even home party baskets, to middle management decisions like allocating money to refurbish the cafeteria or the chemicals laboratory, to more sweeping practices like ensuring that two employees will sit on the company board and participate from the first moment a plant closure or lay-off plan is discussed.

Very few companies desire this kind of self-management, of course. As very few Generals would want soldiers voting on tactical moves. Recently, in a difficult negotiation with a joint venture partner, the director at the other end said: 'Ricardo, make no mistake about it, this company is not pretending to be a democracy. We are not, and do not want to be.'

Many of Cushman & Wakefield Semco's customers feel the same way. As one of our newest units, it's in a unique position. Because it manages customer facilities, its people are usually working on-site and not at Semco. Also, Cushman & Wakefield Semco has added hundreds of new employees. Some of those workers went home on a Friday employed by one company and came back on Monday morning to find they were working for us.

Stela Maris Hirata is a 40-year-old architect who was a building manager at Itaú Bank when it became Cushman & Wakefield Semco's first big contract. All the employees were turned over to Semco. Stela, a small, trim Japanese-Brazilian, had worked for Itaú for seven years, and found herself suddenly facing unemployment.

'When Semco won the Itaú contract, we all felt unsafe,' she says now. 'Communications within the bank were terrible. My boss had no information about what was going on, so I went to his boss. He told me he'd heard that Semco would keep the good people.

'The day before the management change, I was told to move our department to another floor of the bank,' she says. 'When I got the blueprint, I was surprised. There were no walls. And that wasn't all. It didn't tell me who would sit where. At the bank, bosses were always entitled to the corner offices – you know, those with status. Next to them we'd put supervisors, in offices that had to be smaller than the bosses offices. And so on down the line, following a hierarchical order. The Semco blueprint not only had no private offices, but they also didn't say anything about which tables the bosses should sit at.'

On a Friday, about 20 people gathered together in Stela's department for the first meeting with Semco managers.

'The atmosphere was so tense you could have cut it with a knife,' she says. 'But then the Semco reps told us how their company worked, and I was surprised. No one spoke of themselves, only about the company.'

On Monday the bank workers returned to their new space, each with a résumé tucked under their arm. Their bank boss had told them to bring it.

'Laura Barros conducted my interview, and mainly she wanted to listen to me,' Stela says. 'Nobody asked me for my *curriculum vitae*.'

Slowly she began to notice 'the easy going-way Semco people acted with each other, the lack of autocracy and hierarchical thinking, the focus on innovation, and mostly, the way people listened to each other.' It was not Itaú Bank.

'My former boss at Itaú didn't have the Semco style, but he stayed for a while,' she says. Soon Stela was asked to manage Itaú Bank's receptionists. 'My former boss got jealous. He wasn't really organized, and when the Semco people needed information they were coming straight to me. And he noticed that. When Alignani asked what was the problem between us, my former boss said he didn't like the idea of me taking over the receptionists. Alignani answered that he'd better get used to it, because I would become his boss. He answered that he would think about it. Actually he left.'

This tremendous influx of new people, workers from different companies, and employees who spend all their time at customer facilities all challenge Semco's culture.

'Since the day we hired 100 employees, we've been discussing how hard is to spread our ideals through a fast growing company,' says the CEO, José Alignani. 'Now we have more than a thousand people working at Cushman and it is even harder. But I can't stop the company to solve this problem.

'I have to admit, we have a few autocratic managers in some positions,' he says. 'But is due to lack of option. They have technical qualities that are not easy to find. Some of them will change with time. If they are changing at a speed that we find acceptable, they shall stay.'

Some years ago I spoke to the joint chiefs of staff of Brazil and the Supreme War College. Hundreds of senior military officers – generals, admirals and brigadiers – filled the room. There were so many polished buttons, starched uniforms and rows of shiny medals that I shuddered to think how many orderlies awoke at 5a.m. that morning with flannel cloths and steaming irons in their hands.

I'd spoken against army rule at massive rallies since my university days, when Brazil was a military dictatorship. For years I'd criticized the military in Brazil's main daily newspaper. Surely everyone in my audience knew how little enamoured I was with their worldview.

After some remarks about Brazil as a whole, I dived into the issue of hierarchy and organizational rule. Some 40 minutes later, three of the officers had gotten up and left – all I saw was many stars rippling toward the auditorium doors as they made their clear dissatisfaction known. Before the question and answer session we lost another few dozen stars. And then the debate raged – the remaining officers were one in their belief that where there is no clear order, there is no progress, only confusion, and thus the road to disobedience and chaos is paved. In other words, if people are left to their own devices, they will become an amorphous group with no sense of direction. They'll turn into an undisciplined mass.

This line of thought has been driven home to me hundreds of times over the years, in talks with leaders from all walks of organizational life. Speaking to a group of executives at MIT's Sloan Fellows Program in late 2001, I encountered the same incredulity over self-management that I heard from the Brazilian military leaders. One participant, a highly placed colonel in Singapore's government, wanted to talk about breaking unions. He asked whether Margaret Thatcher's philosophy of an iron rule wasn't the best approach.

Yes, I answered, if you want to 'break' unions. Then force is a good tactic to employ. If you recognize, however, that labour unions play a role, your strategy will change.

But in most conventional organizations, management is the prerogative of the upper echelons only. Such thinking can lead to extremist views. People begin to believe that the whole is more important than the parts. Workers get the message: If you happen to be one of the parts, or you are in the bottom 10 percent of performance, you can be amputated, presto. That does little for morale and much to instil a reign of terror, however subtle, which says: 'It's a cruel world out there, buddy – the enemy is out to kill us, and in order to continue fighting, I may have to leave you here to die.'

Right.

The same tactics in business – cost-cutting, weeding out, downsizing, layoffs, re-engineering – amount to a loss of 'life' in the form of employees, jobs and livelihood. And they're a lousy way to accomplish organizational goals.

The Jack Welchian eradication of weeds (or nuking the tumour) is not only ineffective, it's harmful. No amount of chemical weapons will kill weeds without harming the grass. And weeds scorched in one place will sprout somewhere else until a method that respects nature is achieved. Not that the nuking won't work for a while. Sure it will, and Welch himself is a tremendous example of leadership and success. Except that such forms of leadership do not create sustainability – and what's better in the long run? A charismatic central figure, or a sustainable organization? Rarely do the two coincide. Only grand statesmen will take any but the easiest ways out – and they're few and far between.

Most managers rarely stop to think about the military-inspired policies or strategies that seem so straightforward. Rather than being the most direct or most efficient action, they're usually unsuitable for the workplace. But no one thinks about that. They leap to tactics that merely play to the personal insecurities of board members or shareholders, or to the mass concerns of employees. Unfortunately, those tactics are just a show of force, never a meaningful solution.

If humans are organized in a huge, complex group, they'll need complex regulations and procedures to govern them. But if their organization is simplified, the way they're managed can be simplified, too. Best of all, they can manage themselves. If you want to know what time 40,000 individual employees arrived in the morning, you will need a complex system of time clocks, cameras, penalties and rewards. But if you have groups of ten people each, those clusters can be counted on to monitor themselves.

It is a question of respecting the basic atomic structure. In my Internet ramblings I've been constantly amazed at the way atoms are organized. Putting that together with the anthropologist Margaret Mead's concept of nuclear family, it becomes clear that people do not relate to more than an atomic family. In other words, no one deals with dozens of people. The maximum anyone is able to regularly deal with is a half dozen people. So groups of between six and 10 people know all about each other, and don't need outside control. All you have to do is divide in this organic fashion – respecting nature makes for easy control systems.

At Semco, our units are no bigger than a few hundred people. The maximum is always whatever number permits people to know each other, understand the whole, and undo the need for excessive control. At any rate, they will be organized along the lines of the half dozen to ten people who directly interact.

At Semco-RGIS the groups don't exceed a hundred or so. They're responsible for a geographical area or a customer. That way they concentrate on their world, have a permanent idea of what is needed in their area of expertise, and escape the need for control by thinking small.

That human interaction functions best on that small scale anyway is evidenced by basketball teams, church groups or military units. Or in large families. The members meet at Thanksgiving or when Grandma is 80, but don't regularly deal with more than a half dozen relatives – most don't even like a lot of their own family. Which is why I always find it comical that business owners are looking for a company that is 'one big family'.

Rather than seeing 40,000 employees, look at 4,000 groups of ten people each. Those ten will always know what's going on within their group, where the problems are, whether the people they work with are doing their jobs on time and in tune.

Take the way we do budgets at Semco. Each group of six to 10 people, once every six months, puts together their numbers. If they need help, they easily get it from the financial types. They organize their work for the next semester. Whether they are biologists at ERM, engineers or plant assembly mechanics in manufacturing, or inventory counters, they know what's going to be needed in the coming months.

Adrisia Moreira, a logistics manager in the Semco RGIS inventory unit recently defined it like this: 'We encourage everyone to come and look at the numbers, and some do. Most don't however, and I think it's because they know they could if they wanted to. Numbers can be very boring, and they trust us, in any case.'

Trust or indifference aside, the fact is that the cellular principle is respected. People are free to feel secure or bored. Of course, when push comes to shove, and budgets have to come out positive, the vocal disagreements and heated arguments sometimes fill the air at budget meetings.

The same is true when you want hundreds of workers to agree on the decor of the factory – it works better to use self-management to create separate worlds. If this looks strange, or makes one think that an artistic opportunity of creating a handsome whole was lost, it's worth remembering that people who choose their immediate surroundings are more inspired than those working in a building that is artistically grand.

Sure, beautiful buildings or surroundings can cheer, encourage, even alleviate mental pressures. And there's no debating that work in a wonderful, open space with a view of green is preferable to labouring in the dank corridor of a third world government shack. But that's not the point. The issue is that self-designed workplaces are even better. The grandeur of a lobby, open spaces or striking architecture wears off. Soon the rooms and spaces feel ordinary. They can never satisfy every worker's tastes or preferences.

Allowing employees to design their workplace may be cosmetic, but it's essential. So is letting them change those same surroundings, almost at will. Sometimes this is possible only in small ways, given that office towers cannot easily be designed by three hundred pairs of hands. But the degree of customization and the amount of employee involvement in the process is largely underrated by management.

When Semco decided to set up new non-territorial offices, we did it in a long series of open meetings. We asked 15 architect and design offices for proposals. A dozen bid on the project. They visited us over two days, making half hour presentations. Everyone at Semco was invited to participate, and the decision was to be taken by a vote of those present. The project was awarded to three young women architects with a lot of enthusiasm but little experience. Nevertheless, they quickly grasped what we were after, and were sincere when they said they couldn't imagine completing the project on our budget. But they'd try. Their innocence and straightforwardness got them the job.

We told them we would be building with a unique method: Every Wednesday morning we'd call a general meeting, and those present would make the pending decisions. Their firm, however, would be responsible for final decisions. The budget was finite, but they could distribute the funds anyway they wanted, including deciding how high or low their profit would be. They would choose the materials and suppliers. They'd also earn a bonus for finishing the offices on time.

Our process followed the philosophy of what architects call 'charrettes,' or short, intensive brainstorming sessions that create multi-talent synergy. We furthered the process by distributing the weekly agenda before the Wednesday meeting, soliciting comments via e-mail, and sent out the minutes right after the meeting ended. Anyone who was interested in the process had several opportunities to comment.

Pierina Piemonte, the architect who ran the day-to-day business of the firm, is an elegant, fashionably up-to-the-minute clotheshorse who looks for balance and minimalism in everything she does. This project was a parting of the waters for her. It was written up in many papers and magazines, and was chosen from among dozens for a special piece in Steelcase's world-wide magazine.

She ran into the usual delays, obstacles and blank walls during the Semco project: heavy-handed engineers, ludicrous city building codes, greedy suppliers who saw in the rush an opportunity to overcharge. One way or the other, all these hurdles were overcome with grace.

In the end, the offices were completed one day early and $2,000 under the $300,000 budget. At first people were sceptical – as Moises Assayag said, 'This will only work if we're Danish or Japanese! We Latins talk too loud!' Some people proved to be louder than others, so everyone learned to scope out on the kiosk screen where the most voluble people were sitting – and then try to choose a spot as far away as possible. With time, of course, people learned to co-habit – and moderate decibel levels (one group even set up a training course on the use of voice in common areas).

Most everyone grew to love the non-territorial offices. It became difficult to reserve a spot there, and other parts of the building became under-utilized. Soon, four other floors were redesigned to emulate the space. When Semco people talk about the biggest changes at the company in the last couple of years, they mention the non-territorial office.

'You're forced to change your habits,' says Edi Lima, an administrative assistant at our headquarters. 'You have to adapt to a smaller space, you have to learn how to speak in a lower voice on the phone. But you're free to do whatever you want. You can work at home, or come in only after lunch to do the rest.

'And it improves relations between people because you are sitting right next to them,' she adds. 'There's an openness, you have more time to talk, more integration. You are freer, can be more creative, more innovative in what you do.'

'People are happier,' says Auro Alves, a sales manager. 'And when they're happier, they produce more.'

Certainly, non-territorial offices can cause confusion, even after people have gotten used to them. The non-territorial office can result in the non-territorial suit.

Jorge Lima's job requires him to spend time in customer offices, and some of those are more traditional than others. One bank is particularly scrupulous about employee dress – all the men wear suits and ties every day, they all wear blue or dark gray, and they don't remove their suit coats even on sweltering days. So when in Rome, Jorge does as the Romans do.

On one of the first days that he used a satellite office, Jorge also had a major meeting scheduled at the bank. As he rushed off, he snatched up his suit coat from the back of his chair. He didn't plan to put it on until the last minute – so only when he was riding in the bank's elevator did he discover that he'd grabbed another executive's coat by mistake – and that guy was 35 pounds heavier than Jorge.

Caught between the easy-going satellite office and the rigors of the bank, Jorge bent to the bank's culture – and wore the wrong coat, hoping that the sceptical bankers would buy his explanation that he'd recently been on a crash diet.

Minor mix-ups like that are bound to happen. But most of the fears over satellite and non-territorial offices have proved unfounded. I've used our outside café many times, pulling my e-mail from a modem in the terracotta floor while sipping a cappuccino. Nothing came of the dire predictions that it would be impossible to work without confidentiality. I've conducted two very difficult negotiations while sitting two feet from employees that I'd never met. I've met with bank directors at the coffee tables by the espresso machine, smack in the middle of the offices. Recently the president of one of our major customers, Unibanco, came to visit, and we never left those round coffee tables. People stopped to say hello, even interrupted for a moment. Pedro Moreira Salles, the president and owner of Unibanco, sat, bemused, as our conversation was interrupted, or as I waved to passers-by. He's a loyal customer and an enthusiast of constantly re-thinking life. Not everyone can imagine living and working like this.

That day, Paulo Camara stopped to say hello. He's a very tall, lanky fellow, a senior broker who speaks english like a native without ever having lived outside Brazil. He's also a conservative and a gentleman at heart. He worked with Cushman & Wakefield Semco from its conception, and is an icon of class in a business not known for these qualities – a gray whale among sharks. At several meetings with customers, I've heard Paulo rattle off the exact names of tenants in nearby buildings, floor by floor, condominium costs included. Hewlett Packard, Lucent and other large customers go to lengths to be served by him directly.

Paulo was dead set against the non-territorial system. Self-management, in his case, meant being close to his staff, monitoring their work, and looking for synergy. An impeccably dressed man who crosses rooms while speaking on two cell phones at the same time, Paulo needed the seclusion of separate offices and the prestige of dedicated space.

Paulo participated in some of the architect's 'charrettes,' or brainstorming sessions, and fought for private spaces. He gained some yardage this way – two individual, non-territorial offices were created in the new space. Of course Semco's methods meant plurality, so anyone who chose to could keep their private offices. At the beginning, Paulo did so.

Months later Paulo came around. He set himself up to work from several different Semco satellite offices as well as his own home. His private area is gone, and he has realized that self-management works for his people as well. He knows that someone who speaks on two phones at once shouldn't really care much where they do so.

Later, he became interested in becoming an independent consultant, to have even more flexibility. So now he works at the virtual office that is closest to his home, and has started doing completely different things for us. Paradoxically, he's running the infamous HomeWorks project, the one where some large companies share a collection of virtual offices around town. What an about-face!

But anyone at a much larger company could be forgiven for asking: How do you allow tens of thousands of people to self-organize? How do you do it at a place like Boeing, GM or a Post Office?

The same way we do it at Semco. It's not a question of size – it's a question of relinquishing control, trusting workers to pursue their own best interests, sitting back and letting nature take its course. This isn't an academic exercise for us. Self-management at Semco has been tested many times, often in tricky and unexpected ways that would be complicated no matter how big the company.

In 2001 we had a problem with theft at Semco headquarters. Someone targeted personal belongings – purses, jackets, laptops, cell phones. So many were stolen that it had to be an 'inside job'. The thought that someone inside the company was preying on everyone else was disconcerting and infuriating.

People became so upset they began clamouring for searches and then security cameras. Clovis, many directors and I resisted making any changes – I think measures designed to monitor people's activities are far more dangerous than any thief. But we knew that the workers were going to self-manage in this situation. They'd decide for themselves how they wanted to deal with it. If they choose to install cameras, that decision would come in a company-wide referendum. I was convinced that cameras wouldn't solve the problem and would raise new debates about privacy issues. But I am always willing to let the process play itself out, to see what will happen, because everyone learns best if they participate in real events.

In any case, the system at Semco does not allow for me to impose my will on the company, even if I wanted to. Sure, I'm the main shareholder, so I always have a loaded gun in a drawer and the right to fire it. Worker self-management can't stop me. Understanding the benefits of our system is my self-restraint. I know that there is only one bullet in that gun, and if I fire it off in a fit of pique, I'll only get one shot. One shot at overriding a popular decision, after which I'll be disarmed. I'll have lost everything I've worked for. People will know that democracy at Semco was fleeting, insincere, unreliable. That's too high a price to pay.

Considering that I haven't pulled out my big guns in worse economic times, I wasn't about to use them over the hidden camera issue. As it turned out, the thefts stopped without my intervention or the use of security cameras.

The most critical self-management point came in the early 1990s, when the Brazilian government enacted several emergency plans (such as one that froze people's bank accounts) that wreaked havoc on our economy. We lost contracts in droves, and couldn't meet payroll for two consecutive months. Banks failed, and times were desperate. Our workers gathered at company meetings in the cafeteria. Many took turns at a microphone for long, emotional debates over the fate of Semco – the same cafeteria where many had collectively interviewed their CEO and machine tool operators had shouted technical questions to gauge their future boss's knowledge. Now they wanted to understand the options for Semco's future.

They'd already tried everything they could think of to avert layoffs and closures – they'd left their machines to sell spare parts on the road, had severed the contracts with maintenance, cleaning and even security providers to take those jobs on themselves, they'd driven company trucks in shifts, had taken turns doing kitchen duty.

We had long been practising what we preach with open, shared information. We'd also been co-managing with the union (a system under which every cheque required a signature from management and one from the union). So Semco's numbers were well known to everyone, and workers and management trusted each other.

There was no denying economic reality in Brazil. The market was unyielding, and sales were down too far. Whatever heroic measures the workers had undertaken couldn't be sustained indefinitely. More drastic measures were necessary, and a decision had to be made. We'd have to close a factory, and let go the people who worked there. The employee commission studied our numbers carefully and concluded that there was just enough money left in the till for a generous severance package.

The workers in the cafeteria voted. They shut down the factory. Two hundred souls lost jobs. They elected to distribute the remaining cash between them.

Throughout this process, I opposed closing the plant. I didn't want to empty the till in one stroke, and I was concerned about the emotional shock of padlocking a factory we had worked long and hard to build. I spoke against it, and tried to persuade the workers to keep it open, to hang on by our teeth for a few more months. But when pressed I had to confess that our cash cushion would only continue to shrink, so the risk that the workers would get no severance at all would increase. After much debate, they chose to shutter the plant. Their pay at termination included our very generous terms (six to 14 months severance, nearly double the amount required by law.) Many of those who voted to end their own jobs wanted to take their severance pay to start small businesses of their own; many started working for us. We even leased machinery from the closed factory to some who started machine shops (and we contract some of them to this day).

I still feel pangs of sorrow when I think of those painful circumstances. But the workers were ultimately right. The Brazilian economy worsened. Had we extended our goodwill indefinitely, the workers would have been even more financially unstable in the end. They exercised their right to self-management in the most trying circumstances, when it meant eliminating their own jobs.

As sorry as I was over the end result, I had to admit that the employees were also exercising self-interest – choosing a course of action with the absolute conviction that they knew best how to manage themselves.

Self-management isn't limited to major decisions. Take a simple security guard. We could have opted to train a particularly scrupulous one who one afternoon turned away a Semco employee who came to work in shorts. The guard refused him entry, pointedly declaring that shorts were not acceptable. In fact, Semco has no such rule. But the worker returned home as instructed and changed his clothes. The story got around, and soon everyone was asking whether we had a dress code. Should we have reprimanded the guard? Should we have clarified our dress code, or stated that we don't have one at all, and sent the guard for training (in whichever policy was the true one)?

No to all of the above. The only policy we have is to take no position in any of these issues. We let the debate be the teacher.

Three guys from the ERM unit, who were adept at coming to work at odd hours, told the guards that there was no such policy, and if there was one, they'd like to see it in writing. That ended that.

Good thing, actually. Because Rafael Tinoco, the 18-year-old hacker, refuses to wear much other than shorts. According to Danilo Saicali, there are plans underway to teach him to put his underwear inside said shorts, but no one has had the guts to start this conversation with him yet. Further, Rafael has started an entirely new fad within Semco, of using tiaras on uncombed hair.

Paulo Valle, from ERM, caught on quickly. He particularly dislikes combing his hair, and has, as far as anyone can tell from afar, never yet done so in his years at Semco. The impeccably groomed guards, standing at military attention at the entrance may not be the best judges of what clothing works for other walks of life. So to each his own, and sometimes one tribe oversteps its freedom to interfere with another. At Semco that always generates a reaction. So we do what we do best: you guessed it . . . nothing.

Recently, it became clear that the Cushman & Wakefield Semco unit was spending a lot of money on supplies, ranging from photocopying to disks, stationery, and petty items such as paper clips. None of our directors approves supply purchases, but the people in the unit wanted to control these costs. We could have made a rule to limit the amount of supplies. But employees decided instead to divide into groups, and then continue using supplies as they saw fit. They'd tally the amount, and the group that spent the most on supplies would 'lose', and have to buy afternoon coffee and snacks for everyone else.

The project management group lost the first round, and during the five o'clock coffee break (which they paid for), they presented a plan to reduce office supply costs. After much debate, the other groups decided to adopt the 'losing' group's plan. The net result was a 21 percent reduction in supply costs, and the camaraderie and lightweight method served the unit well. If costs creep up again, a new humorous solution may come into play once more. It's already proved to work better than unpopular and ineffective campaigns or management chiding.

Our inventory unit frequently practices this sort of self-management. When they are sent to conduct counts at Wal-Mart stores, they know they will need, for example, an administrative staff of 15 people and a temporary staff of 20. Once the group is established, a lead person might be sent from São Paulo to the store's location. He will hire his Number Two, and together they will choose the third, fourth, fifth and so on, employees. The assembled group can then decide what sort of leader they need, and then hire that person. In practice, employee Number One usually becomes the designated leader.

If the Number One is a general manager, and his department gets another big contract, then the selection process changes somewhat. The group may now need a financial manager or a sales manager, too. That means they have to recruit. People from inside Semco can apply, and the managers will place a public ad, as well. The candidates are subject to our collective interview process through which anyone hired is chosen democratically. The leaders, however, will be subject to the twice-yearly reviews that anonymous employees fill out.

There are other forms of democracy and freedom for lower level workers. They can attend any meeting they are interested in, read all reports and memos, participate in budget forecasts and preparations, and sign up for board meetings.

No one is obligated to attend any meeting at Semco. They're all voluntary. Everyone is invited, and people can come and go as they wish – it's not improper to get up in the middle of a meeting and leave. No one will stop the meeting to ask why. If someone's self-interest is served by skipping a meeting or leaving early, then they'll do that. If it's served by staying to the end, then that's what will happen. There is a constant ebb and flow at Semco meetings – people open the door and plunk down their things, or gather papers and notebooks together, smile around the room, and make their way elsewhere.

It leaves our international partners somewhat bewildered, and sometimes offended when someone skips out of a meeting – at what seems to be a critical moment. Or when someone waltzes into a meeting one hour after it started, listens for a while, puts in a comment, goes outside to answer their cell phone, and never returns. If a Semco employee needs to spend an hour and a half talking on the phone to her teenage daughter instead of attending the pow-wow, no one has a problem with that. If she doesn't feel a sense of proportion between her personal and professional life, she's not going to do either well. While she may stay in the job because she needs the money, she will quickly become one of those disillusioned people who does only what she must to earn her paycheque. Plus she'll be the disillusioned mother of a troubled child. What's the point in that?

We know when and if people are really interested. We also know that people who pretend to be interested, or who show up out of necessity will never be the ones with the energy and drive that we need. If they're not interested in this particular project or meeting, we'd much rather they conserve their energy for something else.

If Semco forced workers to attend meetings, we'd never learn when projects or subjects are of no interest to the company's employees. If no one signs up to take part in a collective interview, then we know that Semco employees didn't think the job we were trying to fill was important or necessary. So we'd eliminate it. But if eight people were compelled by an order to show up, we might never find out that we were hiring an unwanted and unneeded new person. Until it was too late. And what if we attempt a new project, but no one wants to work on it? Then that new service or product shouldn't exist. Not until someone really wants to see it happen – then it'll take off in no time. It's that simple.

So if people aren't interested in being at a meeting, we don't want them there.

This extends to self-managing the operations. Everyone at the company is invited to participate in preparing the rolling six-month budget. Cynics say that it's impossible to put a budget together with input from dozens of people. The good news is that we don't have dozens of people in every business unit who want to play with Excel tables, HP calculators and spreadsheets galore. So it is coincidentally the financial types who always show up at budget meetings. The others are comfortable knowing they could have shown up if they'd wanted, and that they'll nevertheless see the results, understand and still be able to question them.

During these budget sessions, each unit plans how many people it will need for the upcoming six months, and they are included in the proposed payroll. There is quite a bit of open debate on these occasions, and it is not an easy time if business is down. Often we end up with employees who are not on anyone's payroll. These usually become non-traditional employees like reps, out-taskers, consultants or part-timers.

It was during one of these sessions that we examined what really defines an employee. Marcio Batoni, CEO of the inventory business, asked an unexpected question: Why should our people be formal employees at all?

Celso Violin, who has run our personnel area for 20 years answered immediately: 'We need formal employees because then workers will feel safer.'

'But why, if we can fire them at any time?' Marcio retorted, warming up to his next why.

'Because as formal employees they'll have a more stable connection to the company,' Clovis Bojikian, the current Guardian of Our Way of Doing Things broke in. That prompted someone else to speak up.

'Why should they feel more secure as an employee than as one of the independent contractors who have been receiving paycheques from us every month for ten years?'

Once more, the debate was really about conditioning. We take certain procedures for granted and cease to question them. But once we asked ourselves why, we discovered many ways to create a permanent relationship with workers without making them staff employees. We just had to give up control over them, and determine the characteristics a job must have for someone to be an employee.

After Cecília Balby suffered a miscarriage, she returned to work at ERM but made it clear her priority was having a family. She didn't plan to work full-time, but she also wanted to buy an apartment. She decided to create her own company and 'sell' her time to us as a consultant. Once she set herself up, she even got a promotion and began managing a new area for Semco.

Soon Cecília was pregnant again, and her doctors advised her to take it easy.

'I went to the office only for the monthly meetings, and the rest of my job I did at home,' Cecília says. 'People would come to my place for meetings that we held at the candy-store by the corner of my building. Our sales goal was $300,000, and I reached half a million while working from home.'

After much soul-searching we concluded that a full-time employee only had to have one prerequisite – a material connection with the very heart of the business that makes us unique. We decided that the job had to be a central part of the difference between us and our competitors; the person had to be more useful as a full-time, exclusive Semco worker, rather than as a part-timer who gains knowledge and vision by also working for other companies; and the connection between the company and the job has to be intrinsic and obvious.

This list generated much debate, and not a little screaming.

As usual, these ideas were not reached by consensus, or set out as policy, or carved in stone. When we don't have full agreement on something, we often leave the issue unsettled by accepting that some people will follow the list while others ignore it. It's arcane to believe that every issue requires a company policy. That's just someone's need for rules and regulations. We don't go in for those.

This process has set many people free, and opened entirely new horizons for others – just as surely as it cost us some first rate collaborators.

Pedro Gardesani is one we gained. After working for several years as a Semco accountant, he hit a ceiling. Pedro was a shy, thoughtful manager, but unsure of his opinions, and often unclear when expressing them. We couldn't offer him the career choices he deserved, so we set him free with a retainer and helped him open his own business.

Now Pedro is instrumental to Semco as the author of very complex cost calculation software that we needed when we created HomeWorks, a new business unit out of an idea for a virtual office.

Combining our expertise in commercial real estate and human resources practices, we can offer companies the opportunity to share VIP-type lounges throughout the city. The plan requires 15 to 30 such offices, where employees of member companies can drop in, swipe a magnetic card, and use the space. They'd be a mix of cyber café, airport lounge, pit stop, conference centre and video-conferencing unit. We'd distribute them all over São Paulo, so traffic wouldn't be an issue and they'd be convenient to a worker's home, client locations or other needs, like training. The centres would have Intranets, daily mail service and specialized hardware and connections, so they'd be more valuable to members than an independent lounge. Yet they wouldn't compete with the service providers who set up temporary offices around the globe because there would be dozens in one city, against the one or two premium locations that the service providers offer.

Pedro Gardesani was indispensable in putting together the virtual office network. His software integrated immensely complex variables, something that off-the-shelf software couldn't do. His program took into account geographical particulars, the wishes of the member companies (which never coincided), the location of the homes of the executives who would use them, the time and traffic calculations, the amount of investment in each, and the end gain per member company. He made hundreds of business plan calculations, and came up with an ideal of 22 virtual offices. For this, he charged us on a consulting basis (and made out quite well). Over the years, he has served us in similar situations. He's become a seasoned executive who sees the world in a much broader perspective. He is just as shy as before, but now he speaks assertively, and everyone tunes in.

Fully half of all the people who wander our buildings and facilities are no longer traditional employees.

We've found that our litmus test for full-time workers – that their jobs be central to what sets us apart from our competitors – doesn't usually apply to accountants like Pedro, or marketing assistants, most human resources types, and all our support services personnel. Most manufacturing positions don't qualify either, as well as almost all repetitive functions, such as inventory counters. On the other hand, changing light bulbs in the commercial buildings we manage might be considered the heart of what we do there.

The positions that do connect to our core businesses and should therefore be held by staff employees include specialized engineering and product application tasks, strategy thinkers, geology and remediation experts, final assembly workers, or the supervisors who oversee third parties in facilities management.

That narrows down the kinds of jobs that can be filled creatively. It's not the entire company roster. But we do have directors in support areas who are no longer formal employees. They're all free to work for other companies – although many don't have the time or the desire to do so. They are also free to work for our competitors, and a few do. After all, if we cannot trust someone to be ethical and decide what information is confidential, we shouldn't be working with them in first place.

When we line up a few whys in a row, we find no pat answers – and not even lasting replies. You never know when someone will ask why we need balance sheets at all, or headquarters, or safety regulations. Come to think of it, all three of these issues have come up in earnest, and there are people searching for the answer to each of them.

Over the years, this conceptual flexibility has come to mean that Semco employees self-manage so many things that they have reached the point where they auto-regulate the way they are paid.

There are 11 compensation options: fixed salary, bonuses, profit-sharing, commission, royalties on sales, royalties on profits, commission on gross margin, stock or stock options, IPO or sale (which warrants that an executive cashes-in when a business unit goes public or is sold), self-set annual review/compensation (in which an executive is paid for meeting self-set goals), or added-value, a commission on the difference between the current and the future, three-year, value of the company.

The options can be combined in different ways. This flexible reward system mirrors our philosophy that people should be innovative in their jobs. They understand that it's in their best interest to choose compensation packages that maximize both their own pay and the company's returns.

We offer these variations so we have the flexibility to hire the people we need, even when times are hard, and we tie this to our practice of deciding at each budget-setting session how many employees will be needed in the near future, and what the options are. Since they have a large role in setting their own salaries, the self-interest of Semco people really shines through. It's self-regulating in a way that most wouldn't expect.

Anyone who requests too large a salary or too big a raise runs the risk of being rejected by their colleagues. So self-interest almost always prevents them from asking for excessive paycheques. We also encourage people to set their own salaries without creating a deficit in their departments. That's why monthly revenue reports, budget, costs, salaries (if you don't understand it you can't be part of the rules), profit sharing, and transparent numbers (publishing salaries) are so important at Semco. If workers understand the big picture, they'll know how their salaries fit.

Many people at Semco choose to invest part of their salaries in our profit-sharing plans – to believe that our profits will be enough to earn them a greater return on their money than if they simply took it home in a paycheque.

Francisco Alves Pereira, a mechanical assembly technician at Semco Processes, invested two-thirds of his last few raises in a variable mode. If his unit's earnings goals are met, Francisco can take home the equivalent of three extra paycheques. On the other hand, he may lose the entire sum of the raises, some 10 percent of his income. So Francisco takes an active role in how his unit performs. Like many employees, he knows his unit's numbers better than I do. Production costs are on the tip of his tongue. He decides which equipment the factory will assemble, rather than a more senior engineer who doesn't actually work on the shop floor.

And like others at Semco, Francisco has had tempting offers to work elsewhere. He was once offered a 20 percent raise to help run a Semco unit that was sold off – to a former boss of Francisco's. He turned it down, and didn't ask for a raise from us, either. He stays at Semco because it offers him flexibility and a chance to grow.

'I like the environment at Semco,' Francisco says, because 'I wouldn't like to risk this at a traditional company.'

Francisco could be making a mistake, if his unit doesn't come up to par. Semco could be making a mistake by letting people plunge into unknown waters. But mistakes are as inevitable in self-management as they are in 'command and execute' structures; they'd happen even if the Superior Beings who run Semco announced from on high that they'd chosen a route for everyone to follow.

The real significance of mistakes is not that they occur, but how they're handled.

Jaime Minquini Perroti was 25-years-old when he was chosen during a collective interview for a job at Semco MAQ. He'd worked at Fiat, 'where things were more bureaucratic and communication was difficult,' and was thrilled with Semco from the first moment.

'At my first interview, I looked around and was the only one wearing a suit in the whole office. I came more casually dressed to the second interview, and that helped me calm down before talking to the engineers responsible for the area where I wanted to work.'

He also loved the leeway he was automatically given to deal with customers – Semco 'gives you lots of freedom, and sometimes you feel like you can do things you actually haven't learned yet.' He'd only been on the job for a few months when he sold three $25,000 machines. Only after the deal was finalized did he realize he'd forgotten to add sales tax to the promised price. The mistake amounted to about 20 percent of the equipment's value.

Desperate, Jaime went to his boss with his error – and was calmly instructed to call the clients and explain. Fortunately, the customer was understanding, and agreed to correct the price. Jaime figures he would have found only cold shoulders at companies he had worked for in the past.

At ERM, one of our energy company's customers became upset when we missed a project deadline. We were late because one of our junior engineers sent samples for identification to a lab not certified for that kind of testing. We'd worked successfully with this lab many times in the past, but this time it mistakenly classified a residue as 'Level 1' instead of 'Level 3'.

Level 3 waste costs some $30 per ton of earth to clean up, whereas Level 1 costs over $300 per ton. The energy company had 30,000 tons to clean up. Needless to say, the customer was not amused when we discovered the mistake. Our ERM partners in the UK demanded that heads roll – they wanted to know who would be fired as an example of our contrition. Our answer wasn't the one they wanted: active omission. We told them we would immediately do . . . nothing.

It took a lot of effort to convince them that our people learn from these mistakes, and that Semco groups create a peer pressure that prevents the mistakes recurring. We wanted them to understand why we would do nothing – because the situation would remedy itself. This was particularly unnerving for them because the customer was pressurizing them by threatening to cancel business in European countries.

In the end we did nothing to the employees involved. Our managers stepped in, sought help from experts in Argentina, and fixed the problem. But when asked, our ERM CEO has a hard time explaining what controls are in place to avoid such mishaps in the future. The answer, of course, is none. We'd rather screw-up once or twice a year than curb the energy, creativity and drive that comes from freedom and lack of control. For anyone who thinks this is an absurd way to conduct business, let them consider these more conventional benefits of our system: In 250 projects a year, Semco ERM records one or two errors like the one made with the energy company. That client eventually became a repeat customer; in fact, ERM's repeat business indicator is the highest of all ERM companies world-wide (86 percent.) Nine out of every 10 customers is a return customer. Semco ERM's customer satisfaction rate is over 85 percent. And our ERM company has shown the greatest growth and increased profit since 1996 of all ERM partners worldwide (a measurement that is a more important indicator of success to others than to us).

The same is true at Cushman & Wakefield, for example, where our joint company in Brazil is the largest Cushman & Wakefield employer outside the US, and the fastest growing. But it's probably also the most laid-back Cushman & Wakefield company in the world, as is our ERM unit in comparison to ERM world-wide. Apparently, our strength lies in our weakness.

Sometimes it's not a question of avoiding mistakes, but of devolving power. Of letting people exercise their potential, at our risk.

One afternoon, Francisco Alvim burst into a meeting looking for José Alignani. Alvim is in charge of a loading dock at one of Semco's facilities. Every time it rained (as it had that morning), the receiving dock flooded. Francisco was red with outrage. It was a disgrace that a respectable company like Semco didn't have a better loading dock, he nearly shouted. Startled, Alignani heard him out and then said:

You're responsible, Francisco. You should have had that docking area set in concrete long ago. Alvim was speechless. He didn't understand how a low-level employee like himself was supposed to bid for concrete sub-contractors and approve a construction project. He walked away in a daze. Another employee from the purchasing department, who'd overheard the conversation, offered to help Alvim put the project together. Within a few days, a winning bid was chosen, the dock was cemented, and the bill sent to Alignani.

Alvim learned that when he trusted his own judgement, others would too – and that he could make decisions without paperwork, internal procedures and layers of management approvals. He learned one of our unofficial mottoes: Always beg forgiveness rather than ask permission.

At Semco, we identify with Kafka's parable about the man who approached an open door where a vigilant guard stood. He asked the guard many questions. Years passed, and when the man was old and dying, he finally asked the guard why he had never been allowed to pass. The guard responded that the door was there exclusively for the man, who could have entered any time he'd asked. Now, said the guard, the door would be permanently closed.

At Semco, this reminds us that doors are always open – it just takes the courage to walk through them.

On another occasion, Nilton Morais, a purchasing manager, and Armando Ceccone, the sales manager of our industrial machinery division, took it upon themselves to rent a helicopter for a day when the president of one of our American partners came to Brazil. He only had two days to spare, but insisted on visiting all of our sub-contractors. So without consulting anyone, Nilton and Armando decided the only way to manage the trip was to hire a helicopter. In corporations worth multiple billions, it sometimes takes a director to approve the rental of a chopper, at the tiny machinery unit of Semco a manager can make this decision on the spot, even if the thousands of dollars involved will show up on that month's profit and loss statement.

Izak Santos, an RGIS manager, is also accustomed to improvising. At one point, he was in charge of an inventory count at a pharmacy chain. One or two people can usually complete these counts in a few hours. The person responsible for doing this particular count was a 'Carioca', or someone who lives in Rio de Janeiro. Every good Carioca takes Carnival most seriously, and this Carioca was no exception. It happened that this inventory was the night before Carnival began. So just as he started the count, the lights went out in the little town. A phone call to the energy company brought the bad news of maintenance schedules.

The Carioca didn't blink an eye – he just parked his car in front of the pharmacy, started the engine and directed the headlights into the storefront, and finished the count. He got to Carnival in time. But his count was off, and the customer was less than happy. We lost their business for eight months, until finally we were hired under the condition that we don't send any Cariocas to his stores!

By definition, self-management means the freedom to do good work – or not. It's the freedom to be actively involved in shaping the company or to simply report to work every day and do an assigned job. Freedom to be a 'nine-to-fiver' is also freedom.

Remember, business culture is like a long-simmering stew. The right mix of people is essential. As is an understanding that every organization needs its share of indifferent and uninterested workers to balance its leaders, joiners and activists.

Adir Fassina is such a person. He's been with the company for 42 years. He started out as a mechanical assistant, and soon went on to selling a mixer for paint factories. When I was a summer intern at Semco – I was 16 at the time – he reminded me of how he used to come over to the house, at my mother's request, to fix my train set.

Adir has always been the methodical type. A tall, germanic looking fellow with a booming voice, Adir is well-liked – especially by his clients – for his tell-it-like-it-is attitude. Adir has a set schedule, and very little can make him swerve from it. In at eightish and out by the end of the afternoon. He has lived through Semco's momentous changes – without a hitch, or a change in schedule. He avoided promotions – I'm a simple man, he says, and I'm happy doing what I do – and sold the same product for years. For almost 30 years he sold a particular mixer, known as a Cowles, which blends paint components. This product survives on the basis of mature technology – there are not many ways to mix paint, apparently. Sure, there have been some electronic controls added for good measure, but basically the drawings he uses are firmly rooted in the 1950s.

So Adir has come in at about the same time, to sell approximately the same product, for a similar pay and commission, for decades. Fine with us, and fine with him. He officially retired many years ago, but he's still around – and it is always a pleasure to pass him in the corridors and ask about his daughters. I took them in my arms when they were babies, then heard about them through their school years, and now all of them have children themselves.

Accepting that there is no such thing as a 'special worker' perfectly suited for one company means accepting worker individuality. And once you do that, you set the stage for making the most of that individuality by encouraging workers to tap their inner reservoir and find a balance between their aspirations and the company's.

The mix of people can be an upset if a company grows too fast, or aims for skyrocketing results, or merges prematurely with another. The culture of the company will be diluted until it has no flavour of its own. We are wary of this at Semco, too. We've seen enormous growth of 30 to 40 percent annually for many, many years.

We cope with this rate of change by specializing. Adir goes on his merry way each afternoon while dot.com kids go crazy during the wee hours. Each is trusted to do their thing. And we take stock of the whole.

But joining Adirs with 'Cariocas,' Izaks with Armandos still doesn't turn enough control over their own destiny to our workers. We need more ideas for programs that will expand self-determination for employees.

A great deal of employee satisfaction comes from giving individuals some control over the logistics of their job. At Semco we set the stage for that by foregoing formal job descriptions, career plans or organizational charts. We don't dictate to people what their responsibilities are – we assume that, as adults, they can figure out for themselves what it takes to do their job, and that without guidelines to adhere to, they're more likely to test the boundaries of what they do. That testing often leads to new business practices or new ventures for the company, and new challenges for employees.

Without a formal job description, people can wander into neighbouring work activities without hitting a wall. Semco has a slew of assistants and junior personnel who regularly meander among tasks and projects. In 1999, when we founded our dot.com venture unit, SemcoNet, we hired Lucia Kobayashi, the woman with the blue hair. When the *Kursk* project drowned her she started working for different units, and it soon became unclear where she officially belonged. The answer, of course, was nowhere specific. But because people like Lucia work without a checklist of tasks or responsibilities, they have the freedom to decide for themselves what their job entails. They self-manage. They also control where they work, when they work and how much they are paid for their work. Finally, several of the managers Lucia worked for got together and . . . split up the cost of her job. The solution suited both Lucia and the managers perfectly, and lasted for more than a year. We've concocted solutions to the limitations of worklife. Semco is experimenting with various ideas, but they're still just blueprints for returning control over their destinies to our people.

One is for a plan called *Up'n Down Pay*. It's a program where employees flexibly manage their pay. The idea is that moments in people's lives are very different, one from the other – and that making it possible for them to adapt their pay and work hours accordingly will be a plus. Employees would look to balance the company's present needs with their own, and adjust the pay package accordingly.

If someone is going through a phase in which they would rather work less – and lower their pay accordingly – the company would do its best to adapt. A mother who wants more time for her children would turn to a committee for help in locating another person who would gladly take over 30 percent of her job responsibilities (assuming that the person's business unit cannot do without 100 percent of their time). Both men and women could reduce their work hours and pay to address childcare or parenting needs, for study or simply for a need to step away for a period of time.

Sabbaticals would fall under this program, but would be only one of the variations on the theme. The committee would have a database of candidates to fill our constant demand for part-time work. Or it could turn to the full 3,000 employees and appeal to anyone interested in switching jobs or sharing tasks. This flexibility would make it possible for people with temporary interests – or problems, or sicknesses, or with family issues – to scale back or freshen their minds, knowing that they are not in danger of derailing their career.

We don't come up with these ideas in a vacuum – they're prompted by the seven-day weekend, and by the fact that like it or not, we're facing a new world of 'multiple careers' for most professionals. And they dovetail nicely with our *Retire-A-Little* concept.

Another plan, called *Work'n Stop Plan*, would complement the first two. Under it, employees could take off longer periods (up to three years) for similar reasons (to realize a dream, study, travel or re-evaluate life). The committee would act almost like an internal head-hunter. If someone within Semco could be found to take a job for six months or a year, the employee who wants a break would be fairly certain he could return. Along with our 11 ways to remunerate people, these programs make it easy to stay at Semco for decades, without forcing difficult choices on people when they yearn to take a break, go back to school, or have a family.

Up'n Down Pay and *Work'n Stop* encompass sabbaticals in a much broader sense, and they're open to everyone. But let's take it a step further – a program providing minimal pay for these phases could be set up in advance. Anyone who is interested could set aside a monthly sum for these situations. The company would keep the money, but release it whenever the employee asks. The company might even keep 30 percent until the person returns to work. For the employee, it'd be a golden opportunity to self-manage, and to balance work and personal lives. For the company, it'd be an incentive to break with routine. The amount put aside by the company (which could have a minimum and a maximum) would be a worthwhile investment in employees. They'd come back refreshed and invigorated by the outside world. It would pay for itself in productivity and longevity. Not to mention the decrease in turnover – after all, it costs companies between $22,000 and $45,000 (according to a study from the University of Pennsylvania) to fully train an average new employee! The money set aside for this program would be much less, would pay people a 'survival' income while they pursue their dreams, and would certainly keep turnover down.

These ideas could be expanded to training, too. A company would set aside a sum, per year, for every employee's training. Companies already allocate 1-3 percent of their revenue for this, but leave it up to HR to distribute these monies.

But don't forget – we're talking about self-directed careers here.

People would take their allocation – which would be different per person according to the job held – and 'buy' training from the company menu. In this manner, the company would extract itself from the paternalistic position of planning people's careers for them.

If someone is a check-in agent at an airport, for example, and the company feels that 50 hours of classroom explanation are necessary for that job, they'll indicate this. But it will be up to that agent to take those classes or not. If that agent applies the allocation towards management training, or foreign language classes, that would be neutral – as far as the company was concerned.

In our system, where people only survive by performing, that employee would be responsible for making things happen at the check-in counter, for example. If he or she learns quickly on the job, for example, those 50 hours would have been a waste. Time spent learning a language, computer skills or baggage handling may be much more valuable to the company.

Again, all it takes is confidence that employees are responsible adults, and not ignorant newcomers who know next to nothing about what their jobs require. This system would also reveal an employee's real interests – and any changes in those. Which in turn makes alterations in the employee's and company's courses, in relation to each other, much more effective.

These concepts should also apply to benefits. Flexible benefits are just becoming an option for some workers. More creativity is needed to take benefits to their natural end in organizations looking for self-determination and self-management.

Employees should be able to customize their health plans, pension fund contributions, insurance, meal tickets and even health club or collective purchasing programs. For example: A healthy 40-year-old's basic health insurance risk is death by car accident. The other risks are negligible, but the averages are computed, and they take cancer, heart attacks and a good dose of Parkinson's and Alzheimer's comes into consideration. Health plans are not effectively customized to every company's real situation and profile, meaning that the provider must use averages, and these must be above the real risk.

Similar things happen with life insurance and pension funds.

In any case, companies can band together to exploit tax and economy of scale advantages. A few large companies negotiating medical coverage for 50,000 lives (Semco alone has 11,000 lives insured), can easily maximize volume discounting.

By letting the employees make their own calculations, and freely choose their own health benefits, we transfer responsibility to our people. We hand them their freedom.

These are examples from our Why sessions. We only want to make self-management the norm at Semco. But that doesn't mean we disdain leaders. We don't pretend that organizations, cooperatives or even communes can be run without leaders. Human anthropological history proves otherwise. We want people to self-manage as intensely as possible, leaving leadership to those whose talent resides in helping others get where they want to go.

Self-management may require courage from those practicing it, as well as those who bite their lips while waiting to see how it will all turn out. In almost all cases, though, it beats the military legacy hands down.

CHAPTER 2

Seducing Row Boats Onto The High Seas

I WAS AT A LOSS. I reminded myself that CEOs, generals and maestros all complain of the same thing: It's lonely at the top. Oh, you poor souls, the people at the base will say, with an appropriate degree of sarcasm in their voice. How we'd love the loneliness of the top honcho, The One, El Comandante.

None of us pity millionaires – even when they're kidnapped, discover cancer in the family, or turn out to be totally dysfunctional. So it is difficult to write a manifesto about life being very confusing, unhappy, or lonely on the tip of the triangle. But, believe me, it is.

My drive to Semco takes me past a cemetery – it's our next door neighbour, and my parents are buried there. The sight often gets me thinking. When I enter the lobby of our building, I pass a small bronze bust of my father, and I invariably greet him with a nod. As I climb the stairs, I try to measure how happy he'd be with Semco today. Sometimes I know he would be very satisfied, other times I'm not so sure. My therapist of course explains to me about always having to feel that I've lived up to his expectations.

My mother had a Freudian streak. More than one, actually. She fit Freud's description of the mother who teaches her son he can be anything in the world that he wants. Sigmund said his mother gave him that kind of self-confidence, and I clearly see that my mother had that gift. Both my parents talked constantly about how I was going to achieve great things. I remember my father waiting for me in our living room at 2a.m., patiently anticipating my return from a late night at a disco. I was 16 at the time. He waited for me so we could talk about his business problems. I also remember my mother discussing my sister's problems with me when I was still in my teens myself. I always felt that my parents expected me to be more mature than I was. They imagined I was much more prescient than a teenager could be.

It's a challenge to live up to such high expectations. Especially those of a father who was a beacon of self-discipline. Antonio Curt Semler always stood ramrod straight, was always on time, always carried out his week in precisely the same way. Without fail, he arrived at the downtown office at 8:15a.m., he returned home for dinner at 7:45p.m., he appeared at the golf club to tee off on Wednesdays at 6:50p.m., and he could be expected at the front steps of the Suvretta Hotel in Switzerland every December 27th.

This routine gave him a sense of security and solidity. Which explained his bouncy step, and his can-do attitude. Nowadays his rigid schedule would get him kidnapped in São Paulo – which had 1400 such incidents between 2000 and 2002.

But Dr Semler, although repetitive, was not a limited person. He was an avid reader, and a stock market player of some skill. He would take up opportunities at dinner – which we always ate as a family – to turn homework into a discussion about Roman aqueducts or world wars. In the 1930s in Vienna he had seen a colleague of Dr Freud's to try the new fad of the time, psychoanalysis. He was at it again in the last years of his life – although the family found out only after he had passed away. Perhaps he'd was battling the demons of the difficult succession to me. It was, as Freud would have guessed, nothing like he imagined or dreamed.

He'd be proud today, I say to myself as I climb the office stairs. And I like to think he would make it less lonely at the top. But of course that would have been improbable – we didn't see eye to eye in terms of how a business should be run. I do, however, feel myself becoming slightly more conservative, and I am constantly surprised how alike we look when I ponder old photographs of him. We must be getting more similar with age – mine of course.

Compared to him, however, I am a frisbee in the park. I never know where I'm going to land next. I copy from him the habit of waking early, and the routines that start the day. Thereafter, no one, including myself, knows what's going to happen. Even if I have set appointments. Because I will sit down, after breakfast, to list by hand the things I must get done that day, and start crossing out what I think can wait or be cancelled, that day or that week. On the same day, I will easily demur from going to a scheduled meeting at Semco if I know that many other people will be present – and my presence now doesn't seem as vital as it did when I agreed to attend. I rarely need to cancel appointments with outside third parties because I rarely set anything up.

Having got through my e-bike by 7:00 a.m., and having made my list of what needs to be done, I now have the day to look forward to. And that's when I practice my quirky type of leadership. Firstly, I rarely do anything that someone else can do – and I do have a lot of faith in what other people can do, as the employees at Semco will attest. I'm also a bit short on explanations and instructions, so it is typical for Semco employees to receive a curt e-mail requesting that they find someone at a given company, and sell them a certain service, because it occurred to me the timing is right. Hmmm . . .

Many times I'm wrong, of course, so there's quite a bit of salt that people take with my advice and e-mails. But I'm also right more often than not. Mostly, however, I insist that we constantly re-think everything. That's what's most valuable about my contribution. As I said, I'm a catalyst. And catalysts don't have to keep exact office hours.

How many hours a day do I work? Too many. That might seem like a pat and self-serving reply, but I am wired into Semco issues for the most part of any 24-hour period. The actual amount of butt-in-the-chair is not much – maybe 4-5 hours per day.

The rest includes picking up my little one from school and taking him to the pond to feed the ducks, or going out for a long and lazy lunch. Or, once a week or so, taking a nap mid-afternoon, lying next to little Felipe, who looks just like his grandfather and me, hugging him while he's watching *Bob the Builder*.

But the mind is always working in the background, like a software program that never stops. And that can be unnerving. Suddenly I'll make a comment about Bob's earth-moving machinery to Felipe while I jot something down about a new product, something we can change, or some woolly idea that has occurred to me.

Much of leadership involves instilling ideas and processes, and carefully choosing people who will want to champion them. The ideas serve as launching pads, the processes ensure that other ideas emerge and bloom (if the timing is right). Passion, of course, is something that a leader is always desperately searching for in others.

This particular time, as I was saying, I was at a loss. We had spent six years trying to take Semco Johnson Controls to its full potential. And we'd failed. Our US partner was a powerhouse, a $16 billion company with 170,000 employees. We thought we were pretty good at taking companies from nothing to fair size. We had good customers and good people. But the revenues were slim.

We had managed to keep our noses above water, so that the business still had cash in the till. It hovered around break even. But that had been true for years. On many occasions the board had made it clear that there was really no future in Semco Johnson Controls. Firstly, because the Americans were much too busy with their own explosive growth. And secondly, because the parent company's CEO in charge of South America kept changing. We'd run through seven different liaison persons in seven years, and were starting to look as if we would challenge the Italian government for revolving door leadership.

Every new CEO that arrived on the scene would begin by explaining why the former had left – and why his theories and directives had been wrong. So we moved in and out of car manu-facturing ('good business, we're heavily in it' to 'we're moving out of the auto business, they squeeze the providers too hard') and retail ('that's a penny pincher business, we don't want to be in it' to 'we just sold JC Penney an integrated service for 4,100 stores') and were thus at a perennial loss as to what customers and industries to pursue.

We had plenty of our own faults, as well. We'd backed a project for a third-party administrator which wouldn't actually provide any maintenance, cleaning or security – just the intelligence behind them and the supervision of the service vendor. Nobody was interested. We'd packaged the deal so we'd be paid a success fee, instead of fixed income – in other words, we wouldn't make any money unless we provided verifiable savings for the customer. But the market didn't seem ready for that either.

Marcio Batoni had already tried to run this business for us – he was our first CEO there – but he had given up. He was unsure of the exact product, as were we. We had run through another two CEOs, and were beginning to emulate the Johnson Control's italianate style of constant new leadership for an old problem.

So the top of that particular pyramid was lonely indeed.

And now I was at a loss – because it was 2002, and six years had gone by, and this business still, uh, er . . . how should I say . . . sucked. After several long sessions, most of the directors felt we should give up. The business was beginning to lose money and Johnson Controls in Milwaukee still wasn't enthused about South America. As a final word, everyone agreed we'd done everything we knew how to do.

And so I was between a rock and a hard place. On the one side, I should heed the directors who had a balanced sense of reality. Stop the losses now, re-focus management energy somewhere else, and let go. My therapist would have backed this theory – he thinks I don't know how to let go, that I only accumulate. (And knowing how to let go is a wise thing indeed. To be fair to myself – someone has to – I did sell the Hobart dishwashing business and chunks of stock in Cushman & Wakefield Semco and ERM. Congratulations, Dickie.)

On the other hand, persistence is a singular quality of entrepreneurs. One cannot expect executives to have the broad sense of balance that they need, and still be obsessive. A certain compulsion is necessary for the entrepreneurial spirit, and one could argue that this is the ingrained characteristic that makes for bang or bust. It's the psychological pattern (almost certainly a deviant one) of those who want to see something magnificent where there was once nothing.

But executives need to be sanguine as well. They need to know how to let go, to plough limited resources and energy into sure results. Executives may steer big ships in and out of dangerous harbours, and away from shoals, but only real entrepreneurs listen to their belly and head for the open sea. And a balance between these types of leadership is essential.

So I convinced one and all to head for the open sea. In a rowboat. But I knew I had to find a motor somewhere. And that motor was Notker Raschle. It took months to woo Notker from ABB, but he adapted to Semco like Lake Geneva fish to Evian water. After a few days he felt at ease in the non-territorial areas. We gave Notker 10 percent of Semco Johnson Controls, so now he thinks like an entrepreneur. And the naysayers who warned that his 25 years at a huge company made him impermeable to the workings of a business owner's mind are probably in for a surprise. At least I'm betting on this. Notker will come away with a small personal fortune if things go well. And I think they will.

Semco Johnson Controls is starting to take off now. And Notker has a firm grip on where the company is going. With this, I no longer feel lost. That doesn't guarantee that the company is headed in the right direction, or that I'll be vindicated in the end. But my record as an entrepreneur comes from having lived as one and taking all the chances I can – and arriving safely at port more times than I get lost at sea. Making sure that I never sink comes from my father's post-war conservatism – which I think is slowly growing on me. In my youth I would simply have turned the boat to the high seas, with no regard for the waves. That was my attitude in my first days at Semco, when I fired almost the entire management team, thinking they would sabotage all my turnaround efforts.

But can leadership be structured in such a chaotic mix of self-management and isolated talents? Can Semco serve as inspiration for other companies if it believes that an organization's greatest enemy is traditional leadership? If it directly contradicts the prevailing leadership model – the military?

Traditional companies and organizations have been well served by a military structure. It consolidates power in a few hands, creates a chain of command that eliminates uncertainty, and makes the rules of behaviour and engagement clear to all.

Not surprisingly, it also stifles free thought and free speech, two pillars of creativity that we have come to count on at Semco. Cowering before a chain of command where the plea, 'Permission to speak freely, sir!' is fraught with risk isn't exactly the best way to inspire openness, confidence and potential in employees.

A company like Semco cannot survive if it relies on single leaders, even with Notkers aboard. Successful business owners and leaders often fall prey to their own egos – if their company is successful because of what they've done, then they must know best. Giving up control will mean turning it over to someone who necessarily knows less.

Even though I have a sizeable ego myself, I'm not convinced that I always know best, so I don't subject my organization to the belief that I'm the most knowledgeable person in the place. But the people around me should be, especially if we have the benefit of their collective wisdom. Once I accept their expertise as valuable, I definitely want some form of democracy. I want to be disagreed with, criticized, voted down.

At Semco we don't just voice opinions about leaders at meetings – we also evaluate them in a process called *Seen From Below*. We use a criteria based on 36 unchanging questions. Every six months, workers fill out a questionnaire that asks things like: Does your boss treat his subordinates the same way he treats other managers?

Workers answer each one with a number from a possible 100. We don't change the template because we're interested only in relative ratings. A 70 score is good if that's the range a manager always receives. But that same 70 might be worrisome if the manager had previously always earned a 90. Everyone sees their own scores, as well as everyone else's. They can compare their results with those of others. The average score of our people has increased by two or three points every year for the last six – an indication that attention is paid to the survey.

Clovis Bojikian – who is evaluated himself – calls it a 'rich experience', even though he was apprehensive about his first review.

'We knew we needed to conduct evaluations from below just as well as from above,' he says now. 'A 360 degree assessment would have been best, but that was impossible. So we decided to concentrate on the most important, the ones coming from below.

'When we started evaluations by subordinates, the only thing I worried about was that they wouldn't evaluate me highly,' Clovis admitted after the questionnaires had been in use for a while. 'They gave me high evaluations, but also attacked my weakest point, time management.

'It's a very rich experience because it identifies points that the normal process doesn't,' he explained. 'For instance, in a regular company people treat their superiors one way, their colleagues another way, subordinates in a third way. The questionnaire has a question – how does the boss treat subordinates? If he treats others differently, that's a barrier to participating in the process.

'But some people can't imagine that they differentiate between people,' he said. 'But their subordinates see it. And so he's un-covered.'

For over two decades, Clovis has consistently received ratings of 90 or above (his average is 94). Violi always gets between 94 and 96, while Alignani and several other top executives always score in the 90s. My own scores have never been as high as theirs – I've had a maximum of 92, and an average of 87. In any case, I think these ratings are extremely and uncharacteristically high for anonymous evaluations from subordinates of company brass, honchos and suits.

Yet leaders are not obligated to act on their scores. They can do nothing – they don't even have to meet with the workers who rated them. But that assumes they can continue to do their job effectively. But if a crisis looms, we believe in letting it play out. People who care about how they are led and about the company's productivity will not quietly endure a leader they disdain. Self-interest will prevail – especially since we encourage it. Elsewhere the workers might just fill out the review forms and then wait for more senior management or the human resources department to do something.

At workshops outside Semco, participants tell me that they'd expect workers to choose leaders who are nice to them, even if those managers are ineffective. They also question whether people won't choose bosses who are politically able but technically weak. But I know that people will not follow someone they don't respect for long. Semco's history has proven that many times. Also, our employees participate in profit sharing, so they know that their livelihood depends on the company doing well. They won't support someone who is a nice but ineffective leader.

The leaders of substance who stick in our minds are larger than life. They're a hard act to follow; which begs the questions: Does good leadership necessarily have to allow for continuity, sustainability, and heritage? In other words, future? Must an especially charismatic and successful leader amortize himself (or, in business-speak, depreciate present value) to allow for systemic success?

People expect someone to embody a new revolution, and I've felt the danger in this. When Semco became well-known in Brazil, I began receiving requests to consider a political career. At about that time, I decided to speak publicly in São Paulo about business, life and politics. We rented an auditorium that held 200. It quickly sold out, so we moved to a 400-seat theatre. The same thing happened, and in the end, we moved the venue several times before settling on the largest auditorium in town (a 5,000-seat hall). On the day of my speech, it took me 40 minutes to push my way through the crowd and onto the stage. Twenty-five hundred people were unable to enter (last minute video screens had to be set up outside), and masses of people sat with their backs to the stage. Parts of the crowd grew restless and unruly; turnstiles were ripped from the ground and two large windows were smashed.

The next day a similar thing happened in Recife, 3,000 miles away in the north of Brazil, when some 1,500 people were left outside a 2,500-seat hall. A series of talks to students was also overcrowded. In one of these, at the University of St Judas in São Paulo, I was forced to stop the talk due to the chanting of the 1,200 students who didn't make it inside – they set up an ad-hoc committee to negotiate a second talk, immediately following the first.

I realized that people were projecting their frustrations onto me. They desperately wanted a new form of leadership, and were pinning all their hopes on novelty. Sure, what I had to say was new in many respects – but that did not mean that I had the slightest competence to run entire cities or, Lord forbid, countries. I know that Brazil's structural problems can't be solved through charismatic leadership. So those were the last talks I ever gave in public in Brazil.

I mention these events because it is always easy to project onto public, or organizational figures, the responsibility for bringing the future to roost. We do it in our companies, cities and countries. We continuously ask why. Why doesn't 'somebody' do 'something' about this, that or the other? But just thinking about the heroic character that is built into this aspiration will prove that there is no such thing.

I've ridden the media waves in the years since *Maverick!* was published. On the one hand, I want to garner attention for Semco. Executives alone cannot easily do that. On the other hand, I want to fortify Semco, and the greater my personal image, the harder that is to do. I also ask myself why Semco needs the attention. The obvious first responses – client awareness and greater ability to attract people – don't always add up when I ask additional whys.

I was 21 when I effectively took over from my father and became CEO. Shortly after I began working, an incident occurred that left its mark. A trusted and highly valued manager was said to be having an affair with the telephone operator. The employees expected action from me. I agreed wholeheartedly, puffed up my chest, took a deep breath, and fired the telephone operator, who had been with us for many years. After all, the manager was much too valuable.

Years went by before I realized my mistake. I learned the hard way that leaders don't always know best. How arrogant of me to take a moral position, to believe that the company needed that sort of leadership.

Since then I've heard many tales of affairs, drug use and other so-called illicit behaviour inside and outside the company. I'm sure it's only a small part of what really goes on. But I have never again considered taking a position. It's abundantly clear to me that our employees are responsible adults who make their own choices about their lives. That's their business.

If drug or alcohol abuse contaminates a person's work, or disturbs the work environment of others, someone will act. It's rarely the company, however. I know of at least one instance at Semco where marijuana users routinely lit up during their lunch break, away from the plant, and then returned to work stoned. They performed their tasks well, but nevertheless were on drugs, and we fought off many requests from other employees to take disciplinary measures. Only when the drug use compromised two machine operations and put the people involved at risk of injury did the company approach the people.

But who is The Company, after all? Is it the owners only? Who sets the standards? Should there be standards at all? Should the minority of people be forced to live by the standards of the majority?

Would those who don't want to conform just leave the company, until all we have left is a like-minded and thoroughly submissive group? Next they'll be composing a simplistic credo to hang above the receptionist's desk.

At Semco we have no such standards, only our cartoon-illustrated *Survival Manual* designed to let new employees know that all we really care about is freedom seasoned with respect and trust.

That effort includes me. Oftentimes, company-wide votes result in decisions that I don't believe in – and that makes me very angry. When we had the rash of insider thefts, for example, workers overrode my wishes and debated installing mini-cameras. I also disagreed with decisions regarding parking, dress code and e-mail policies, such as rules that chats groups couldn't be accessed from company computers. But my anger is irrelevant to the process. Like everyone, I vote, and when my side wins, I smile, when it loses, I sulk.

In many corporate settings, the employees wholeheartedly agree with the direction and moral tone of top management. This could be an example of homogeneity, of wonderful cohesiveness and positive uniformity. But, of course, it's probably because people who work in such places are self-selecting – they go there because they are predisposed to share the company's beliefs. Anyone who can't tolerate the system has no option but to leave. How effectively they do their job is secondary to conformity.

It all comes back to a simple formula: Democracy requires freedom, which requires acceptance of diversity, which cannot happen without respect. And this sequence defines leadership at Semco.

*

216

I never wanted Semco to be heavily associated with me as an individual, but I knew that if we did well, outsiders as well as employees would credit me with more than my share of the success and less than my share of the blame. The charismatic leader has two options – embrace that image and live the rest of life trying to shore it up, feeding the monster and being a slave to a theatre character and a Jungian persona. Or move away from the company and leave some breathing space between that persona and you. The latter involves physically distancing yourself from day-to-day company workings and continually decreasing your influence. I choose the second option.

I stepped back from Semco because I had evidence that anything else would strangle it. In the 1980s, when Semco was growing and I was well-known, we could rarely close a deal without my presence. Everyone thought they had to talk to me. But the company suffered from these displays of ego. What if I got hit by a bus, shot in one of my quirky trips through Afghanistan, or drowned in a felucca slithering down the Nile in the Sudan? Semco had to be able to function without me. I like my trips – they're my opportunity to better understand how tribes work, to discover where people get their world view, and to gain some perspective on humanity. They also test survival skills, which are vital if you are going to live as an alert and inquisitive person.

Another way I distance myself is to frustrate customers. One experience was a watershed. A client owned a large chain of diners, and he bought his dishwashers from us at a heavy discount for quantity. He was a ferocious bargainer and known to go up the corporate ladder for even more rebates. When the unit general manager passed him onto me, I listened at length to his tale of loyalty and commitment. When he finished, I asked him what discount he had been given. When he told me, I exclaimed in shock at the size. I immediately promised to honour the discount but also have a stern talk with the manager who'd authorized it. The diner owner hung up, relieved but uncertain.

After I'd done the same to a half dozen customers, they stopped calling me.

It has been 12 years since I put my signature to anything – contracts, cheques, powers of attorney. At the same time, I've never approved any expenditure, capital project or plan. I lobby for the things I believe in or would like to see happen. I participate when I have something to add to discussions of strategy or positioning. But most importantly, I continuously try to remove obstacles and create mechanisms that will reinforce what contributes to Semco's success – lack of control, freedom, democracy. I work on the mechanisms and not on the final results.

That means I get involved in the newer businesses, and perhaps those employees get the impression that I'm important because I'm around. But the risk is bigger at first in those units, so people want to see that the major shareholder shares their burden. It's a bit like preschoolers and separation anxiety – they don't want mommy to leave them in unknown territory. As they get older they'll continue to want a leader, but they won't be so upset when he leaves. They'll come to realize that I am as fallible as they are – I'm just as much of a toddler and sometimes have to learn things the hard way, as we did during the dot.com cycle.

When Danilo joined the Internet Ventures unit, I went to a few meetings to smooth his transition period. But I stopped when I quickly realized that everyone directed their questions at me.

I let Danilo work his magic alone, and now, just 18 months later, Danilo is the acting president and CEO of the entire company.

But it's ironic that I should be credited with success or vision when in our first year and a half, all our new ventures lost money. Our people blamed the market, the economy – everything but me. Fact is, some of the things I believed in did not become businesses. I was wrong. But they will never blame me, because they need a charismatic leader. They pretend I have the golden touch, and I pretend to be Midas.

Next door to the Ventures unit, the head of Semco BAC complains that it has been ages since I've stepped into his offices. But he's run that business well for many years, and he doesn't need me. We haven't talked on the phone for over 12 months, and we send one another only a handful of e-mails a year. So for him, that bus has already hit me.

Every time I find myself obliged to do something for the company, I work very hard to get out of it. Nobody cancels meetings as much as I do, nobody avoids projects as often as I. I've been known to decide at the last minute that an important international conference call scheduled two months in advance was no longer appealing. If six people are slated to participate in a conference call, can we ensure that all six will have their hearts in it? No. That's why all of our meetings are voluntary, and anyone can leave as soon as they grow bored. Will that conference call go sour because I wasn't there? Will the deal go south because I wasn't on the line? Who knows?

It's arrogant of executives to believe that the company will do better if they are involved. Thinking you can do something better than anyone else is irresponsible. The company will be weaker if I think only I can make decisions, for example, and customers or partners believe they need me more than anyone else. Unless you have arrogance borne of 100 percent success rate you have no business making colleagues or employees do something that they don't heartily support.

Anyone can fall into the trap. Celina Antunes, our director of facility management at Cushman & Wakefield Semco, is perpetually in a good mood. She's intelligent, she's thoughtful, and she makes people feel like a best friend inside 15 minutes. Her lunch hour is spent with people every day – there aren't enough lunches in the week for all the people who want to eat with her. But her charm has created a tremendous problem, because every customer wants to know if Celina will be at the office or joining a meeting. I say, forget Celina, focus on the product, if the service and the price are right, we won't lose the customer because Celina isn't there. But some people became very worried that ultimately we'll be at a disadvantage without her presence.

Whether they realize it or not, they believe they don't need to work as hard or as creatively as long as Celina has the customer in the bag.

But what happens when Celina decides to take a year's sabbatical?

Of course that is exactly what she did. In 2001 Celina moved to Palo Alto, California to attend Stanford for a year. We missed her plenty, but corporate life went on. Not a single customer canceled because she was no longer around. A year later she returned, wiser for the year she spent away – in a larger role, as COO – basically running all the operations and marketing as well.

The same situation occurred with one of our biggest customers. Unibanco is Brazil's third largest bank, with many hundreds of branches. We'd tried for months to see the bank director about managing his real estate and other businesses. We knew the bank's contract was up for renewal, but the director put us off time and time again.

Enter Jorge Lima, then operational director and our most relentless executive. After weeks of waiting for an opportunity to meet the bank director, Jorge decided on an unorthodox approach. He monitored the man's movements, waiting for nature to call. When the bank director visited the men's room, he found himself washing up next to Jorge Lima. Jorge introduced himself, they became friendly, and Jorge won the Unibanco contract for Semco (and ultimately was named godfather of the bank director's son). Jorge increased the Unibanco contract sevenfold, making Semco the bank's largest supplier. We run all of Unibanco's non-core business, and make decisions regarding their 450 properties in Brazil. We manage their data centres, support services, transportation fleets, security, mail services, and procurement. Some 250 Semco managers work in Unibanco buildings.

But we had to create a year-and-a-half project to excise Jorge from the bank. We needed him elsewhere – to run the new mobile outsourcing unit that we'd been attempting to start for years. But we had to postpone his move. Unibanco and the director didn't want to lose him. So what did Semco provide to Unibanco? Was it Jorge, or a product they would buy no matter what? We have 16 other customers. How many of them are being ignored because Jorge is not available? We'd rather have an institutional presence – something a little less heroic than Jorge on his own. It was difficult to wean Unibanco from Jorge, but in the end, the company continued to increase its contracts with us after he moved on. Our relationship was healthy enough that post-Jorge, Semco and Unibanco became institutional partners.

We are taught to look for a saviour or a father figure in business. Our herd mentality prompts us to line up behind leaders like Lee Iaccoca, Jack Welch or Lew Gerstner.

People want one person to lead them, and to save them.

But two things happen very quickly when a leader becomes a hero. People will delegate upward when they believe the CEO is important. In turn, the CEO begins to believe his own press. He feels like Superman when he has such a large impact on the people and events around him. He begins to view the masses in the company as people who are going to execute his mission, his values. He'll leave his executive suite for a weekend at a resort, where he will put together a new business plan, come back to the office and inform everyone of what they're going to be doing. It won't matter if the workers cannot find anything in the new plan that intersects with their interests, talents or skills. They'll just do their jobs, however unenthusiastically.

Modern leaders often don't realize this is happening, or are very subtle about executing this course – they go through the motions of listening to the ranks, allowing lower echelons to meet and formulate plans, and then taking only their own advice.

How many times have I heard managers say that they are 'participatory' – that they listen to their subordinates, and only then decide?

Most experts on leadership agree that it is situational. If it becomes evident that a leader isn't performing well in a given situation, how do you move him out if he still has strong qualities? And how do you promote him downwards? How do you merge him once more into the ranks, once he's been a boss, and has tasted the good life with plush carpeting and embossed business cards? How do you reconcile a management salary package with a rank-and-file job?

If a manager is an important and central player, replacing him will rock the boat. In that case, change becomes upheaval.

Long-term leaders can also be too deeply connected to board members. Board members may have no connection to a company other than sitting on its board. What they know they learn through senior management; the information is filtered through a few people. They direct the board from a personal point of view, with the help of a few people they know and trust. Since their time is limited, they rely disproportionately on one or two people at the company. That may be the most comfortable way to deal with a situation where you don't know what you're talking about. The point man has already filtered the information and ideas. That makes the CEO a hero.

I've found that the time spent on any given item on a board's agenda is inversely proportional to its importance. People can only competently debate issues they understand intimately.

For example, a capital allocation of $150 million is usually a one-hour item at a board meeting. Management doesn't want too many probing questions, and board members are loath to question such a large project. After all, thousands of man-hours have gone into preparing it, including much soul-searching, careful planning and expensive consulting. The project wouldn't come before the board if it wasn't important and worthwhile, right?

So deciding whether to invest $150 million is a 60-minute item. Want to see a three hour discussion? Try parking! That is something every board member understands intimately, cares about profoundly, and is willing to fight for. A debate about first-come, first-served parking, for example, will guarantee many hours of animated hollering. Once people see themselves walking in the rain to the building when a trainee has parked by the door, you have a hot board item. The members can understand the implications – personally. And they can visualize them. After all, $150 million is just paper, like Monopoly money. No one has ever seen $150 million, so no one can relate to it on a human level.

But parking . . . anyone can picture that, right away.

Senseless as many board agendas are, at Semco we have created a good symbolic tool for preventing the deification of our board and our CEO. We sometimes rotate the CEO job every six months, each March and September – as we did for eight years, until 2002. Other times we try a fixed president and CEO – as we are doing now, with Danilo Saicali. Or we might try yet another undecided method – rotation isn't the only way, and fixed CEOs aren't either.

The rotation method renders the CEO a temporary figure. That way the CEO's office is not responsible for the budget or performance on a fiscal calendar. The acting CEO cannot be blamed or credited for performance. And that makes the system independent of the CEO. And it makes us like Notker's Switzerland, where many citizens have a hard time remembering their president's name. Solidity comes as a consequence of action, and not from one personality.

We have a practical method of ensuring that our board members do not become idols, either. Boards of directors have made a name for themselves as a group of overdressed, overly serious, over elderly males (mostly) who meet opposing members of identical background in overly oak-panelled meeting rooms. Why? Because someone has to be in charge, goes the line, and someone has to represent the shareholders' interest. Why only the shareholders' interest? Because the union looks after the employee, the government looks after the consumer and the other stakeholders can look out for themselves. Can you think of a more outdated way to run a company, museum or school? Have you ever heard of a board that is in touch with the reality of the organization? Or one that doesn't rely almost entirely on one person only, the CEO?

So why do they exist in this format? To assure shareholder representation, for one. And to give the company direction. And why can't the people involved in day-to-day operations participate? Because the board needs to see the forest from the trees, and in their eyes, employees are but monkeys in the branches.

Plus there is the issue of confidentiality. Why? Because certain things are said at board meetings that no one else should know. Why? Because they'll worry too much if they do, they'll overreact, or plan a counter strategy. Why? Because they are children, and for the same reason you don't explain a divorce quarrel to a seven-year-old, you don't want workers worried about a possible merger or downsizing. Ah.

At Semco we have put together a mixed board, one that we feel has the most chance of understanding the company, and helping it make choices. We want our board to make tribal decisions around a fire, not technical ones with more attention to motions and voting procedure. So we stack the deck. I hold one seat and three are permanently filled with senior executives. Two rotate among senior managers, and two are given over on a first-come, first-served basis to any worker in the company. Whoever signs up first gets to sit in on the next board meeting. Effectively it means a messenger and a secretary might leave their workplace saying, 'Sorry, I'm late for my board meeting.' We provide information about what will be discussed, so they're prepared to participate. We expect them to vote, and to cast ballots as much as possible in the name of the people they represent.

Everyone at the meeting has an equal voice. The workers are represented, and the board never gets too lofty or too far removed from reality. The workers are there to bring them back to earth and add a point of view they may be missing. Nothing is confidential. That means there's no point in denying the same information to the rest of the company. Anyone can request to see a copy of the minutes. They can't take it away with them, but they're free to examine it.

Semco's board has nine seats. For 20 years it gathered around an enormous table in a sombre, impressive boardroom with dark walnut panelling. The table was removed when I was out of town. No one asked me first, they simply decided they needed the space for a more productive purpose. I was determined to move the meeting into our company garden, to open the board gathering even further. Bringing the board into the light was more than symbolic for us.

But as I've said before, I don't always get my way.

On the first day the board was to meet in the garden, I could tell trouble was brewing as I arrived. As usual, there hadn't been a great rush to sign up. Minutes of the meeting are available to all (though they have to stop by to read them. Many people would like to get the minutes via e-mail, but there are legal issues, questions of board members' fiduciary responsibility, and some concerns about strategy sessions to iron out first).

José Violi, our CFO and acting president, and several others thought it was unrealistic to hold a board meeting in the garden.

They didn't quibble with my desire to 'undo' the boardroom mentality, or to make the meeting 'open', but they thought the garden was going too far. They felt silly. Further, they were armed with all kinds of PowerPoint presentations, which require darkness. Of course it all could have been put on paper, but that was beside the point in the face of discomfort over the garden. After a few minutes, all 16 of us adjourned to a free meeting room.

Five or six of the faces were new faces to me, so I introduced myself. I explained that everyone in the room had a vote, and that anyone new to the proceedings was welcome to interrupt at any time. Don't be shy, I said. Among the newcomers were an administrative assistant from the inventory business unit, a purchasing person from the machinery manufacturing area, a building manager from the facilities management unit and someone from corporate accounting. Violi chaired the meeting, and opened with a pretty traditional agenda – future funding for under-performing units; namely, Semco Ventures, which had invested in software and Internet businesses and had lost over a million dollars in 14 months. Several board members felt we should cut our losses. After a lot of debate, however, we voted to continue financing the unit, but also to look for outside investors to take a stake in some of the companies. We wanted Semco Ventures to increase its scope because it had already initiated a dozen strong business possibilities. The board simply didn't want to pay for it all. Representatives from the Ventures unit explained that they were actually doing well compared to the rest of the high-tech sector, but that did little to assuage misgivings.

The meeting continued with budget discussions – our rolling 6-month forecast – cash flow projections, and the state of negotiations with our British partners in one of the environmental companies. We were 50-50 partners with the British firm. They planned an IPO in London, and wanted to buy some stock from us in order to be a clear owner. We tossed all sorts of ideas around, but the best one came from the young facilities management guy. His creative solution was to tie half the buy option to a price/earnings multiplier (which was what the British wanted) and the other half to a minimum floor (which made us secure).

Some might argue that this (or any) solution could easily have come from a staid, traditional board, as well. That's surely true. The question is whether all traditional boards would guess that solutions could also, just as easily, come from the young employee attending his first board meeting. We don't advocate eliminating leadership. Leadership is important, but it's equally critical to ensure that the leaders are wanted. They have to be legitimate for the situation, but they can't become cult figures.

Marcio Batoni is a good example of that. In the 19 years that he's been with Semco, he's held many positions and made many lateral moves. He joined Semco as a production manager, quickly rose to business unit CEO, and has subsequently been CEO at many of our companies, ending up as the Inventory unit CEO.

In the early 1990s, Marcio was running our traditional manufacturing business when his subordinates began to question his leadership qualities. People found him excessively driven and pushy. His rating in the bi-annual *Seen From Below* evaluation fell consistently. Where he once won a score in the high 70s, he'd dropped to the 60s and finally to a low of 52. It was, in fact, the worst score of all our executives.

In social settings, Marcio is a humorous man, renowned for telling strings of jokes followed by his own easy, boisterous laughter. But Marcio at work is a different man. He's tense, impatient, unable to delegate, unwilling to believe anything will be done right unless he does it himself. He micro-manages, and that creates a dangerous set of alignments.

The situation quickly became untenable. Employees in the Industrial Equipment unit didn't want Marcio as their manager – and told him so. Times were difficult, Marcio was increasingly testy and demanding, and his scores continued to drop.

It was obvious that Marcio wasn't going to change overnight, even though he sincerely wanted to. He enrolled in management courses, tried to adapt a more 'Zen' approach to life, and began swimming every morning to alleviate tension. But it was all to no avail.

When his review score reached 52, everyone knew he would have to step aside. Marcio knew this too – and he resigned, confessing that he saw it as the best solution for the business. He was homeless at Semco for a while, filling odd jobs until he took over as CEO of

Semco Johnson Controls. He remained in that job for several years. But even there he was unable to make the business take-off, and our US partners began to clamour for a new CEO. In fairness to Marcio, none of his replacements were able to maximize that business's potential – I know firsthand because I was one of them.

By this time, Marcio's star was tarnished with the stain of ineffective leadership. He'd had eight different jobs with us, was successful in two or three, had started a series of companies for us, including a business importing machinery from Europe, and SemcoEnergy, where we developed and sold systems for alternative energy sources. The latter was far ahead of its time, and became feasible only eight years later.

Executives are famous for declaring the importance of mistakes. They profess generosity toward those who err in the course of taking action. But still, nearly all believe that 'one mistake is acceptable, two is just stupidity.'

At Semco we understand multiple mistakes, even when they're repetitive or come in rapid succession. We're more interested in the process. When those who work above, below and next to the person making the mistakes emerge from the rubble, they'll be wiser and more experienced. They just need the guts to wait it out.

In most companies, I imagine that Marcio would either have been left for dead after one or two trials at CEOship, or maintained his Number One job by virtue of slowly replacing people below him until the team was comfortable with his type of strong leadership.

But not at Semco. First, Marcio himself held a healthy respect for freedom, democracy and participatory management. Second, employees have the power to undermine their bosses, and in Marcio's case, they exercised it.

When executives, consultants and professors in the world at large agree that leadership is situational, mostly they are preaching something they do not practice. Those same CEOs strive to remain in their jobs for years, the consultants hold tightly to the reigns of their companies, and the professors clutch desperately at tenure.

The same is true in organizations. There are no methods for alternating power and leadership at the same speed at which the world changes.

I once conducted a series of workshops for the Australian Management Institute. My favourite exercise was to invite half-a-dozen volunteers to the stage for a leadership skit. I asked them to consider that they were the few surviving passengers in a plane that had crashed in the Himalayas. I designated one as the captain, and then asked the group to enact what they would do over the next 20 minutes. Within a few moments, a leader would emerge – and it was never the captain I'd anointed. Someone else would start dividing the people into teams of two or three. One team would be assigned to look for water, the other to fixing the radio or signaling passing ships, the third to tending to the wounded, and so on.

After a while, I would interrupt and ask them to consider another scenario. The same group would now be an environmental activist group that had heard that a large chemical plant was going to dump toxic waste into the river that afternoon. What were they going to do about it?

Almost immediately someone would take over as leader, and it was never the same person who had led the plane crash survivors. In a few minutes, the new leader would suggest that one of them contact the press, the other rally the workers, a third get in touch with management, and still another organize a protest boat. On two occasions, the person I had chosen as aeroplane captain came through as environmental leader in this second exercise.

People sometimes later asked me whether this wasn't a risky exercise. Couldn't it easily happen that the person I had appointed captain would turn out to be the natural leader, and also repeat the leadership in the second exercise? To me, there is no risk. I'm confident that leadership is, indeed, situational, and a terrific coincidence would have to occur for the same person to be the correct leader in these two different scenarios.

Sure, a pushy or very vocal person may try to lead the group in these exercises, as might the person I named as captain. But if they're not the natural leader, their dominance doesn't last for more than a few minutes.

The exercise also raises another question – why is leadership necessary at all? Can't self-management take over – doesn't it in any event? I've studied 19th century Italian anarchists, Bakunin's work (the mentor of anarchic organization at the turn of the century), and worker's cooperatives in Yugoslavia or Mondragon. In all cases, leadership could be derived from a worker's power, on a rotating basis, and with flexible governance *per se*.

In many respects, I think Semco accomplishes most of the goals of a worker's cooperative with our rotating CEOship, worker freedom and participation, lack of policies and procedures, and profit-sharing. The difference is that our goal is capitalist in mind and Socialist at heart – sustainability with gratification.

Once, as often happens, I was late – this time for a flight to Dublin from London. When I arrived at the check-in counter, the agent offered to call the gate and ask them to hold the plane. She urged me to run like crazy, which I did.

I must have broken the concourse speed record. Corridor after endless corridor, skipping along empty greenish tubes and hopping over the construction materials that seem to have a permanent home at that airport. When I finally ran breathlessly up to the gate, the bemused agents looked at their watches, glanced out at the plane, and again at their watches. To my huffing I added my best 'aunt died and the funeral is at six' face. The agents sighed, looked at their watches once more, and reopened the plane door.

Thanks to the check-in woman's initiative, I made the flight.

When I returned, however, even though I arrived much earlier at the counter, the agent informed me I'd overstepped the official check-in deadline by ten minutes. I argued with her; there was plenty of time to walk leisurely to the gate and board the plane. But she was unmoved. Rules were rules.

Until that moment, the airline's organizational chart was of absolutely no relevance to me. The woman at the check-in counter on my flight to Ireland had helped me, so the buck had stopped with her. But the minute the second agent refused to solve my problem, I suddenly became keenly interested in the airline's organizational chart. I wanted to know the name of the agent's supervisor, the airport manager, and everyone else up the chain of command. I demanded the airline's entire organization chart because that agent did not permit me to make my flight.

That experience taught me that the chart is only important when things go wrong. So now whenever someone asks me for ours, I say: 'Why do you want to know?'

Revering boxes on a chart is no longer any way to run a company. Situational leadership and rapid change have seen to that. Instead, leaders should listen to the wind. Self-management should play a greater role. Executives should give up their attachment to long tenures. The only advantage of entrenched leadership is the image of stability it creates for the board. But the greatest gain may be the increased chance of ramming into a brick wall that shows up out of nowhere.

Leaders at Semco respect the wishes of those who really count – our employees. Even on those days when my people kick me to the curb, I enjoy knowing Semco is propelling itself into the future.

If you asked four people in a Semco unit to sketch their group's organizational chart, you'd be likely to get four different versions. But some form of hierarchy is inevitable. Democracy, freedom, and distribution of power are not synonymous with lack of hierarchy. A company can have all of the above without engendering conflict. Hierarchies will spring up wherever there are leaders, whether or not there is formal structure or an organizational chart.

Richard Mariana is a salesman at Cushman & Wakefield who enjoys bringing colleagues along to visit prospective clients. He spends so much time with clients and at their facilities that he may be out of the Semco offices every day of the week. Since we don't care about control and reporting to a traditional workplace, his style is perfectly suited to ours.

Richard often takes facilities managers along because he believes it benefits both the worker and the client. The employee gets to see Semco's entire operation beyond the part he handles directly. And the client gets to ask the person who will actually be managing his property exactly how the service works.

On a visit to a bank called ABN Amro, Richard brought along Rogerio Mattos, who had run property management operations at Itaú Bank for seven years without hitch. When ABN Amro's maintenance director questioned him closely about electrical systems, Rogerio was ready to explain how repairs at Itaú Bank were handled within hours. His teams worked whenever necessary – even if that meant at night. They were all committed to their jobs, of course, but also understood that they could compensate for that time with flexible work schedules.

Hierarchies evolve into a problem when people draw power from their box on the organizational chart. That's why we avoid the rights and perks that usually accompany the box – the corner office, the parking space, the executive secretary. We're in favour of hierarchy and opposed to everything that comes with it.

One reason is that 30 percent of all issues in organizations are what I call 'boarding school' issues. How we dress, what time we show up, how we address superiors, how we should behave. What are our rewards and punishments. What we're supposed to do next.

And worse – like, why did he get something I didn't? Why did she get a higher grade when my test results were better? Why does the teacher like them better than us? Why do they pick on me?

One of my least favourite boarding school issues is the argument over titles and business cards. In hiring at a traditional company, that point alone can be a subject for serious negotiation. What will it say on the new person's business card?

Salary is another one. People want to compare salaries and then hear justifications for them.

If we could just get over these boarding school issues, we'd regain a hell of lot of time that is wasted on them.

At Semco, we've done away with these discussions. We tell people, write anything you want on your business card. Figure out why you need a business card in the first place, what's its purpose, and who is going to read it? Then put anything you like on it. For example, most Semco executives avoid the title 'president'. At other companies, it is traditionally reserved for someone like me (I don't use a business card, so I don't need a title. On the other hand, João Vendramim's card read, as a gentle joke: 'Royal Pharaoh in Charge of Supplies.') José Alignani had nothing written on his card beyond his name. Most people did the same. But when Ubirajara Freitas joined Semco, he decided on his own that he was a 'president'. Soon customers and suppliers were tsk-tsking over what a shame it was that José Alignani, CEO at Cushman & Wakefield Semco, had been demoted. They wondered about his new boss. It was so unfair, they decided.

This commentary reached enough of a pitch that people inside Semco began urging Alignani to put 'president' on his business card, too. But it wasn't important to him. The issue came to a head when customers began calling Bira but not Alignani because they wanted to talk to the president. Finally, I sent Alignani an e-mail suggesting that if his customers found it so important, he should print a card that says president, because the function of the card is to give the customers what they want. 'If the customers need a president,' I said, 'we'll get them a president.' But Alignani's card means nothing inside the company. And that's true for everyone's titles and cards.

At Semco you are what you do.

Leadership that is subject to anonymous evaluation depends on enchanting not only your customer, but also your employees.

Workers can throw you out, as Marcio Batoni discovered.

Not only Marcio, by the way. On at least two occasions my evaluation score showed that a different form of leadership from mine would have better served Semco. One that would stabilize instead of discombobulating (what I do best). One that would lead the company more gently, more carefully into harbour. People tire of being tossed around the high seas for too long. That is why Danilo took over as president and CEO in 2002. We don't know if he has rotated into the job or not – he was, after all, acting CEO for six months, and the 12 CEOs of the business units agreed unanimously that he should be the president for an indeterminate period. Why do we need to know if this is the right answer? If it works, it becomes more long term – if it doesn't, we don't want to lose a wonderful executive like Danilo. So we'll see. Hopefully the boat doesn't rock too much. I love to watch the view from the upper deck.

When we sent out e-mails about Danilo's ascension to CEO, an endless stream of responses complimented us on the great move. Dan Sheffield at RGIS, a model executive and an extraordinary partner, said that Violi (who now runs the holding company that owns Semco) was usually described as our most intelligent person. To which I responded, in jest, that I resented that comment profoundly. Dan told me to chill out, that the best leaders choose people better than themselves as their subordinates. So there you are.

Part Five

Rambling Into The Future

'*Alice:*   *Would you tell me, please, which way I ought to go*
                 from here?
Cheshire Cat: *That depends a good deal on where you want to go.*
Alice: *I don't much care where –*
Cheshire Cat: *Then it doesn't matter which way you go.*
Alice: *– as long as I get somewhere.*
Cheshire Cat: *Oh, you're sure to do that, if you only walk long*
                 enough.'
                 Alice in Wonderland, by Lewis Carroll

1. Why do we think that the future 'is in God's hands' and then
   pre-plan every moment of it?

2. Why do we think intuition is so valuable and unique – and find
   no place for it as an official business instrument?

3. Why do we agree that living well is living every moment,
   without reinforcing past or future – but then spend most of our
   work lives dealing with historical data and future budgets?

CHAPTER 1

Management By Debating Your Dog

WHILE WRITING PARTS of this book, I sat in the grounds of a 14th century monastery in Sicily, watching two elderly gentlemen tend the ornate and precise gardens. Silence, of course, was the order of the day. Yet in the little nearby village I was always under the impression that a rabid family feud was in progress – but it was of course nothing more than Sicilians heatedly debating the relative merits of hanging clothes from the bedroom window or from the roof.

At the monastery I would read at night – a book about the migratory navigation methods of geese, another about the patterns of brainwave flow that ensure motivation, and a third about *Paideia*, the Greek concept of a full education towards life. When I read like this, I don't necessarily finish all the books – the same way that I'll happily walk out of a movie, concert or theatre performance that doesn't grab me.

This time I was just indulging my endless curiosity, and constantly shifting my position as an onlooker in the world. It's akin to changing my seat in the auditorium of life, where the stage is in the middle of a round theatre. Sometimes I sit up front, and see all the minute details, sometimes so far up and away that the stage is but a little box and my mind wanders. And sometimes directly on the stage, wondering what I'm doing there.

At home, I navigate books and the Internet for one or two hours a day.

I like to sit with the books in the garden or by a fire, or in front of a computer, and study in a rambling fashion. Serendipity is my guide. My interests change from day-to-day. I may study the planets one afternoon, but a word I stumble across may lead me to a subject in Renaissance Italy, or molecular theories. Key words can lead me anywhere when I'm at the computer. There is no set curriculum, no controlled pattern.

Have I been thrown off my original road? Yes. But like Alice, in my life, anywhere I end up is somewhere I want to be.

For most people, this is fairytale talk. But I take it literally. Twice in my life I've gone to an airport, and only then chosen a destination. If I don't know where I'm going, any road is interesting.

After floating down the Nile from Sudan, riding a dogsled to the magnetic North Pole and retracing Marco Polo's route through Iran, Afghanistan, Kazakhstan and Mongolia, I am now preparing for my fifth trip to Africa. Having gone from Zanzibar to Uganda, Congo to Madagascar, I am now off for two weeks of gorilla-viewing in Rwanda and pigmy contact in Cameroon.

Each of these ramblings brings unexpected dividends, from throwing my watch from a camel's back 15 years ago in mid-Sahara Chad, to viewing eremitism at a French Trappist monastery in the Atlas Mountains. In Rwanda, an insight into humankind might arise from contact with the Hutus, or a simple visit to the Nyamata genocide museum in Kigali.

In an organization, the road taken can also permit ambling and rambling – and unexpected learning. It just requires losing control. As I've said, most business leaders find that difficult, if not painful. But it is also profoundly rewarding.

If I'm building an inventory-counting business and I rely only on inventory specialists to guide me, I'm not going to stumble across an idea for a web inventory clearinghouse, or for the possibility of clearing checks on that site. I'll never develop fourth generation supply chains, which Semco is doing now, or a plan to bundle re-stocking, re-ordering, inventory management and loss prevention.

We could have relied only on our partner's specialists in the inventory business. Did we want to specialize like them? Then we should follow their model. It's a fine one, at that. But if we want to split things up, explore ways to use the technology for other purposes, we have to be open to employing people who understand the Internet or supply chains. They'll create different businesses. By the second or third derivative, Semco's unit will become a company that our own partners don't recognize. Otherwise, the inventory business risks the same fate as the tram car business that once had a lock on city transportation – it becomes obsolete in the face of changing times, technology and demand. And that's scary to anyone responsible for planning.

Yet most people prefer control, rather than rambling and staring straight into the unknown.

Parents certainly take some comfort in knowing there is a curriculum governing what their children learn in school. If they were told the teacher was going to let their son or daughter ramble unsupervised through the library, they might protest. They'd object, even knowing that rambling through history or science might ignite their child's passion. Parents prefer the comfortable and the familiar, even if it means their child will learn less (and become like the rest of us, who retain only 6.8 percent of what we learned in school, according to the University of Chicago). Doubters should take the SAT, A-levels or a baccalaureate exam. I have, and my pitiful score would not have won me a place at any university.

Rogerio Ottolia, the 43-year-old electrical engineer who is CEO of Semco's machinery manufacturing business, exists in a whirlwind of activity. He reads other people's reports upside down, dictates e-mail while standing metres away from his computer, delegates everything so he'll have time to pursue new ideas. He's developed eight new products for Semco.

He chased new businesses for our industrial scales unit, refusing to give up after a potential customer decided on a competitor. He worked through a weekend to develop a scale and a software program from scratch that would satisfy a customer. His efforts led to a new unit at Semco – the Nucleus for Technological Innovation, NTI. Three engineers gave up their jobs to join in the effort to find new business ventures, and Rogerio eventually met two more working in environmental consulting. That relationship became Semco's environmental business, which in turn acquired Eugenio Singer's consulting company that later became our ERM unit.

By relinquishing control over management in the office, Rogerio freed himself to pour his abundance of energy into something that really interested him – developing new technologies. New challenges to him meant new businesses and new sources of revenue for Semco.

All this makes Laura Barros a bit dizzy. A soft-voiced but strong-willed woman who spends weekends at Zen monasteries and once took two weeks to trek the length of Spain's Santiago de Compostela passage, Laura has been with us in human resources for nearly 20 years. She left Semco for three years in the early 1990s, then came back (like so many others). Laura wanted to be a line manager, and we tried her out as head of an engineering-based operation that outsourced services at a bank.

'I believed I could do it because I had management experience,' Laura says now. 'The important point in our business is if you get the right opportunity, you can manage anything. If you have a good team, and good technical support, if you ask the right questions and are open to learning from people, you can be successful.'

She laughs at the memory of her first days.

'The first two months I couldn't sleep at night. I'm not an engineer. I thought the air conditioners could explode at any moment. Then I began to learn. Now I can talk about AC all day.' After several years at Cushman & Wakefield Semco running several such engineering operations, she rambled into helping launch a new business called SemcoHR, which outsources the intellectual part of human resources for companies.

At SemcoHR she went crazy with six-month forecasts. Not only were her business plans constantly re-written at strategy meetings, but she also found that six-month budgets gave her no feeling of security whatever. Exactly our intention. When you have a one-year plan in front of you, you can relax to a degree. After all, executives find that all good things in a budget are meant to happen in the second half of the year! Then some three months before the end of the year everyone goes crazy to meet the budget. Laura discovered that in a six-month budget, three months is halfway, and comes darn quickly. She really needed her Zen teachings, reinforced at regular retreats high up in the mountains at a Japanese monastery, to find the peace of mind to make her budget work.

To fly freely anywhere within Semco, people must navigate constantly and precisely. Much as the exact movements and rituals of a Zen existence set the mind free.

When you know you've reached altitude, your fuel tank is full, and your wing lights are working, then you can sit back, enjoy the flight, and concentrate on where you are going. Rigid mechanical checks prepare you to roam freely. Failing to address them beforehand, then trying to fix them en route, is a silly and unnerving way to spend the trip. People like Laura can take their companies anywhere they want, as long as they've arranged for fuel, checked their gauges, and tell us every so often where in the sky they are.

Yet even for us, freedom isn't easy to do.

Paulo Valle is a 29-year-old geologist at ERM. He calls himself a 'dreamer who likes to look at things from all sides, and let imagination fly.' Before coming to Semco, he freelanced for one of our competitors. Just as he was preparing to sign a contract to join their permanent staff, he broke his neck in a car accident. Paulo wore an orthopaedic brace for three months, racked up huge medical bills and grew fundamentally depressed. So naturally our competitor rescinded their job offer.

'They wouldn't hire me because they were afraid I'd have limitations as a field researcher. It broke my heart.'

But a head-hunter working for us contacted him that same week. He showed up for his Semco interview still wearing his neck brace.

'The company that knew my work wouldn't hire me, but these people at Semco who had never seen me before were betting on me,' Paulo says. 'I've been working here – on a flexible schedule that lets me balance my needs – ever since.'

From the first day, he noticed things were different at Semco. 'With the horizontal structure that we've got, it's not always clear who is responsible for what,' Paulo says. 'Once in a while something is not done during a project and we are not sure who is the one responsible.

'But on the other hand,' he says, 'I have the freedom to decide what to do by myself. I have the freedom to make mistakes here. And that means I have the freedom to do the job right, too.'

Is there any way to reduce the risk that comes with freedom? Can a computer replace gut instinct? Can numbers and financial discipline tell you where to go? Many people will tell you that if change is a constant, then strategy is the solution. This has been scientifically and laboriously tested.

In the early 1970s, a group of German professors in Munich decided to test the concept and execution of strategy. They used an early Cray supercomputer to monitor an activity that had specific strategic goals and very limited variables – football. They spent over a year inputting all of the data available on the German football championship.

They studied player height, weight, and force of kick. They input the strategy of the coaches, various athletic techniques, differences between the playing fields, the mass of fans, the effect of salaries, press coverage and even wind speed.

They used the current and former tactics of each coach, the weight of the ball, player substitution, and even meteorological conditions to determine each team's strategy and its effect on the game. They conducted countless simulations. Then they followed one full season of the German football league.

After it was over, the researchers conceded that not once were they able to predict a goal or a winning team. But in the same season, a punter at a traditional bookmaker in London had been right in 11 out of 13 matches!

A similar situation affected Gary Kasparov. Anyone who has played chess surely watched the progression of games between the champion and a computer. (I used to sneak into the Chess Club at high school, slinking along the corridor, pulling my baseball cap low over my eyes so that the girls would think I was lifting weights with the machos in the gym, instead of playing board games with four-eyed nerds named Christian and Rudolph. Even then there were small computer games that played chess.)

Some 25 years went by before a computer was able to defeat man in chess. If you stop to think about it, this has no logical explanation. A normal chess player thinks forward two or three moves in the space of one minute. The dumb computer at my high school could do that.

Ten years later, the computer was pondering 150 future moves in a minute's time. By the 1980s, it was 10,000 moves per minute! All the while, man had been represented by the world's best, Gary Kasparov. He resisted bravely. He had come to enjoy the blank look of Deep Blue from IBM, a mega-computer with every Grand Master game ever played stored in its 'brain'. By the late 1990s, Deep Blue was also able to pre-plan and consider 200 million plays before making a move. Kasparov could contemplate two in the same time. Until then, Kasparov had always beat the machine. Only when it was armed with a million moves did the machine finally beat Kasparov. (He asked for a rematch, but IBM declined, and retired Deep Blue instead.)

The extraordinary news is not that the machine could out-think man, but that man had beat this Argonaut of mechanics when it was processing several hundred thousand moves a minute and its memory contained all the strategies of the Grand Master games.

Intellect, memory, agility, strategic vision, complex mathematical capacity. None of this justifies the victory of man over the machine for 30 years. Kasparov certainly has all of these, but the machine always had more of it. So what explains Kasparov defeating the behemoth of one hundred thousand moves?

In my eyes, Kasparov had only one thing that the machine did not. It's the same advantage that the London bookmaker had over the Cray supercomputer. Intuition.

And intuition is the fuel of choice for rambling.

Sometimes, it's just plain common sense as well. But people have to know they can act on their instincts. In the summer of 2001, Semco was attacked by a computer virus. It swarmed through our entire network. No one could stop it, but several of our IT managers could see that it was going to destroy our system in more than one unit. Still, they hesitated to shut down the main server for fear of causing worse damage or being reprimanded for crippling the entire company. The only person who took the initiative was a young girl who manages ERM's network. She couldn't help thinking that the best thing to do was simply to shut down everything until someone could stop the virus. She didn't ask anyone's opinion or permission.

When the dust settled, it took two days to clean up Semco's main computers. The ERM system needed only a few hours of repairs.

Once people learn to rely on intuition – and learn that it is welcome in the workplace – they can use it to guide their ambitions, as well. Since there are no rules to using intuition, the quest can easily take a rambling form.

I once spent a few hours with the planning director of a major oil company. He explained the intricate process of collecting data that went into their analyses. With 110 people in his department, and a bank of computers to support him, he produced five- and 10-year plans, as well as 20-year outlooks.

Geopolitical criteria, geological surveys, chances of war, drilling and transportation variables were put into the system.

I asked this man what their five-year plan of five years ago had predicted as the price of a barrel of Brent crude oil for that month. He replied: $38.40. A barrel actually cost $18 at the time, less than half. Which made a slight $22 billion difference in his company's budget.

I then asked him whether intuition couldn't play a part in his calculations. Ah, but I do use mine, he said. He kept a notebook for his feelings about where the barrel price of oil will be. And what was your prediction for this month, I immediately asked. $23, was the reply.

Why couldn't he rely on the intuition bolstered by his experience in the oil industry? It was certainly superior to manipulating a mountain of data, I suggested.

He cocked his head like a mystified poodle and said, imagine me telling a board that I've been sitting by the pool, debating with my dog and concluding that oil will be $23 in five years time?

But why are you still in your job, I asked, if your official forecasts are so off the mark? Ah, said the man with silver hair and thick eyeglasses, I have the right to be wrong – but only so long as I am Precisely Wrong!

If you throw out controls and the long-range business plan and base your strategy on rambling, you've got to trust your intuition. At Semco we do. Intuition is a fundamental tenet of how we conduct business, so we not only welcome it, but we look for ways to increase the frequency of its appearance around the office.

One forum for intuition is our *Go/No Go* meeting. The purpose of the meeting is exactly what the name implies – we gather once a month to hear new ideas, and at the end of the session, everyone casts a 'go' or 'no go' vote for potential ventures.

The idea is that if employees are free to pursue any project, they must be able to propose a concept and begin the process of turning it into a business. At *Go/No Go*, anyone with control over budget, anyone who has an idea or is looking for a new project, and anyone who is just plain interested, can show up and participate. There's no studying or setting up commissions. There's a discussion, and at the end of the meeting, a vote – go, or no go. We've had evenings where people in attendance knew that if the vote went against their project, they'd be out of a job.

And when the people at Semco speak, it applies just as equally to me as the owner as it does to any other employee. I have one vote, after all.

At one point, I had what I thought was a brilliant idea: To adapt the technology used in heavy-duty, express industrial dishwashers to a home model that could wash everyday dishes in no more than 90 seconds. I called a meeting to discuss this ingenious new business plan – and no one showed up. Not a single person at Semco shared my interest or enthusiasm for this new marvel in home dishwashing. Even though I still thought it was a great idea, I had to shelve it. If I ordered people to work on the project, they'd do so only under duress, perhaps ensuring that it wouldn't succeed.

Some months later, a competitor produced a similar machine, and presented it with a blast of fanfare at a trade show. 'You see, you see!' I would think (but never saying it aloud!) as I prowled the corridors with their new brochures, on the 'coincidental' lookout for anyone who hadn't shown up at my meeting.

A year and a half later that competitor gave up on the dishwasher, and I quickly threw away the brochures. As I walked the halls of Semco again, I could see people's demeanour shouting: 'You see, you see?!'

The fact is that only the very arrogant imagine that decisions have to be made at the top, or close to Numero Uno. Numero Unos are not infallible, or even the best thinkers. And democracy, of course, entitles people to disagree. It means that the intuition of the majority overrides the power of the One. You could argue that Thomas Edison's assistants would have killed many of his inventions (and GE along with it), but we don't know how many bad ideas were indeed aborted by assistants, how much of that energy was refocused on something feasible. Or how much support was needed for his inventions to finally succeed. Take Bell Labs – no one has taken out as many patents, developed so many Edison-like inventions from scratch – and yet, a ludicrously small percentage became something useful.

So it is in business – one cannot imagine that every 'bright' idea has merit just because it came from the owner or from someone else at the top. When collective work is necessary for a product to succeed, the best approach is to lobby as ferociously as possible for an idea. If no one buys into it, to leave it on the back burner and return to it. In the end, if no one takes a passionate liking to it, it won't become anything.

I could, of course, get someone else to champion my ideas. But I like collective projects – if the other people aren't excited, the concept can probably wait.

Sometimes, when I am adamant, and think that no one is seeing the merits of the new idea due to conservatism, I go to kooks. I love kooks.

Anyone who visits my garden at home realizes this. John Brookes, one of England's leading garden experts, was so struck that he spent hours photographing it from every angle. The woman who planned and executed it, a 70-year-old architect of Russian origin, had asked for 90 days and one assistant to create it. I gladly accepted, even though I had heard that she was quirky, unstable and suffered from manic-depression. Twenty-six months and 29 workers later, the garden was ready. As a CEO, I would have been fired eight times in the two years she worked on that garden, for allowing her to miss eight clear deadlines. But it is now a model for landscapers as well as an endless source of pleasure, with its 200-million-year-old boulders, underground waterways and 300-year-old elephant paw trees.

The same is true for the intricate music listening room that I built in the back of that garden – it took a group of specialists in Oregon and a zany acoustic expert in Brazil a full 17 months to tune the room with blue and pink noise generators and create a Mecca for audiophiles.

Sometimes, to execute cutting-edge ideas, you must be open to unorthodox people (kooks). True, these are the workings of an eccentric mind. Peter Kuhlmann of RGIS remembered sitting in my sound room: 'You went to great length to explain the system as well as it's unique components. Then you had each of us sit in what you called the "sweet spot". I was thrilled when it was my turn and you were about to put on some music. I envisioned some Mozart or Liszt, maybe the Beatles, or – would I be lucky enough to hear Elvis? Nooooo! You played a friggin' garage door opening and closing. This I will never forget.'

The danger with rambling and engaging kooks to bring dreams to life is the possibility of losing contact with reality. But then, sometimes that is necessary, too. Mistaking sound effects for music – or obsessing over the logistical nightmare of moving 30 ton rocks by crane over an existing house – may overtake the ultimate pleasure of simple things. It may obscure the ultimate goal, such as a soft passage of Mozart or the discrete gurgling of a stream in the garden.

It takes a bit of both to create the extraordinary. So although I've ceased playing garage doors for people (a well-known test for audiophiles) I still look for slightly crazy people to mix with our sane ones. Then intuition comes to the fore, and supplants the safe path. Excellence depends on following intuition to strange places.

Intuition is responsible for two Semco businesses that I wouldn't have invested in, but other people felt strongly about – namely, Danilo Saicali, Eugenio Singer and Zeca.

Zeca has always believed there was a need for cell tower management, and I found it interesting. This led to Semco Site Master, a venture that manages cellular antenna sites for customers like Bell

South or Portugal Telecom. Initially, however, as we went through the business plan at a *Go/No Go* meeting, several grandiose assumptions struck me as too optimistic and I lost faith in the project. The business plan was approved without me, and the unit exists. It still hasn't proved itself, but we continue to invest. We're investing in the gut feeling, the intuition about this venture.

But then I believe in a project we call Concierge, and no one else does. In essence, I've always believed in a service that would substitute a new 'concierge' for the old 'secretary'. People would pay to use a centralized personal assistant. Since we manage buildings where thousands of people work, a concierge-type, Internet-based service seems to make sense. But it just doesn't work. Beats me . . .

No one at Semco will give me latitude to throw money at it – after I lost $200,000 in my initial attempts to create the business. The mathematics don't add up, and now I'm a laughing stock every time I lamely bring it up.

But it's sitting on the back burner. And we have some tests running. One is at the São Luiz building, the one that belongs to the Benedictine Fathers. There, the concierge is a bright girl, Patricia, who takes care of banal, and sometimes quirky, requests. Recently a director of Telefónica de España was at the building and said that he collected interesting rocks and bricks. A part of the building was under construction, so Patricia ran out to the site in skirt and heels, picking through the bricks for a typical Brazilian one. Father Roberto happened to be in the yard and couldn't contain his laughter. But that's what Concierge does; enchanting clients with customized service.

The same was to be true of the larger Concierge services business, which was to centralize all needs of the contemporary professional. Since secretaries are on the wane, and the world has become so complex, Concierge would offer services from A-Z. Buying roses, reserving tables, but also selling a second-hand car, renting a house for vacations, finding bricks(!), and even surfing the Internet for the customer, in search of medical information, insurance plans or curiosities. Wonderful, everyone says, but how do you make money? I, an orphan of the dot.com era, would love to say, 'who cares, the more it loses the better,' but that doesn't – for some odd reason – work any more. So I've shelved it, for now.

Another good example of instinct at work is Semco Econsult. Eugenio Singer, the CEO of Semco ERM, dearly wanted to buy

Econsult in 1998. Established by four environmental engineers, it specialized in air pollution and health and safety standards. But its numbers were poor – it had only 20 employees, and did no more than $300,000 of business per year. I couldn't see much merit in it. There was no material evidence that this would be a good fit. It would cost Semco $150,000 and could mean a deviation of significant management effort. In other words, we could be dedicating management horsepower to something that was never going to be very big. But Eugenio insisted. In his business plan, he declared he could turn Econsult into a $1million-a-year business in five years. We all snorted a bit, and shrugged our shoulders.

There were four partners at Econsult, and one, Marco Fabiani, was especially intuitive. He is also very funny – he and Eugenio dominate conventions with their never-ending jokes. Tears roll from people's eyes and by the end of their over-lapping stories, all our sides are aching. This easy-going attitude caught Eugenio's intuitive attention from the very start. He felt someone like Fabiani could only be very good with people. And it is on people that this business is based.

It turned out to be a good hunch. The warm, friendly and caring atmosphere at Econsult was a greenhouse for talent. Then intuitions clashed. Several Semco corporate leaders (including me) were in favour of moving the Econsult team into the main offices to optimize space and interaction, and to bring their easy-going, can-do culture to the head office. But Eugenio, Fabiani and the others resisted, afraid that their culture would end up being diluted. Whatever culture Semco had that it considered good, they said, was in any case different from theirs, and they saw no reason to comply. There was some acrimonious debate, and Semco energetically did . . . nothing.

So they're in a different building to this day. Who can say who was right? Why does it matter, even?

The essence of the answer is elsewhere. In 2001, ERM Econsult held a conference in Bahia for ERM people from all over the world. It had reached $2 million a year in sales and was the most profitable unit at Semco ERM, and one of the most profitable in the ERM Group world-wide. We can't complain. Eugenio's hunches paid off.

Unfortunately, intuition can't be bottled. So instead, numbers reign supreme, and they can be very misleading. Zeca and our other financial wizards love to use decision trees. They are fun, I concede, and I like to see the exercise. Basically, you input the variables that affect your situation and confer a weight to each. Then you factor in the mathematical probability that the event will occur. (Just like my Brazilian friend at Harvard who used charts and graphs to choose the best job offer.)

Here's the decision tree I'd draw up if I wanted to bet $1,000 on a Formula One driver who is skilled at racing on rain-slicked tracks, but has a cold that week: Chance of driver recovering = medium cycle of cold virus = 7 days. He has had a cold for three days so his chance of getting better in the next two days is 45 percent. The weather forecast says there is a 60 percent chance of rain for the day of the race. Factor in the detail that meteorological forecasts are wrong 25 percent of the time. Add the 15 percent chance of other developments interfering, such as the driver's recurring asthma. Consider the number of times the driver has won in rainy conditions (58 percent). Add the chance of mechanical failure (11 percent), and the chance of human error while changing tires during the race (24 percent).

On the other hand, what is the chance that I can afford a $1,000 loss?

And on and on. All you have to do is input the data into the decision tree and *voilà*! You will of course know as much or as little as the Munich professors did about the football championship. The tree will include all the right variables and chances, and probably provide the wrong answer.

Another way of doing it is looking at a picture of the driver in the newspaper, seeing that he's haggard, remembering that his ex-girlfriend lives near the race track, and figuring that he might get distracted by seeing her apartment building in the distance and imagining her there, with someone else.

I wouldn't bet money on that driver that week, no matter what the numbers tell me.

Companies are the same.

To the dismay of accountants and executives, I've often said that business plans and budgets are nothing more than extrapolations of wishful thinking. I often offer – only half jokingly – to spend 20 minutes putting together a five-year plan for any company. With their last two years' numbers, all I have to do is make the revenue and profit projections rise five to 10 percent per year, every year. Does this seem simplistic or silly? Just look around for a company that forecasts it will grow seven percent, then drop four percent, then merge with a competitor, then rise eight percent, and then fall another 11 percent. I've never seen a business forecast like that, even though that is how most end up. They all show their numbers getting bigger every year – rendering the exercise useless.

They're useful parameters, but that's all. Decision trees, on the other hand, can be very confusing, because, like my physics teacher taught me, you could go only halfway into a forest of decision trees. After that, you're on your way out, and will have no idea you're exiting until you've reached the other side.

Sadly, intuition isn't part of any business school curriculum. MBAs, the standard of the business world, are chosen from specific characteristics. Graduate schools rely intensively on mathematical scores, grade point averages and extra-curricular activities. There are just too many candidates to interview, so the process becomes statistic-driven. And that creates uniformity. If the students are those who did best as undergraduates, on aptitude tests, and have similar backgrounds in terms of apparent leadership interests and skills, then business schools get only the tip of the applicant iceberg. In addition, the age of most graduate school students (two or three years out of college) means they have little work history of any importance. Thus, it is grades, and the capacity to compete in the MBA game that separates one applicant from the pile of applicants. Intuition isn't part of the selection process – there's no attempt to get a feel for a particular candidate, for his persona, for his or her potential to innovate or think outside the box.

As the wise Professor Henry Mintzberg of McGill University said, MBA admission tests reveal not how good a manager a person will be, but how good that person is at getting into MBA programs. So businesses become more exacting, when they should be more flexible and open to new answers to new problems.

In fact, business administration is more of an art than a science. As an art, it requires a long series of personal characteristics, specific talents, and unlimited intuition. And intuition can be a collective feeling. And, contrary to a first glance, intuition does require background training, and information. A doctor evaluating a CAT scan will have a very different intuition than a medical resident looking at the same picture. Just as a De Kooning or Mark Rothko painting required a lot of still life exercises.

Information supports intuition, and that's why we make exact information available to everyone, from assembly-line workers to senior executives. Precise information is vital to intuition, as contra-dictory as this may first sound. Businesses usually want such information to project numbers into the future ('I have the right to be precisely wrong'). But precise facts and numbers are only helpful if they're used to enhance decision-making, not as the basis for it.

I think even less of extrapolating numbers into the future. Casting numbers forward explains business mistakes, but also why economists are so off the mark, and why serious scientists who have forecast population explosions, food shortages and environmental disasters have been wrong so often. At Semco, we use available data scrupulously to avoid gossip, rumour and guesses. But businesses tend to be very insular, and even after decades, I'm continually shocked at how little most companies know about their own industry and their competitors. They don't understand their own partners or suppliers, the size of their market, who are their competitors or what those competitors are going to do next. Wild guesses are more common than solid information. But guessing is not the same thing as using intuition. Still, guesses are often repeated until they become the gospel truth in an industry and the source of imitation among rival organizations. We strive to avoid that trap. We are free to use intuition once we've done our still life paintings, or after we've learned all there is to know about CAT scans.

The dot.com frenzy is a good example of this type of ignorance propelled into lofty concept. The business plans presented in that high-tech gold rush were appallingly primitive. They were all predicated on an 'if this, then that' formula to establish demand for a business idea. They ranged all over the map of dangerous assumptions. And assumptions are not instinct. Most were based on greed and ignorance, not informed intuition. I saw at least a hundred Internet-related business plans, and at Semco we put together about 20 of our own. None were any different, not even ours. We made the same assumptions about that Wild West industry. I told investment bankers that I believed it was all pie-in-the-sky, but it didn't seem to matter to them.

How did a system function with such plainly stupid premises? The venture capitalists couldn't have missed it any more than me. But there were enough early successes that lined the pockets of people looking for an enormous short-term upside. The money was there, it was ready to move, and all the investors needed was a few well-dressed business plans to ferry it, because the assumption was that all past knowledge was suspended. Bad way to begin using intuition.

From our painful dot.com lessons, we learned to rely only on available data. Semco employs an editor to create a daily digest of major business news into a short e-mail of issues and developments that might affect the company or one of its business units. It's easy and quick to read – a headline with a link to a more detailed story.

We track our competitors' hiring practices, scouring newspapers, trade journals and the Internet. We track a lot of their web home pages. We've learned to read between the lines on those sites. In each business unit, one or two people will collect business information on a rotating basis.

Frequently it is the obscure titbits that have a serious impact on an industry or business. The information that really affects an organization is rarely part of a cataclysmic event. Rather it is buried in small developments, like the slight change in direction by scientists whose importance is not understood in time.

But we don't summarize or reach conclusions – we just put the information out for employees to peruse. We also subscribe to investment banker's evaluations of our competitors' companies. We may supply our people with more intelligence than the average company, but it's hard to track how they use it. We're hoping it's nothing more than fodder for intuitive thinking. When we add our own first-hand observations or conversations to the picture, the information becomes three-dimensional. Our people are thus better informed, more conversant in issues important to them, more confident about their knowledge. And that allows them to follow their gut instincts.

Alas, intuition can easily lead to mistakes, although maybe less often than numbers-based decision making. We've made our share of intuitive mistakes. We all like to think that erring is human, but erring twice is not so hot. Right? That is the mantra of new-age management, mixed with old time horse sense. The Age of Aquarius, so anticipated by hippies, was supposed to allow people to follow their instincts, tolerate mistakes, and generally be accepting and kind to one another.

I remember a marine engineer who designed the pumps and motors that we sold to the shipping industry when I started at Semco. He was a wise and experienced manager named Rubin Agater. Many customers would order pumping systems for two or three identical ships at a time. And Rubin would say: 'There are no two things more different than two identical ships.'

The same is true for mistakes. There is nothing more difficult than transmitting experience from one person to another, or from one situation to another. My father was eager for me to take over Semco while he was alive so he could help me learn to run the company. His chief concern was to catch my mistakes before I made them. I made a long series of mistakes, and my father never saw them coming. They were made in different circumstances than those he knew so well.

As it happens, erring once only is itself an erroneous concept. Let's take *tarte tatin* as a business case. This French apple tart is the result of a mistake. In the French village of Lamotte-Beuvron, the Tatin sisters had a little train station bistro, and made a fair apple tart. One day they forgot to make the pastry, but because they were late, they whipped up a batch and stuck it on top of the apples, threw the lot into the oven, and 15 minutes later turned the pie upside down – *voilà! Quelle merveille!*

We know that countless inventions resulted from mistakes, or because people were looking for one thing and tripped over another. But like Isaac Newton sitting under a tree, or Archimedes sitting in the bath when Eureka arrived, an inventor or innovator must be deeply involved in that subject. Laws of gravity, penicillin and gunpowder don't occur to most of us when we sit in the bath. We're thinking instead of cheques in the mail, how far away the shampoo bottle is, and where we mislaid our eyeglasses.

In the same way, luck does not strike all of us equally. Yet it's a most necessary component of success. To 'accuse' people of being lucky is usually unfair. Luck is an add-on to effort – it crowns a compulsion to succeed. Success has a long-term measurement in the form of sustainability. Luck rarely has such longevity. It's like lightning – it may strike, but then it's fast, furious and rare. What you make of that stroke of luck is a result of the diligence you apply after it strikes.

Intuition, luck, active mistakes, serendipity – there you have four vital business concepts that should be entire disciplines in the MBA curriculum.

Of course the using my nose instead of a spreadsheet technique means that people are always asking me whether it makes me nervous to have no idea what the company will amount to in five years time. The truth is, it doesn't. Abraham Lincoln said it best when asked how he planned to guide the US after the Civil War: It's like piloting a riverboat on the Mississippi. You should sit back, relax, and plan only as far ahead as the next bend in the river. And then the one after that, and the one after that. Eventually, you'll get to your destination.

That's why I hold such great admiration for Lewis Carroll's Cheshire Cat. Sure, the cat seems 'lost'. His advice is maddening to those who want to leave a boardroom with the certainty that they know where they are going (though they rarely do). But it is sound technical strategy nevertheless. The cat wants us to accept that it's good that we're not masters of our own destiny – it hones our survival skills and makes us opportunists. His advice won't prevent us from pondering the future (or brainstorming sessions or budget meetings where calculators are endlessly juggled). His kind of rambling is not a cavalier, who-cares approach. It's a keen understanding of human nature.

Debating your dog may not be such a bad idea after all. You'll find it's just another way to ask the why questions that lead to opportunity and innovation. Your dog doesn't have to answer, as long as he's there to prompt the questions. Informed minds heed the grumbling belly, just as sophisticated plans rely on intuitive hunches. Those combinations may be the best way to amble into the right product or service, at the right time.

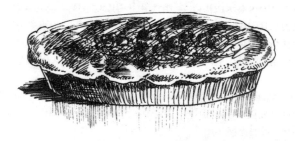

CHAPTER 2

Visiting The Future

IN THE LAST DECADE, Semco has moved smoothly and profitably from the world of bricks and mortar to the world of information and ideas, largely because we already knew how to ramble into strange new worlds.

Naturally, our seat-of-the-pants method led us straight into the dot.com revolution.

In early 1999 one of our senior executives was growing restless. Ricardo Raoul was CFO at Cushman & Wakefield Semco, our property management arm. He was young, had an MBA and a solid computer engineering background, spiced with many years in Alcoa's finance area. He'd done a four-month stint at Harvard Business School, and had returned with many tricks of the trade up his sleeve.

He was also one of the people at Semco who made a career out of 'rambling'. From his first days at the company, when he was still only in his 20s, Ricardo had worked for three business units. Sometimes he contributed to all three simultaneously. He'd worked at Semco Johnson Controls, and had helped launch ERM and Cushman & Wakefield.

But now he wanted a part of something new and different. For some time he'd been watching the gathering dot.com storm, and had become convinced there was a fortune to be made. He wanted a new challenge, something that would take him away from the computers and accounting areas he already knew so well.

Ricardo came to Violi and Clovis and me with the idea of taking Semco into the uncharted Internet waters. We'd already noticed the Internet ourselves, of course, but were somewhat bewildered by it's commercial meaning. Was something huge bypassing us?

Clovis and Violi were sceptical of the web-revolution – they thought there was too much hype and not enough solidity. But we all agreed we should at least investigate. What if our future depended on it?

So Ricardo Raoul and I decided to start a high-tech Ventures unit. There was no formal structure to the new venture. Because Semco lacks rules, established policies and internal controls, we could launch this venture any way we wanted, in any style that fit. We could act like an upstart in someone's garage, even though we are a company with several thousand employees.

Ricardo plunged into the dot.com world. New jargon filled his conversation, to the point that other Semco execs asked for glossaries at the beginnings of meetings. IPO (initial public offering) and DCF (discounted cash flow) were easy. But the other acronyms and jargon were foreign to us all. For example, players had to know that 'pre-money' was the value of the company before its IPO, and that 'concepts' could be sold for unheard of multiples of hard cash. You had to be able to explain to old-time bankers that the normal price/earnings ratio – how many years of profit a company is worth – had been replaced with price/revenue ratios. Under this bizarre convention, a company was worth many times its annual sales (numbers such as 15 and 35 were well accepted).

In the Old World, a company with sales of $10 million and a profit of one million was worth some $10 to $12 million. Under the new philosophy, revenue of $10 million was worth 25 times that, or $250 million! And the owner would be nice enough to sell 20 percent to lucky bankers for only $50 million.

Where did all this come from? That's not difficult to say. Not from the garage kids who did the programming, came up with chatrooms or ultimately geeked themselves into oblivion. The masterminds of the Internet age were smart, arrogant venture capitalists. If I pointed to the thing I encountered most during my two years delving deeply into this world, it would be arrogance. Because they convinced bankers and investors early in the game that they'd found 'gold in them thar hills', these VC players grew increasingly certain that they were going to render the Old World obsolete within five years.

Except that no one talked about precisely how this was going to happen. It was inelegant, a *faux pas* even, to speak of expenses, costs and salaries. Something greater was happening, after all.

The IPO was the ultimate game plan for everyone in this business.

Wasn't it eerie that everyone planned to make a fortune from the IPO, and then leave the company in their dust as they rushed off to do something else with their new-found riches?

No one would ever say that in so many words. But the famous exit strategy went like this: Here's the small boat that we have built so far – in order to make it capable of competing at a world-class level, we need you to give us unlimited amounts of money. We'll soothe your worries by employing an older co-skipper who can show he's bought his wisdom through experience, while the young and ebullient crew will work all night on projects for the boat that you don't really understand. We'll need you to give us your network of contacts too, so we can get more money to buy the fuel to power the boat once it's actually built. On top of your initial investment, we'll call you Angel and you'll help us find friends of yours who will give us the fuel to power the boat.

We'll all agree we're going to an uncharted island in the South Pacific, where low-hanging fruit drips honey, hula dancing rules, and the earth exudes precious metals that we can find on secret maps we've dreamt of but cannot show you now.

If, by any chance, we manage to get the public at large to buy part of this dream, you will excuse us for jumping overboard and swimming to Bora-Bora while you continue your fine journey.

In the midst of the new economy frenzy, AOL merged with Time Warner. Alarm bells rang worldwide. Shock waves reverberated throughout the business world. Time Warner! Old-line content provider meets new economy media giant. The deal seemed to put the stamp of approval on the dot.com furore. And it reminded everyone that if they didn't grab a piece of the action, they'd be left behind altogether, spitting dust. The traditionalists argued that this was craziness. But they were immediately dismissed as, well, traditionalists.

Clovis and Violi could only shake their heads. They tried not to be party poopers. I concurred that it was all crazy, but felt that we needed to be players. We didn't know what would come of it all, but change was in the air.

I do not remember a single time we made plans for a greater fortune, when anyone thought the dot.com venture would mean great profit any time soon. We had hopes, of course, but we never put together a five-year plan showing what we'd be worth if our SemcoNet strategy worked. We never seriously estimated any figures.

We maintained enough healthy scepticism about the absurdity of the entire dot.com sector that we created a cordon sanitaire around SemcoNet. We left Semco to continue business without contamination from the spirit of 'abandon thy heresy-lined ship now, partake in web salvation, for the end is near.'

Start-ups were sprouting from the ground like so many weeds on a lawn. We tried to look at all of them. We favoured those that met our prerequisites of a complex, premium product, built on a solid foundation. We heard the same assurances from every company we investigated – there was always a bank about to pour millions into the company, always an IPO shortly forthcoming, always the famous 'quiet period', when you couldn't breathe a word, even to your wife in the middle of a nightmare.

We invested in metering electricity over the Internet, in one-click utility web bill paying, a business-to-business start-up for food services equipment, and a storage-and-retrieval system whereby a customer could search two billion documents (each within a 40 second time frame at up to 120,000 separate terminals).

We negotiated a food distribution joint venture with the giant Telefónica de España, (a company with tens of billions in revenue). We dabbled in a B-2-B consortium for indirect purchasing with FleetBoston, and dallied with several Fortune 500 companies. We held advanced talks with the likes of PurchasePro, a 'market maker' in the hotel supplies industry.

We juggled myriad deals, sifting through them for our minimum common denominator. Our eyes popped at all the bright ideas.

And then there were our guys from Semco. Not to be outdone by engineers in San Francisco, we came up with our own brilliant plans. None of them have become real businesses, which suggests either that we are too far ahead of our time and will still carve our place in history alongside Ben Franklin and Madame Pasteur, or we just don't get it. Wagers, anyone?

One of the projects was IntelliAgency. This was a business intelligence play ('play' being the key word here). It was the kind of enterprise that investment bankers like Chase Capital Partners snubbed as 'transition plays' because it bridged the gap between old and new economies. They didn't want anything to do with that twilight zone. They were too busy making mega-deals with the so-called 'pure-plays', or the businesses designed for millions of people to access on the Internet.

Meanwhile, Ricardo Raoul was slowly going crazy. His workdays climbed to 12, 14, sometimes 18 hours. His weekends were spent catching up on site visits and finalizing business plans that absolutely, indisputably, had to be ready by 10a.m. on Monday.

I started surfing for real, setting aside two hours daily just for roaming around websites to understand the plays. Ricardo Raoul fed me two or three new companies to look at every day. I always had several hundred sites to visit. There was never enough time.

Every few days, I would receive an e-mail from Ricardo saying, simply: 'So?' This was the standard web fare for engineers. So what did I think, so what should we do next, so how do we jump on this bandwagon? So?

So I would reply. And sometimes I would just delete or throw away. One article that I threw away was about a San Francisco company called Bidcom.com. (Not to be confused with Bid.com, which already existed. This was Bidcom.com.)

It was one of Ricardo's first ideas, a company that created an electronic marketplace on the web for the construction industry. I didn't like the sound of it at first. But considering that I was looking into companies named Razorfish, Tangerine.com, and the infamous Kozmo.com, this bid-something wasn't all bad – at least I knew what a bid was.

The company was ranked by Fortune magazine as one of the most promising Internet ventures. Semco was already managing construction of a new BankBoston building in São Paulo. We had future project agreements with local construction companies. We thought we'd add residential construction to our commercial projects.

So I did the Ricardo-thing. I fired off an e-mail telling the founder that we wanted to talk about joining forces. The two young men who started Bidcom in San Francisco had created software based on an Oracle platform, with Sun support, that made it possible for all the parties involved in a construction project – architects, designers, contractors, building specialists and site managers – to log onto a single website. The site would contain 100 percent of the information pertaining to the project, be it drawings and plans, or schedules and minutes of meetings. One could use a Palmtop to communicate directly from the seventh floor of the site to the architect, or check legislation from up on high.

The backers were heavy hitters. GE Capital, Internet Capital

Group and the huge international developer, Hines. Bidcom was ramping up for its IPO, and the specialized magazines and analysts bet that it would be one of the biggest of 1999. Predictions began at half a billion dollars, then jumped to one billion, then quickly became two. Shortly before the listing at the SEC, magazine articles cited five and six billion dollars – for a company doing no more than $800,000 in revenue that year.

We'd been involved in the dot.com world for a couple of months, and had discovered that our new credentials, plus the right jargon – identifying us as top-secret members of the club – opened doors more quickly than we could handle. Typically, within two or three weeks we would go through a first call with the CEO, then a conference call or two between top management, followed by presentation of an NDA, a non-disclosure agreement.

Secrecy was vital, since everyone thought that they alone had come up with the ultimate game plan. In point of fact, though, there was never as much meat on the bones as one hoped. NDAs flew out of fax machines and as attachments, and people on all sides signed them without any concern for the wording. Oh, an NDA, we would mutter, as we interrupted a meeting to sign yet another one.

Next came the 'term sheet', which was really a 'letter of intent'. The 'term sheet' evolved because language was being overhauled and there was never enough time to do things right. Basically it was an *aide-mémoire*, a statement of the basic terms. Once signatures were affixed, the sides became partners forever more, brethren in religion, friends to the end of time. So personnel made their way to each other's facilities, tech-manuals exchanged hands, and top-secret proprietary software was opened for perusal.

We signed a 'term sheet' with Bidcom, and announced the venture to the press. We'd given interviews, and assigned a number of people to training and development. We had already invested a lot of time and half a million dollars into the Bidcom venture.

As the new Semco Bidcom venture was getting fully underway, we began another joint venture with a Texan company called eTradeShow. Bidcom would still live for a web eternity – a year or so. In the meantime, we were busy replicating our self-image of web success.

A company called Expocentric created eTradeShow as part of their pioneering work in the new speciality of virtual trade fairs. Their technology would bring all the elements of a trade fair to people at home or in their offices. They'd be able to attend the fair without having to get on a plane or train, without having to travel at all.

Conventions and trade fairs being the song, dance and affair-laden events that they are, it was not surprising that all the people that we talked to pooh-poohed our concept. Virtual? Are you nuts, the experts said. That will never take-off. I've been in this business for decades, they said, and I know that people come to trade fairs to see novelty, to press the flesh, to be entertained, to take a break. They'll never exchange that for a cold experience on a monitor, leafing through lifeless catalogues.

You're absolutely right, we'd say. About the people who go to trade fairs. In other words, you know all there is to know about attendees of trade fairs. Now tell me, what percentage of executives in a given industry actually, physically (we loved this word, it was so passé to do anything in person anymore) go to a trade fair? Oh, some five percent they would say. Ah! We would all jump, wave and slap the table, as the old timer recoiled. We're interested in the other 95 percent! You know everything about the five percent, but what do you know about the other 95? Nothing! We would gleefully chant in unison.

Come to think of it, there was merit in our BBP – bullshit business plan. Expocentric's eTradeShow software recreated entire trade fairs in 3D. If they plan to actually attend the show, visitors could go to the eTradeShow website to reserve flights and hotel rooms, set up meetings with sales people, and organize events, cocktail parties and presentations. But even if they weren't going to be there in person, upon opening the home page for a trade show, a visitor would enter a reception hall. He could access webcam images from the show – in real time if the show was going on at the moment, or from archives in the months after the show had closed. Once in the site, he could strut around the fair, going in any direction. He could choose a stand on his left, walk in, and see the promotions, watch their PowerPoint revue, go to their website, ask questions in chat mode, e-mail a salesman, or download catalogues and price lists. The visitor would even have the ubiquitous brochure bag, which he could fill with fliers, leaflets and product descriptions. He'd simply print it all out at the end of his session at the show.

It was fast, incredibly efficient, and should be a Godsend to all the execs who didn't have the time or the patience to go to one of the . . .

physical (oh, how primitive!) events. This was the future, and we were onboard. With the smartest and fastest player as our partner. We approached the largest trade fair people in Brazil, hired one of the most renowned trade fair organizers, a Frenchman who had been CEO in Brazil of Reed and other big exhibition players, added a sales manager and minimal staff, and hit the ground running.

Prospects were brilliant. Everywhere we went (after the initial droning on about how people like to go to fairs), organizers would catch on and not want to be left out. Pilot programs and tests surfaced on all sides. The numbers in our business plan suddenly seemed timid.

At the same time, we had a list of pending start-ups that was 14-strong. All had NDAs, many had 'term sheets', two had final contracts, and two had become joint ventures. They were very diverse ventures, but we always looked for common denominators with Semco's philosophy: Complex or engineered products and services, niches where we could be number one or two in the market, and premium quality products.

Our Bidcom venture was doing well. We had a couple of very big projects, including the new headquarters of a large bank. Our backers were sterling, and onboard were four of the six largest developers and construction companies in Brazil. We had the business wrapped up. Or so we thought.

Other people thought differently. At the same moment, five other ventures were being put together in Brazil to serve the same collaborative tools market. They also planned to piggyback a marketplace where construction materials would be bought and sold.

As we went on with our construction marketplace we constantly added more features to a grand portal that was intended to include real estate sales, a system for finding electricians and contractors on-line, magazines, virtual trade fairs and endless catalogues of goods.

We had added a deal with BuildNet (which was growing astronomically), and also had GE (Appliances this time) and eight out of the 10 biggest residential builders onboard. We played up BuildNet as a big advantage. The other five players were doing the same with their partners. Where we had Oracle, Sun, GE Capital and ICG, they had JP Morgan, BankBoston, Bain and Company. The biggest of the biggies were in the game. And each of us thought that we had the ultimate play, the final word, and the best combination.

So it's not surprising that a reckoning arrived, and that the ground gave way under such lightweight feet. That's how we ended up in the boardroom at Andersen Consulting.

One Sunday morning I opened Brazil's biggest-selling weekly magazine, and stumbled – inevitably, as it were – on five consecutive four-colour full-page ads for a competitor's construction website. Its name, Tecto, meant nothing. It would never stick in people's minds.

That's when I knew that this revolution was going to end badly. So did many other people, of course, which is why it was getting difficult to raise the easy cash that had characterized the Internet wave up until that moment.

Humility was a scarce commodity, and we all needed to eat humble pie, quickly. Even though we at Semco were far from betting the family farm, we were nevertheless diverting huge management attention to something that wasn't standing up to the test of time.

We'd surely tested the limit of our intelligence. We'd been outsmarted. Moreover, perhaps every one of the geniuses we encountered was actually a schmuck.

It was time to examine the sextant to find a way to step off onto firm land.

Why not be less greedy, I thought, and look for a path that would make us a small part of something that succeeds, instead of a big part of something that could be miraculous, but might very well be nothing?

I asked Mario Fleck, the CEO of Andersen Consulting (this was before Accenture) to convene the big portal and website players in the construction field. (None had any websites to speak of yet, but everyone was pouring money into big plans.)

Twelve of us took our seats in the Andersen boardroom in mid-2000. Twelve of the top investment bankers, consultants and service giants of Brazil, and one decision to make: To go forward together, or strike out alone. To believe your own business plans, or to chuck them out the window in favour of a group effort.

'Gentlemen,' I said after a pause. 'We are here for a test. To discover what is greater, our brains or our egos.'

This was going to be tough. We had to choose which way to jump. To be fair, I had opened the Andersen meeting with a prognosis – that our decision would follow my own personal equation: 'IQ+EQ+SQ-EGO.' That formula says the right decision arises from an intelligent thesis, checked by a substantial emotional quotient, tempered by a spiritual quotient that humbles and reminds the players that they're fallible, all of which is discounted by Ego striving to remain in control.

And, once again, the best and the brightest businessmen proved that there is still a long learning curve before this part of society matures. The savage ego is the clear winner, and the dot.com crash was the price we all paid for it. The people in the room had the power to create one single entity that could survive the collapsing Internet economy. We had cleared the concept with our partners, and so had some of the others. Now, we just needed a common measurement tool. If our collective EQ (emotional intelligence) were as high as our IQ, we would leave the room as small but viable players in a beautiful project. If we started a pissing contest, we would probably all lose.

Unfortunately everyone thought they held the winning card. So I started by offering to reduce our cut to a measly 10 percent. That would leave plenty of room for everyone else. Some probably took my opening line as a sign of weakness. Others realized we had a good project and favoured conglomeration. Ultimately, however, they weren't able to convince their partners.

After several hours, the verdict was in: These highly intelligent and successful businessmen had bigger egos than brains. They couldn't strike a deal. We all shook hands glumly and departed in different directions. Fleck and I had a coffee, lamenting the demise of this initiative.

Not long after, the stock market crashed, tech stocks took a dive, investors pulled out of Internet start-ups, and Bidcom, too, disappeared – it merged with another fast-waning company. The new owners demanded that we pay license fees for the software, instead of continuing with our joint-venture agreement. They wanted $2 million in advance. We'd already waved goodbye to six months and $500,000 – so we decided to cut our losses and get out. BuildNet also went bankrupt under the extremely arrogant executives that ran it (Bidcom and BuildNet tried a merger, but each one thought they had the winning strategy). Every one of the smart players around Andersen's table that day lost everything. The figures varied between half a million (Semco and one other company) to $18 million (lost by the two largest companies). It was a blood bath. In the construction sector alone, the Brazilians and Argentines lost $80 million. The big guys in the US lost a collective $600 million. That money will never be seen again.

And then eTradeShow died. We should have seen it coming. Resources dwindled while Expocentric waited to be listed for an IPO.

Managers planned to come to Brazil but never materialized. Offices were merged with others. The final blow came when a competitor cut through Expocentric's proprietary software, raised $80 million of their own, and drove eTradeShow out of business. Expocentric believed it couldn't happen – the software behind its technology was unique, secret, and impossible to steal. No one could copy it. We had a lock on technology critical to a potentially huge market. Thus we discovered the hard way that with software, little is truly proprietary. Someone will always hack a short cut that breaks your programming code. That's just what happened, leaving us orphaned. Dazed and in shock, our team was at least quick enough to humbly call the conquering company and offer to work with them in South America.

Our salvage efforts mean that Semco's surviving web companies have made enough money to cover the investment we lost with the failed start-ups. But we've been lucky. Considering the mistakes made, it could easily have turned out otherwise.

We're still sticking with many of these businesses, hoping that time will vindicate the investments. The pendulum swung too far out, and then came too far back. It will eventually settle into the correct arc. To give up now would show little vision, we think. So we're sticking with our projects, trying to lose as little money as possible.

Organizations must treat mistakes like luck – both are necessary, come at times when they're not expected, and add to existing effort. At Semco, we wander into mistakes with a certain level of comfort. It is very common to hear employees at meetings describe some facet of our business as a big mistake. Because we regularly make mistakes and own up to them, it's all part of learning to use intuition.

With intuition as fuel, we have visited the future – and it is nice. Some day it may even make money for us.

CHAPTER 3

The Wisdom Revolution: freedom, democracy and a new way to live

RECENTLY I SPENT several hours sitting under a tree in my garden with the social anthropologist William Ury, a Harvard University professor who specializes in the art of negotiation and wrote the best-selling book, *Getting to Yes*.

He captivated me with his theory that tribalism protects people from their fear of rapid change. He explained that the pillars of tribalism that humans rely on for security would always counter any significant cultural or social change. In this way, he said, change is never allowed to happen too fast.

For example, technology is a pillar of society. Ury believes that every time technology moves in a new or radical direction, another pillar such as religion or nationalism will grow stronger – in effect, the traditional and familiar will assume greater importance to compensate for the new and untested. In this manner, human tribes avoid rapid change that leaves people insecure and frightened.

But we've all heard that nothing is as permanent as change. Nothing is guaranteed. Pithy expressions, to be sure, but no more than clichés. As Ury says, people don't live that way from day-to-day. On the contrary, they actively seek certainty and stability. They want insurance. Financial security. Five-year plans. To know what's coming. They want to know they'll be safe.

Even so, we scare ourselves constantly with the idea of change. An IBM CEO once said: 'We only re-structure for a good reason, and if we haven't re-structured in a while, that's a good reason.' We are

264

scared that competitors, technology and the consumer will put us out of business – so we have to change all the time just to stay alive.

But if we asked our fathers and grandfathers, would they have said that they lived in a period of little change? Structure may not have changed much. It may just be the speed with which we do things.

Change is over-rated, anyway. Consider the automobile. It's an especially valuable example, because the auto industry has spent tens of billions of dollars on research and product development in the last 100 years.

Henry Ford's first car had a metal chassis with an internal combustion, gasoline-powered engine, four wheels with rubber tires, a foot operated clutch assembly and brake system, a steering wheel, and four seats, and it could safely do 18 miles per hour.

A hundred years and tens of thousands of research hours later, we drive cars with a metal chassis, an internal combustion, gasoline-powered engine, four wheels with rubber tires, a foot operated clutch assembly and brake system, a steering wheel, four seats – and the average speed in London in 2001 was 17.5 miles per hour!

That's not a hell of a lot of return for the money. Ford evidently doesn't have much to teach us about change. The fact that they're still manufacturing cars is not proof that Ford Motor Co. is a sound organization, just proof that it takes very large companies to make cars in great quantities – making for an almost impregnable entry barrier.

Fifty years after the development of the jet engine, planes are also little changed. They've grown bigger, wider and can carry more people. But those are incremental, largely cosmetic changes.

Taken together, this lack of real change has come to mean that in travel – whether driving or flying – time and technology have not combined to make things much better. The safety and design have of course accompanied the times and the new volume of cars and flights, but nothing of any significance has changed in the basic assumptions of the final product.

At the same time, moving around in cars or aeroplanes becomes less and less efficient all the time. Not only has there been no great change, but also both forms of transport have deteriorated as more people clamour to use them.

The same is true for telephones, which took over a hundred years to become mobile, or photographic film, which also required an entire century to change.

The only explanation for this is anthropological. Once established in calcified organizations, humans do two things: sabotage changes that might render people dispensable, and ensure industry-wide emulation.

In the 1960s, German auto companies developed plans to scrap the entire combustion engine for an electrical design. (The same existed in the 1970s in Japan, and in the 1980s in France.) So for 40 years we might have been free of the wasteful and ludicrous dependence on fossil fuels. Why didn't it go anywhere? Because auto executives understood pistons and carburettors, and would be loath to cannibalize their expertise, along with most of their factories.

Entrenched practices led to industry-wide emulation. Think about it – even though auto design changes every few years, the alterations are marginal. And everything that happens converges with industry trends. Line-up eight mid-sized sedans at a distance of 100 feet, and you won't be able to tell which company manufactured which vehicle. Place a Honda, a Ford, a GM, a Renault, and a Peugeot in a row, and you won't be able to distinguish among them unless you happen to own one.

Why? Because their designers all learned from the same books, went to the same schools, meet at the same conventions, attend trade shows together and focus unduly on their competition.

Take the example of parallel parking. You must slide alongside and just beyond an empty spot, and then drive diagonally backwards. I've been doing this for 25 years and am still unsure how it will turn out. Is there a sillier exercise than parallel parking? Yet it remains unchanged for the last 100 years. Why? Because the engineers who design cars understand the basics of the automobile; it goes forwards and backwards, but it doesn't move sideways. Is it so difficult – with billions of dollars available for research – to create a simple mechanism that pivots the front and back wheels at an angle to the car so it can move sideways? Wouldn't I then simply approach a parking spot and, instead of backing up, press the 'swivel' button to rotate the tires, and glide sideways toward the curb?

Is it easier to put a man on the moon than to update parallel parking technology?

Think also about the music industry. Some of the giants around the world have devoted tremendous resources to creating music disks with secure packaging so people can't steal digital recordings from store shelves. While CD manufacturers focused on producing theft-proof boxes, along came an upstart called Napster and a technology known as MP3.

How many people have unopened CDs languishing on a shelf in their original packaging? Whoever invented the shrink-wrap and stickers that protect the disk should be working in Fort Knox by now. Shoplifters, of course, know how to quickly slit open the package and remove the CD. But simple, lower life forms (the customer) must use teeth, pens, razors, paper clips and special openers to get at the CD. The kids at Napster made this feat of safety engineering a milestone in stupidity. And unravelled the music industry while they were at it. But the CDs are still safe in their plastic fortresses.

Examples abound. Take the airline industry. Not only have the executives who run the airlines made flying one of the most painful experiences in history, they've also failed to make sustainable money out of it.

Think, also, of the safety instructions onboard each plane. Ever since I was six years old and flying in Air France's 707s via Dakar to Paris, I've been listening to instructions on how to use the flotation device under my seat. I'm sure I have heard some 500 such presentations. I am equally sure that I would never know which strings to pull when an emergency arose, and would not, for the life of me, know where to blow, and whether to put mine on first, or my child's.

So why not join together two of the most boring activities in modern life? One is safety instruction onboard a plane. The other, sitting around in airports for much longer than necessary, because airlines want you there well before they're ready for you.

Couldn't the airlines arrange to have safety certificates given out in the waiting lounges? All you would have to do is present yourself, and someone would give you a 10-minute course (and you could put the life vest and oxygen mask on yourself). Maybe you'd even have to take a little test – the engineers would love that. Once tested, you'd be issued a certificate that is valid for, say, five years. And you'd show that every time you check in. The crew would thereafter be absolved from the ridicule of waving their arms to passengers who politely ignore them, and the passengers would be saved the irritating repetition.

Or take the outrageous example of Gillette and the razor blade.

King Gillette developed the single razor at the beginning of the

20th century. He had dreams of making a fortune when a friend suggested that he concentrate on a product – any product – that was disposable. Thus the razor. From this early success, Gillette thrived for decades. It was a fabulously successful company – one of the few that Warren Buffet pegged as a solid gamble. Then Gillette concluded that the product required an overhaul, and spent millions on the TracII – basically the same product with an extra blade. But Gillette's executives couldn't leave well enough alone. In the 1990s, they took another unbelievable step: They spent $600 million to develop a completely new razor system. After this vast expenditure (complete with endless meetings, brainstorming sessions and multiple-committee work), they unveiled their new invention: The Mach 3 – a blade inserted between the other two!

I've often asked, in my workshops about corporate architecture and control, whether anyone in the room wouldn't have come up with the same idea if given a couple days to think about it. The price tag would certainly have been a lot less.

Change works well only if it is a non-issue. Because an organization that constantly, and artificially, coaches its people to change (accept change! recognize change!) is like a Darwinist standing next to a giraffe, shouting: 'Stretch that neck! Stretch that neck!'

So how do we suddenly tell people to love risk? To toss aside everything they know about pistons and carburettors, for example, and make a headlong leap into electric cars? By replacing control with democracy, by allowing employees to choose their own managers, and think and act independently. The first step toward creativity and confidence must include internal movement. Move people around from job to job, department to department, unit to unit. Mix and match. This blocks the human tendency to concoct feudal systems and erect fortresses. Those may guarantee security within the group, and protect against the change and risk that might emerge from the outside. But insecurity and change are what we are after at Semco.

Change also means that a company must be willing to shed or undo elements of itself that no longer have a future. It must be ready to unilaterally sell, spin off, or close units – it must be ready to cannibalize itself.

This continues to raise problems even at Semco. Many times when we have elected to cannibalize ourselves, the protective spirit of our employees surges, they close ranks around the relationships they have with one another, and they take the ostrich's approach – let's protect ourselves at all cost. They'll shy away from a new technology if adopting it will destroy their accustomed base.

But then we run another risk – the one that arises when you're too comfortable with what you're doing.

That's why we are dismantling our headquarters, and selling or loaning our industrial machinery to former employees who are now sub-contractors. Keeping either makes no sense as a long-term plan. At the same time, workers inspired by their own cottage industry will take better care of the machinery, the computers, the hardware than if they just passed them every day on our factory floor. If they are producing and delivering parts to us from their own garage shop, they'll understand efficiency and profitability, rather than worrying about the factory, the 60 other lathes, and the 70 people they labour with side-by-side and whose children they've watched grow.

They're not going to cannibalize in that case. But in all likelihood, someone else will.

We learned that in the cooling tower industry. There's an entire market that until recently we were unable to attack. In partnership with Baltimore Air Coil, we manufacture steel cooling towers. That's our entire business. Our American partners have a virtual motto: 'We make steel cooling towers, we don't do anything else.' But it happens that along the lengthy Brazilian coastline, fiberglass is preferred because steel rusts in the ocean air. Yet for 17 years we've sold steel cooling towers, and for 17 years we've done just fine. But there's this entire market for fiberglass cooling towers that we have missed – until we began to shed the machinery and the factory infrastructure for making the steel towers. It's all distributed among our former employees now. They still make the steel towers, but now Semco is free to start producing fiberglass ones because they no longer will threaten the steel production line. We move constantly so that we can't get too comfortable. One facet is to no longer own our production means. Instead we rent out the machinery, by the hour, by the product, by the piece. This forces us to be uncomfortable. We no longer control the machinery, so we must be ready for change at any time.

Many times we begin strategy meetings by asking ourselves what we would do if we were our competitors. Then we look for a way to do whatever it is to ourselves, first. We try to avoid the fate of Ford,

Gillette and the airlines. We can survive by standing still, but we'll never be at the cutting edge of anything. A boat like ours needs someone at the helm wielding a telescope. You can never tell where change may come from.

Take genetics as an unexpected example. Scientists and doctors already predict changes in life expectancy that will force organizations to adapt. And these are changes that we presently ignore.

A little over a century ago, anyone who finished university had dedicated fully half of his life to study. Today that 25 years is no more than a third of a lifetime. Now science predicts that my son, and everyone in his age and socio-economic group, will live to be at least 105, could possibly last to age 115, and has a 40 percent chance of living to be 135! (This based on commercial applications of therapies that delay cell deterioration.)

My first thought is, who wants to be 120? Who wants to hit 90 in a ninety-ish state, and then spend 30 years playing gin rummy and watching TV in a nursing home? Of course the cell deterioration delayers will be administered from an early age, so advanced age status will start only at 90 for my son. At 80 he may be more like today's 55-year-old.

When that happens, work lives will have to be extended, creating a new world for all of us that portent even more important modification.

Today, we spend roughly 25 years getting ready to work, some 35 years working and another 25 in retirement or negligible work activity. Some two thirds of our life, therefore, in the financial auspices of others (parents, the state, company pension funds).

In my son's new world, he might spend 25 years preparing for work, another 60 working, and the same 25 years in retirement. Mandatory retirement may be pushed to 80!

Yet just as people begin to talk about these possibilities, one of Spain's main telecoms is lowering its mandatory retirement age to 52. Most companies view anyone who is 60-plus as a worker ready to be phased out. We ask people at the height of their wisdom, maturity and intellectual prowess to stand down.

Are we so rigid and unthinking that we can find no way for people of that age to merge their interests, physical ability and intellect with our organizational goals? Not only that, but we create a self-fulfilling prophecy: We think the 60-year-old will not last long, so we don't invest in retraining them. We don't include them in the loop as much. So they lose their sense of place. And then we conclude that maybe they should retire.

In early 2001, Clovis, then 67, decided to take a three-month english course in Boston. He'd never mastered english, and it was of little or no importance when he went to school in an insular nation. Now, he needed english because of our many international partners. To prepare for the decade ahead, he invested in a full-time program. Not many companies would pay for that training. We were very happy that we did.

But let's backtrack to where some of these problems begin. It is conventional to ask teenagers just entering college to opt for a profession – doctor, architect, lawyer, historian. Yet at 18, who is prepared to make that choice? Perhaps one-quarter know where their true interests lie. The rest choose from what they perceive. And their perception is incomplete – and influenced by biased advice from parents. How many parents of painters, poets and philosophers, after all, pushed their offspring into those activities?

At 18, a person is only a quarter of the way through their lifetime, and must decide what to do with the remaining three-fourths. That may have been reasonable in the 18th or 19th centuries, but it makes little sense today. If the new life expectancies come to pass, a youngster will be deciding at a time in which 85 percent of his life lies ahead of him. But with 70 years to work fully, why should someone have to choose only one career? Why not be a doctor for 20 years, go back to college for another five, spend 20 years as an architect, and maybe go back to school again to spend two last decades as a biochemist?

Much of the conditioning that makes change so hard for us comes from childhood.

When our toddlers go off to school, we are essentially placing them in an old-fashioned system that is meant to emulate the past and to teach offspring to be like us. We don't stop to ask three whys about its old-fashioned purpose.

Take school holidays. They are a function of an agrarian society, where children were needed during the long summer growing and harvest season. School vacations are a proof that it is much easier to perpetrate a vast revolution via the Internet than to get people to question the simple things that surround them. Why should they make holidays an inferno, in terms of reservations, flight hassles and queues everywhere, just because their kids are on a 1700s harvest schedule?!

My current dream (for the last five years) has been to put together a school based on the Semco rationale; I'm devoting a good part of my midlife crisis to it. I envisage a contemporary education system in which students question everything, where they aim a 'three why gun' at every subject. After all, much as business people look erroneously to revenues, growth and profit for measurements of success, parents and teachers use metrics and grading to rate children.

This is not the right book for the details about Semco Foundation's Educational Project and its school, Lumiar. Suffice to say that the basis of the school is that the teacher is relieved from transmitting information and knowledge. Moises Assayag coined a term for the Semco way of running an organization: 'anthropocentric' – centred on the person. The same is true for the school – the teacher's function is to concentrate on human qualities and development, on transmitting tribal wisdom, on holding hands as the sequential cycles of childhood take place.

Any 'teaching' *per se* is by those with a passion for a subject. To find them, we dip into the pool of parents, neighbours, part-timers, unemployed and, mostly, the retired. From this deep well we fish violinists from the symphony orchestra, carpenters from cabinet makers, plumbers from construction sites, retired ship captains, motorbike test pilots, or pharmacists.

And then we redesign the curriculum.

It should be obvious that interested kids need no more than seven to nine years to learn what kids of a century ago were exposed to in 13 years of schooling.

So what do we do with the rest of the time, if we have to hold youngsters at bay until they're 17? If they're not occupied, it could explain why schools – especially in big urban centres – so often resemble juvenile delinquency institutions. Towering walls, grated windows, and metal detectors are too often features of schools, and not just because of inner city strife, home ambience or social-economic status. These problems arise because the basic assumption that there is enough interesting subject matter to last 15 years is hopelessly flawed.

So the Semco Foundation is redesigning the curriculum from scratch, with the help of several Ivy League universities. At our school, kids 'self-manage' – they exercise their own discipline and set their own schedules. We assume that students can master these aspects of their lives from an early age. They don't need teachers to do it for them. Once freed from these housekeeping tasks, tutors can share their passions with students, and core educators can impart tribal wisdom.

The way we shape our youngsters is the next big step in how organizations will adapt for survival. Flexing the mind and stretching tribal pillars is paramount to finding our way from the industrial revolution to the service era, from the age of knowledge and to the revolution of wisdom. After all, every revolution is 'revolutionary' when it starts!

And a good place to start is with toddlers. Another is to rethink what change is expected from leaders, and how the world currently adapts to change.

Educators today are like the German, French and Japanese executives who did not alter automobiles to solar, electrical or gas power decades ago because it would cannibalize their knowledge. Educators now simply perpetuate a system that produces marginal gains for students. Our experiment with schooling will follow where Semco has already gone.

'What you are essentially advocating at Semco is harnessing the wisdom of people,' Bill Ury told me that day in my garden. 'Their reservoir of talent, the natural wisdom of the system, the wisdom that only comes from freedom, the wisdom that emerges however unevenly from democracy. Wisdom is what you get by asking why. And Semco is a pioneer in the Wisdom Revolution, which comes right after the Knowledge Revolution.'

Much of the world suffers from the same structural crisis – wasn't globalization supposed to create a global village? Free trade, technology and communication would curtail wars, immigration battles and old-fashioned terrorist bombings. Or so we thought.

Instead, the trappings of communism were quickly snapped up by mega-corporations. East Germany may no longer exist, but now we have companies featuring central planning by Troikas, mission statements crafted by apparatchiks, quinquennial planning (or the 'great five year plan'), no right to choose leaders in companies, no democracy in the workplace, a clear distinction between intelligentsia and peasants (top CEOs make 152 times the median salary and enjoy company 'dachas', jets and limos), and 'state' monitoring (time clocks, dress codes, drug-screening, 'employee assistance' plans, e-mail monitoring, smoking and personal conduct rules, as well as family-life audits). Technology hasn't freed more time for leisure. On the contrary – it has eaten away at the 'weekend'.

Global companies don't practice democracy. You might argue that the shareholding structure is democratic, that each share contains the right to vote in an annual assembly of investors. But that's not democracy, and you can tell by sitting at a shareholder's meeting – just look at management's grip over companies, the board's lack of representation and the dictatorship of stronger investors over weaker ones.

Add to that all the family businesses and companies that have one majority partner each – and you've got an overwhelming number of organizations that dispense with democracy as an unnecessary and senseless constraint.

Global capitalism fits Winston Churchill's view on democracy: It's the worst system, except for all the others.

As a consequence, the number of poor people in the world is increasing steadily – despite constant increases in GNP and the lip service about globalization and shared wealth.

The time for organizations designed on the 20th century model is over – especially those based (unknowingly) on the communist or military models. Redesigning the workplace for the 21st century means letting in fresh air. That's easy to say, and hugely difficult to do. Asking why? is terribly distracting for most CEOs. Managers aren't looking for 10- or 20-year change programs – they want simple, objective goals: profit, growth, healthy quarterly reports, trained people, orderly markets, competitive advantage. Until they cease to exist, are merged, or make an embarrassing exit from the business stage (remember that less than half of the companies that were big in the 1990s exist in the same form today).

There could be a better way. Organizations must respect such apparently passé concepts as workplace democracy, the need to question everything, and the search for a more balanced existence. Hopefully Semco's case history and its consistent performance ($100,000 invested in Semco 20 years ago would now be worth $5.4 million) will speak for us. If this book has planted even the smallest seeds of doubt in anyone wedded to the past, and more substantial kernels of hope in those looking for the better way, writing it will have been worthwhile.

Readers who are not managers may be intrigued with what they find here, but I fear that many will be frustrated because they won't believe it applies to them. They're not in a position to adopt the Semco way, they believe. They have no power.

But that frustration is partly anthropological. We all have enormous amounts of latitude, be it with our children, in social gatherings, or at work. Let's apply that to the workplace too. Let's resist the instinct to bow to the military legacy. People who trade rush hour for idleness or who think about what they are doing in a new light can make dramatic difference for themselves as well as for others. People who have two employees working for them can change two, five or ten lives. That's a lot of change.

Semco succeeds in practice, and this book is my attempt to explain the theory behind it. I remember reading about a French company where employees came up with practical solutions to a difficult situation. The director exclaimed: 'Ah, I can see you've come up with a plan that works in practice. But will it work in theory?'

At Semco we're rambling into our future by ending boarding school mentality, having the courage to give up control, asking three successive whys and then going to the movies on Monday afternoons (after feeding the ducks). These practices are justified by the gratification felt among those who make this journey with us.

'The seven-day weekend' is the metaphor and the latest reminder that change is constant. We shouldn't be afraid of it. The seven-day weekend is an opportunity, not a threat.

The world desperately needs an 'Age of Wisdom,' and workplaces would be an inspiring place to start. At Semco we have little to teach and even less to 'sell' in a packaged form. We're just a living experiment in eliminating boredom, routine, and exasperating regulations – an exploration of motivation and passion to free workers from corporate oppression. Our goal is helping people tap their 'reservoir of talent' and find equilibrium among love, liberty and work.

Once people learn to do that . . . I know we'll be alright.